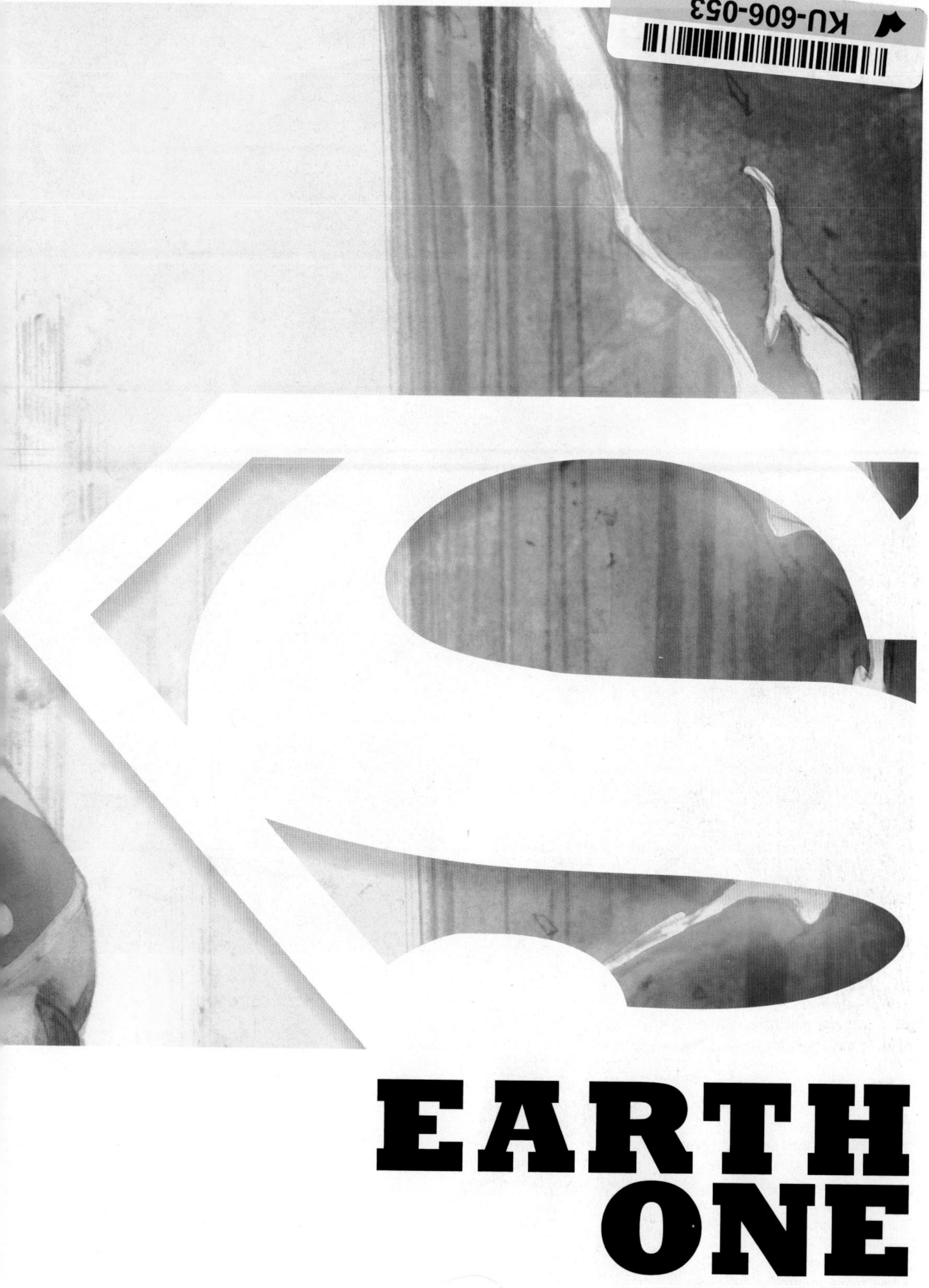

EARTH ONE

Written by J. Michael Straczynski
Pencils by Shane Davis
Inks by Sandra Hope
Colors by Barbara Ciardo
Lettered by Rob Leigh

Superman created by Jerry Siegel and Joe Shuster.

Eddie Berganza & Adam Schlagman Editors
Robbin Brosterman Design Director – Books
Louis Prandi Publication Design

Bob Harras VP – Editor-in-Chief

Diane Nelson President
Dan DiDio and Jim Lee Co-Publishers
Geoff Johns Chief Creative Officer
John Rood Executive VP – Sales, Marketing and Business Development
Amy Genkins Senior VP – Business and Legal Affairs
Nairi Gardiner Senior VP – Finance
Jeff Boison VP – Publishing Operations
Mark Chiarello VP – Art Direction and Design
John Cunningham VP – Marketing
Terri Cunningham VP – Talent Relations and Services
Alison Gill Senior VP – Manufacturing and Operations
Hank Kanalz Senior VP – Digital
Jay Kogan VP – Business and Legal Affairs, Publishing
Jack Mahan VP – Business Affairs, Talent
Nick Napolitano VP – Manufacturing Administration
Sue Pohja VP – Book Sales
Courtney Simmons Senior VP – Publicity
Bob Wayne Senior VP – Sales

 EARTH ONE

Published by DC Comics, 1700 Broadway, New York, NY 10019. Copyright © 2010 by DC Comics. All rights reserved. All characters featured in this publication, the distinctive likenesses thereof and related elements are trademarks of DC Comics. Printed by RR Donnelley, Salem, VA, USA. 3/29/13 First Printing. DC Comics, a Warner Bros. Entertainment Company.
SC ISBN: 978-1-4012-2469-1

Library of Congress Cataloging-in-Publication Data

Straczynski, J. Michael, 1954-
  Superman : Earth One / J. Michael Straczynski, Shane Davis.
    pages cm
  ISBN 978-1-4012-2468-4
  1. Graphic novels. I. Davis, Shane, illustrator. II. Title.
PN6728.S9S77 2013
741.5'973--dc23
                                    2012044878

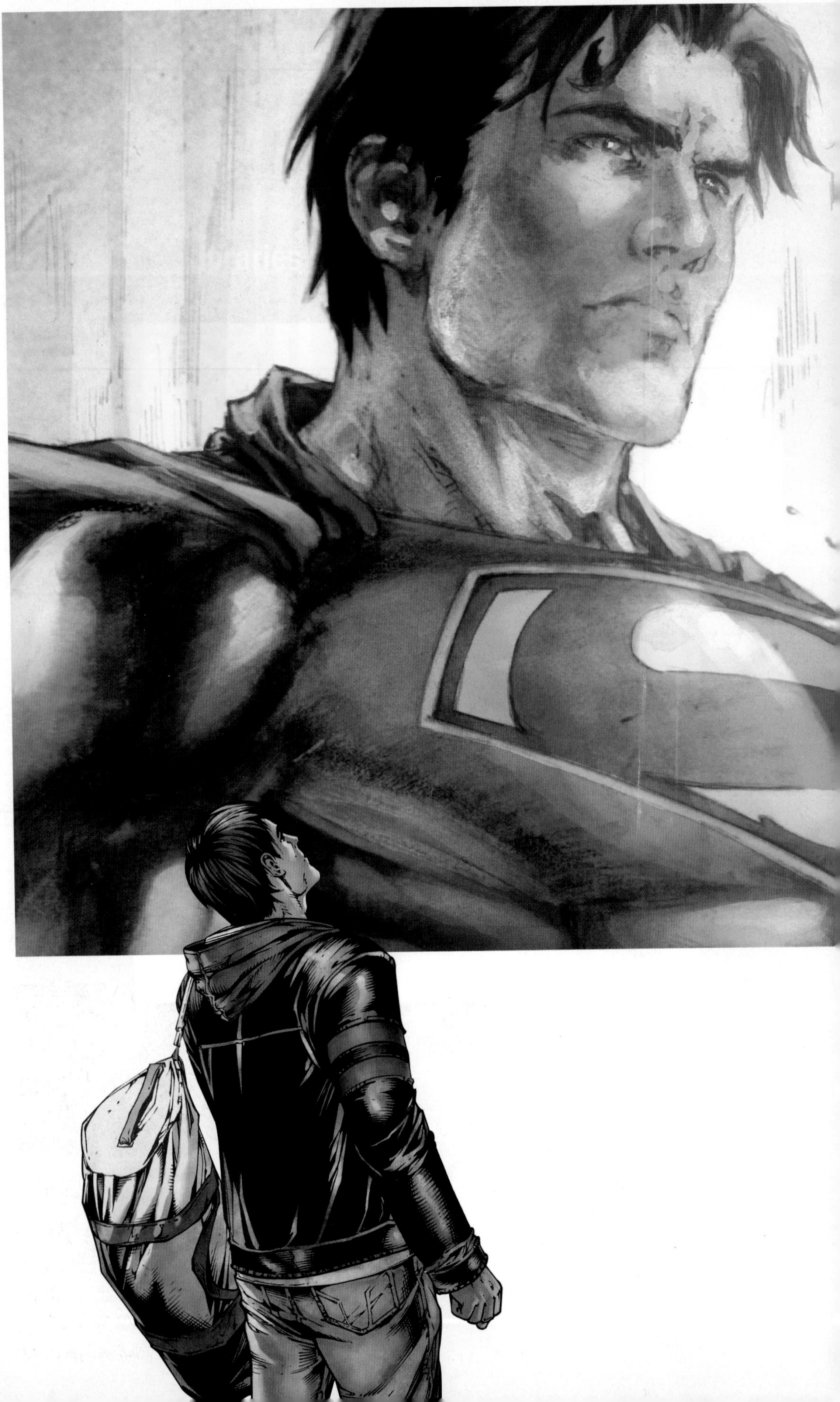

DEDICATIONS

For as far back as I can remember, I would get a thrill of excitement every time I saw this symbol.

If you experienced the same thing, if you've ever worn that symbol on a T-shirt, doodled it on the back of a notebook, or had it tattooed on your arm... if you understand what that symbol means -- that all things are possible -- then this book is dedicated to you.

It is dedicated also to DC's Dan DiDio, who allowed this kid from New Jersey to finally realize the dream of a lifetime.

J. Michael Straczynski
Los Angeles, California
18 June 2010

Shane Davis would like to dedicate his artistic contribution to the memory of Shawn Davis. Shane would also like to give special thanks to Dan, John, Antonio, Michelle, Gabe, Mom and Dad.

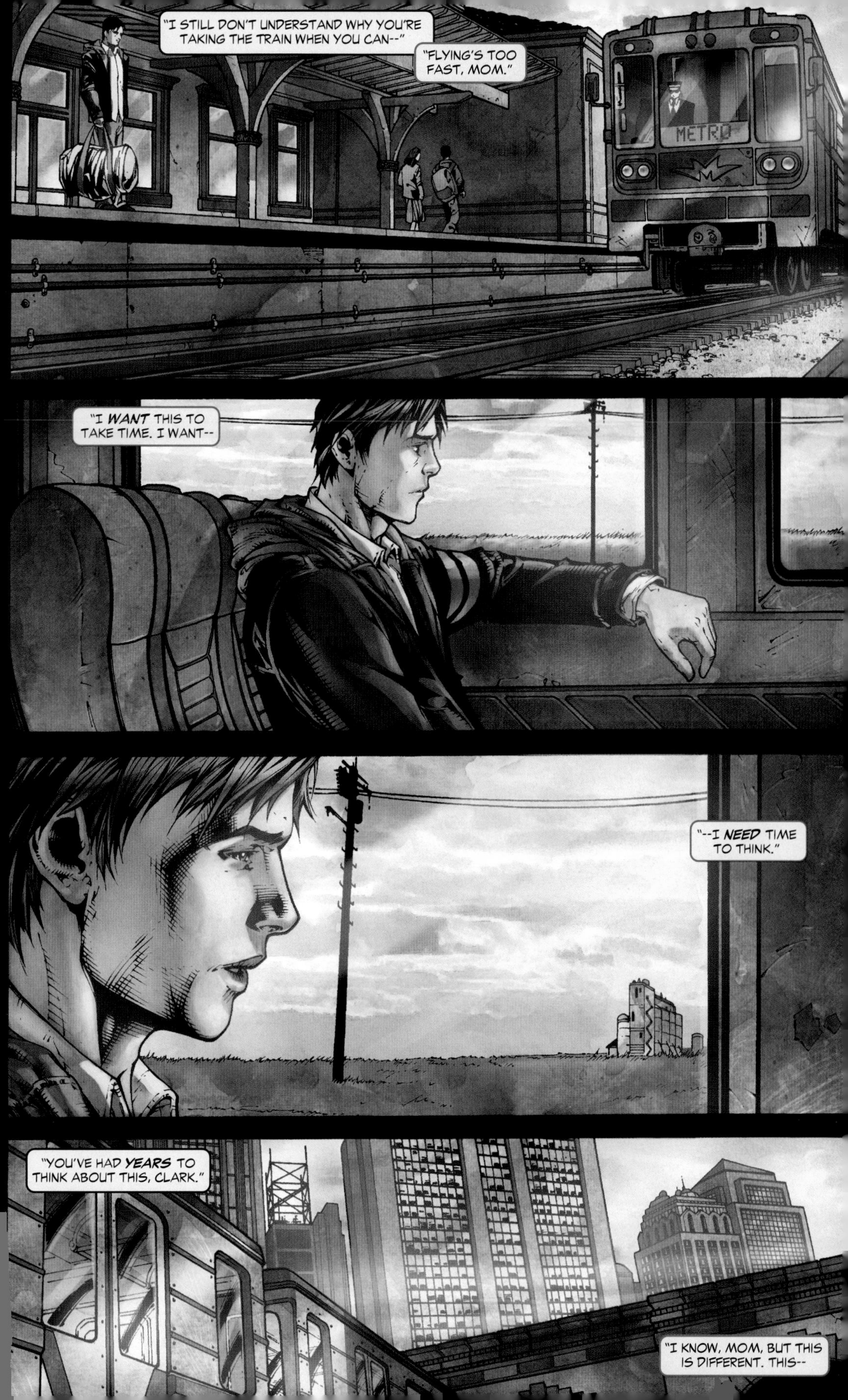
"I STILL DON'T UNDERSTAND WHY YOU'RE TAKING THE TRAIN WHEN YOU CAN--"
"FLYING'S TOO FAST, MOM."
METRO
"I **WANT** THIS TO TAKE TIME. I WANT--
"--I **NEED** TIME TO THINK."
"YOU'VE HAD **YEARS** TO THINK ABOUT THIS, CLARK."
"I KNOW, MOM, BUT THIS IS DIFFERENT. THIS--

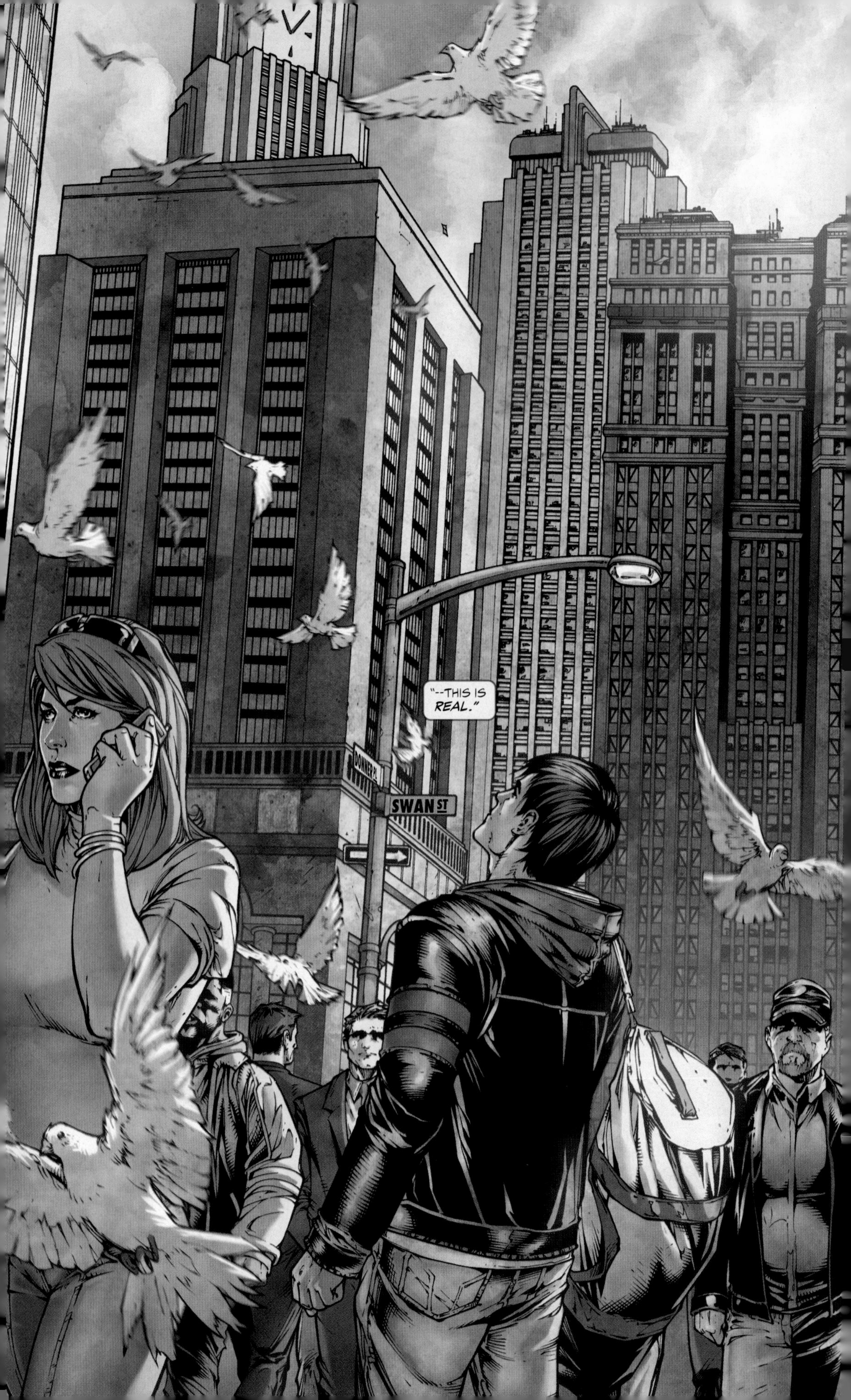
"--THIS IS REAL."
DONNER PL
SWAN ST

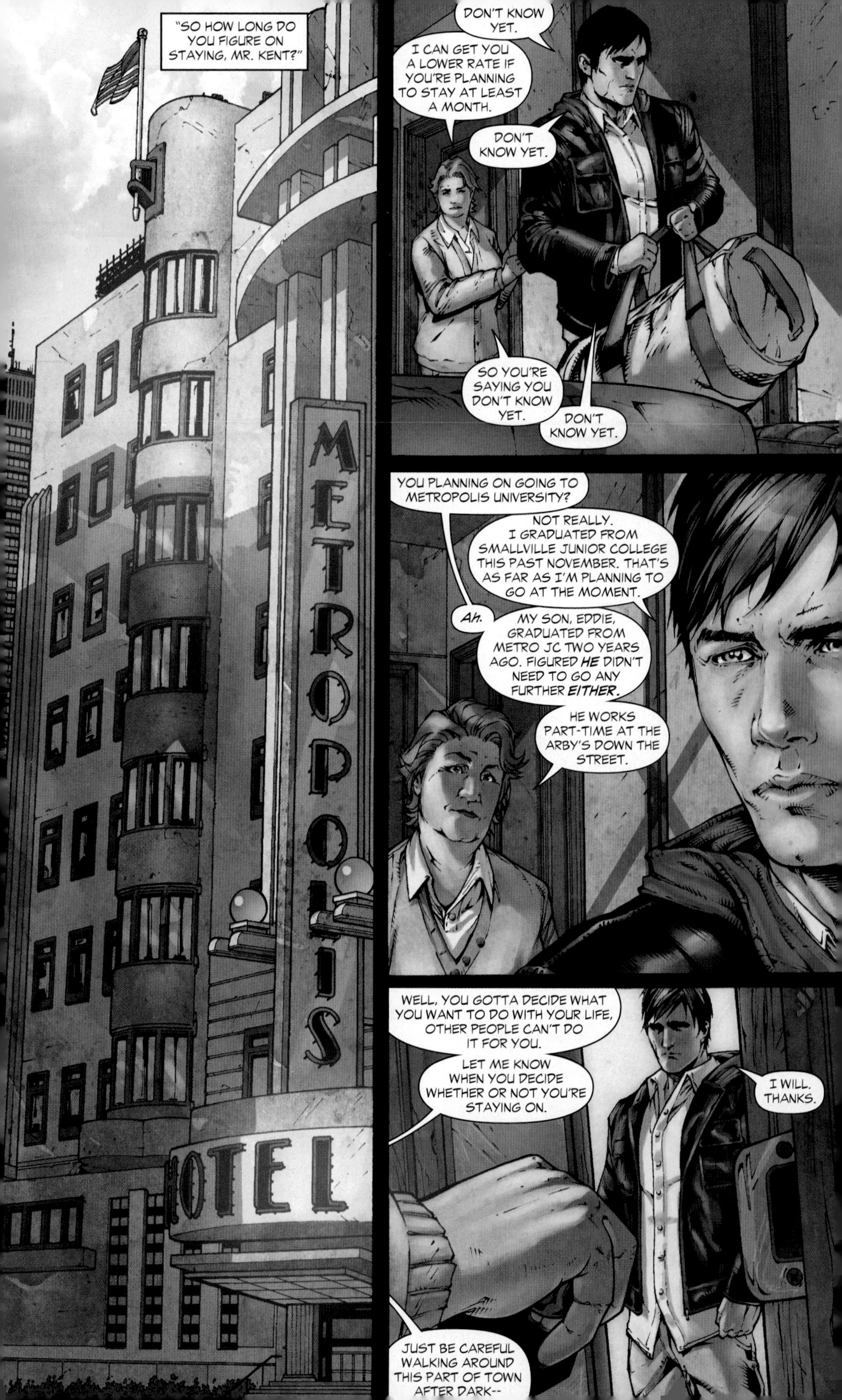
"SO HOW LONG DO YOU FIGURE ON STAYING, MR. KENT?"
METROPOLIS
HOTEL
DON'T KNOW YET.
I CAN GET YOU A LOWER RATE IF YOU'RE PLANNING TO STAY AT LEAST A MONTH.
DON'T KNOW YET.
SO YOU'RE SAYING YOU DON'T KNOW YET.
DON'T KNOW YET.
YOU PLANNING ON GOING TO METROPOLIS UNIVERSITY?
NOT REALLY. I GRADUATED FROM SMALLVILLE JUNIOR COLLEGE THIS PAST NOVEMBER. THAT'S AS FAR AS I'M PLANNING TO GO AT THE MOMENT.
Ah.
MY SON, EDDIE, GRADUATED FROM METRO JC TWO YEARS AGO. FIGURED *HE* DIDN'T NEED TO GO ANY FURTHER *EITHER.*
HE WORKS PART-TIME AT THE ARBY'S DOWN THE STREET.
WELL, YOU GOTTA DECIDE WHAT YOU WANT TO DO WITH YOUR LIFE, OTHER PEOPLE CAN'T DO IT FOR YOU.
LET ME KNOW WHEN YOU DECIDE WHETHER OR NOT YOU'RE STAYING ON.
I WILL. THANKS.
JUST BE CAREFUL WALKING AROUND THIS PART OF TOWN AFTER DARK--

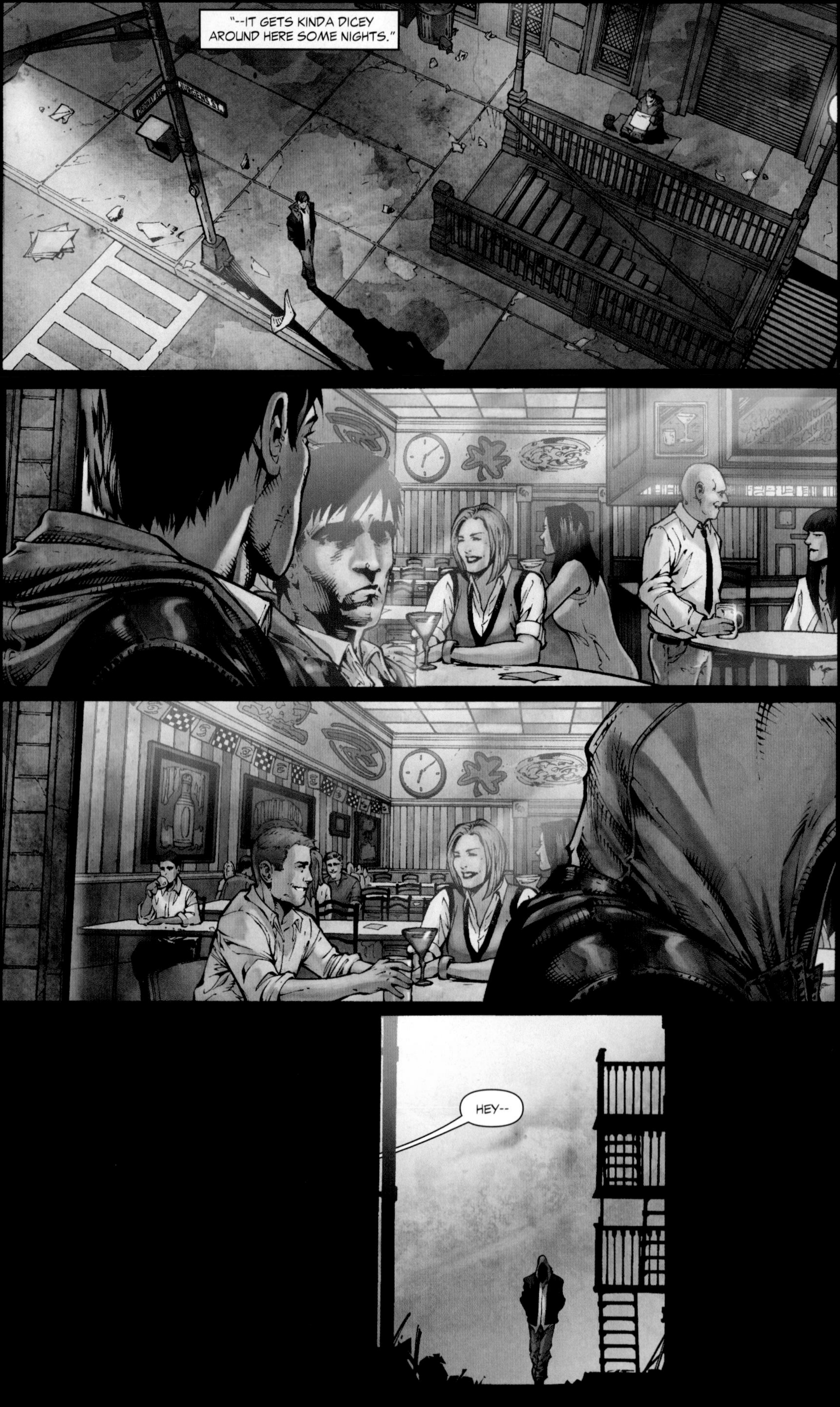
"--IT GETS KINDA DICEY AROUND HERE SOME NIGHTS."
HEY--

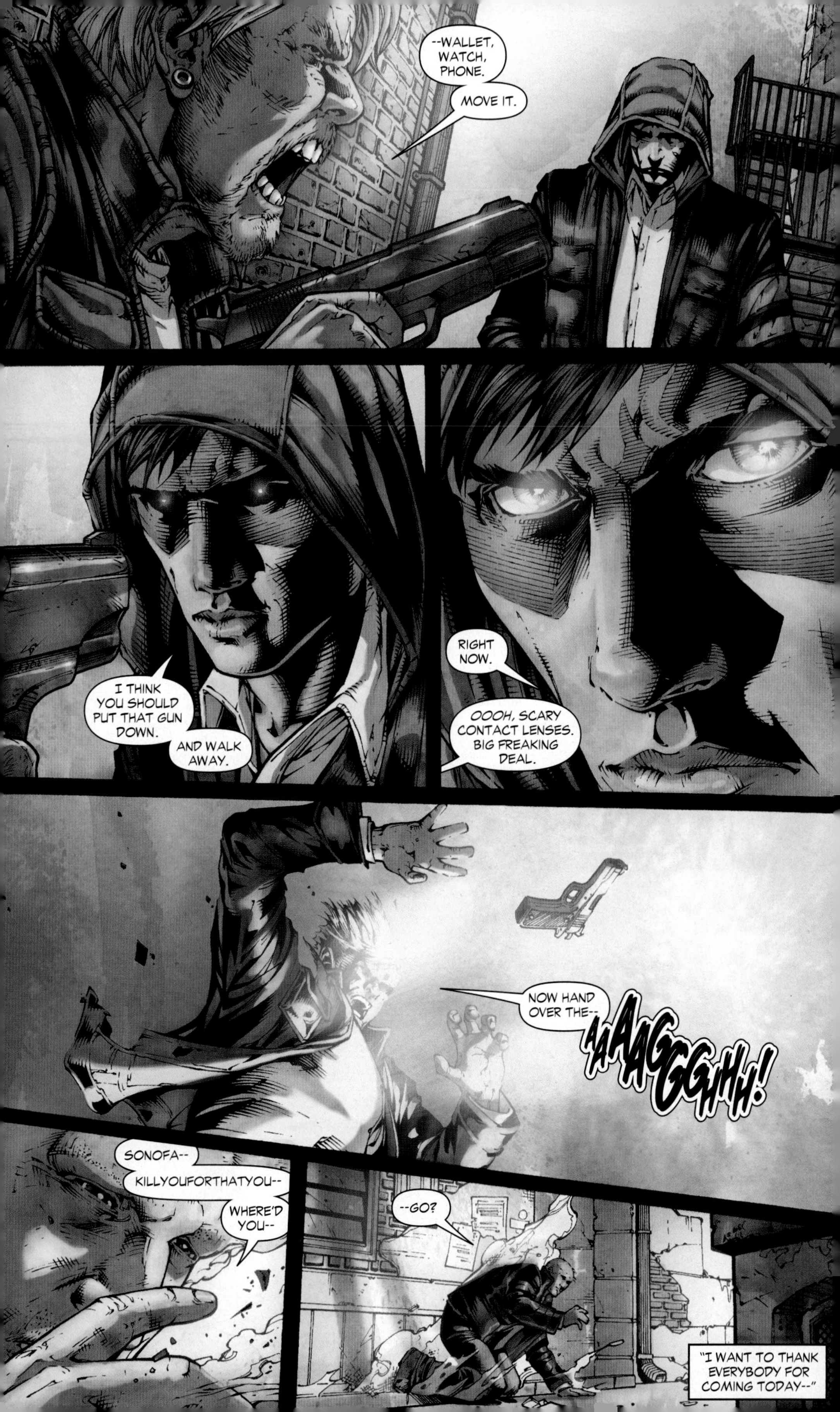

--WALLET, WATCH, PHONE.
MOVE IT.
I THINK YOU SHOULD PUT THAT GUN DOWN.
AND WALK AWAY.
RIGHT NOW.
OOOH, SCARY CONTACT LENSES. BIG FREAKING DEAL.
NOW HAND OVER THE--
AAAAAGGGHHH!
SONOFA--
KILLYOUFORTHATYOU--
WHERE'D YOU--
--GO?
"I WANT TO THANK EVERYBODY FOR COMING TODAY--"

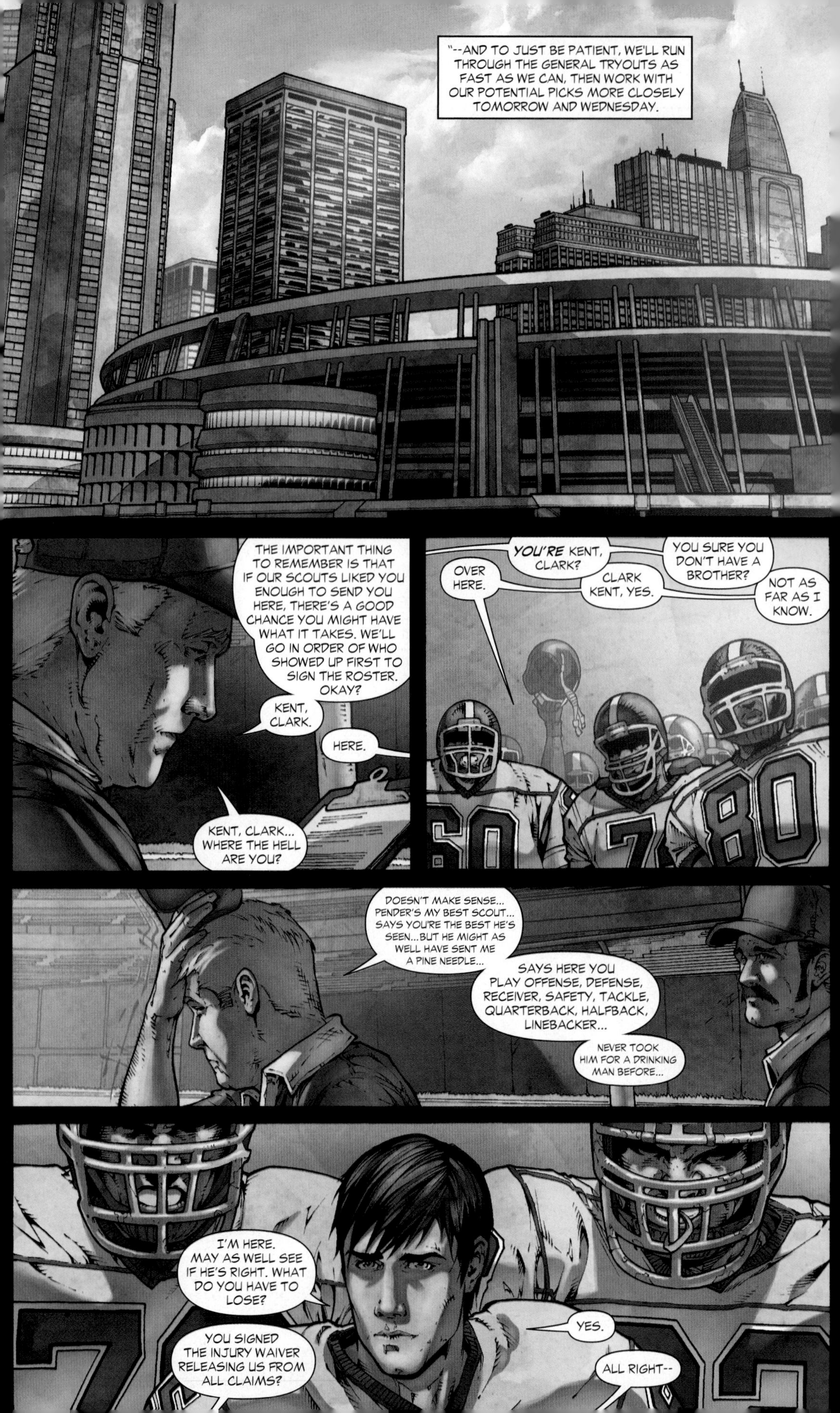
"--AND TO JUST BE PATIENT, WE'LL RUN THROUGH THE GENERAL TRYOUTS AS FAST AS WE CAN, THEN WORK WITH OUR POTENTIAL PICKS MORE CLOSELY TOMORROW AND WEDNESDAY.
THE IMPORTANT THING TO REMEMBER IS THAT IF OUR SCOUTS LIKED YOU ENOUGH TO SEND YOU HERE, THERE'S A GOOD CHANCE YOU MIGHT HAVE WHAT IT TAKES. WE'LL GO IN ORDER OF WHO SHOWED UP FIRST TO SIGN THE ROSTER. OKAY?
KENT, CLARK.
HERE.
KENT, CLARK... WHERE THE HELL ARE YOU?
OVER HERE.
YOU'RE KENT, CLARK?
CLARK KENT, YES.
YOU SURE YOU DON'T HAVE A BROTHER?
NOT AS FAR AS I KNOW.
DOESN'T MAKE SENSE... PENDER'S MY BEST SCOUT... SAYS YOU'RE THE BEST HE'S SEEN...BUT HE MIGHT AS WELL HAVE SENT ME A PINE NEEDLE...
SAYS HERE YOU PLAY OFFENSE, DEFENSE, RECEIVER, SAFETY, TACKLE, QUARTERBACK, HALFBACK, LINEBACKER...
NEVER TOOK HIM FOR A DRINKING MAN BEFORE...
I'M HERE. MAY AS WELL SEE IF HE'S RIGHT. WHAT DO YOU HAVE TO LOSE?
YOU SIGNED THE INJURY WAIVER RELEASING US FROM ALL CLAIMS?
YES.
ALL RIGHT--

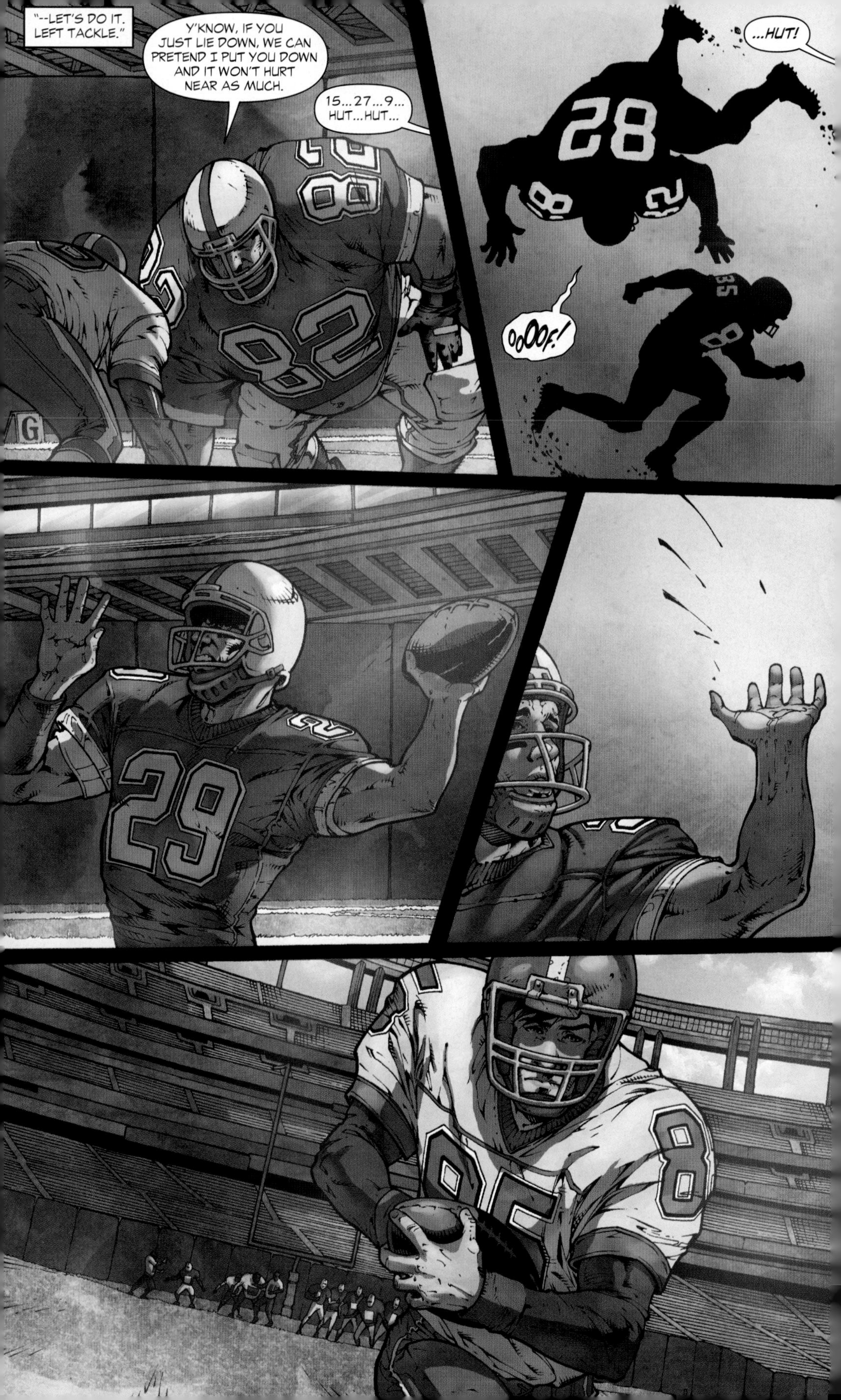
"--LET'S DO IT. LEFT TACKLE."
Y'KNOW, IF YOU JUST LIE DOWN, WE CAN PRETEND I PUT YOU DOWN AND IT WON'T HURT NEAR AS MUCH.
15...27...9... HUT...HUT...
...HUT!
OOOOF!

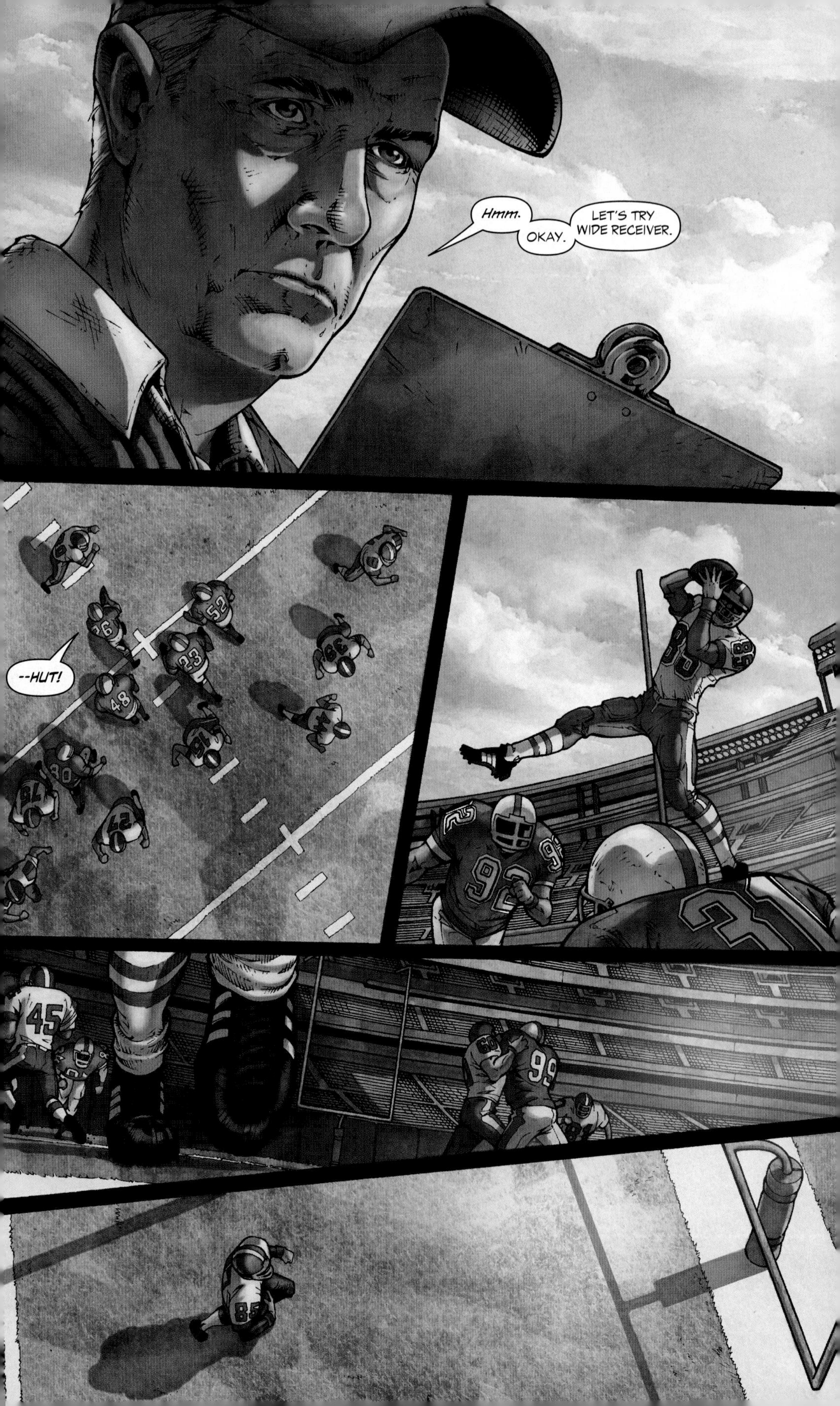
Hmm.
OKAY.
LET'S TRY WIDE RECEIVER.
--HUT!

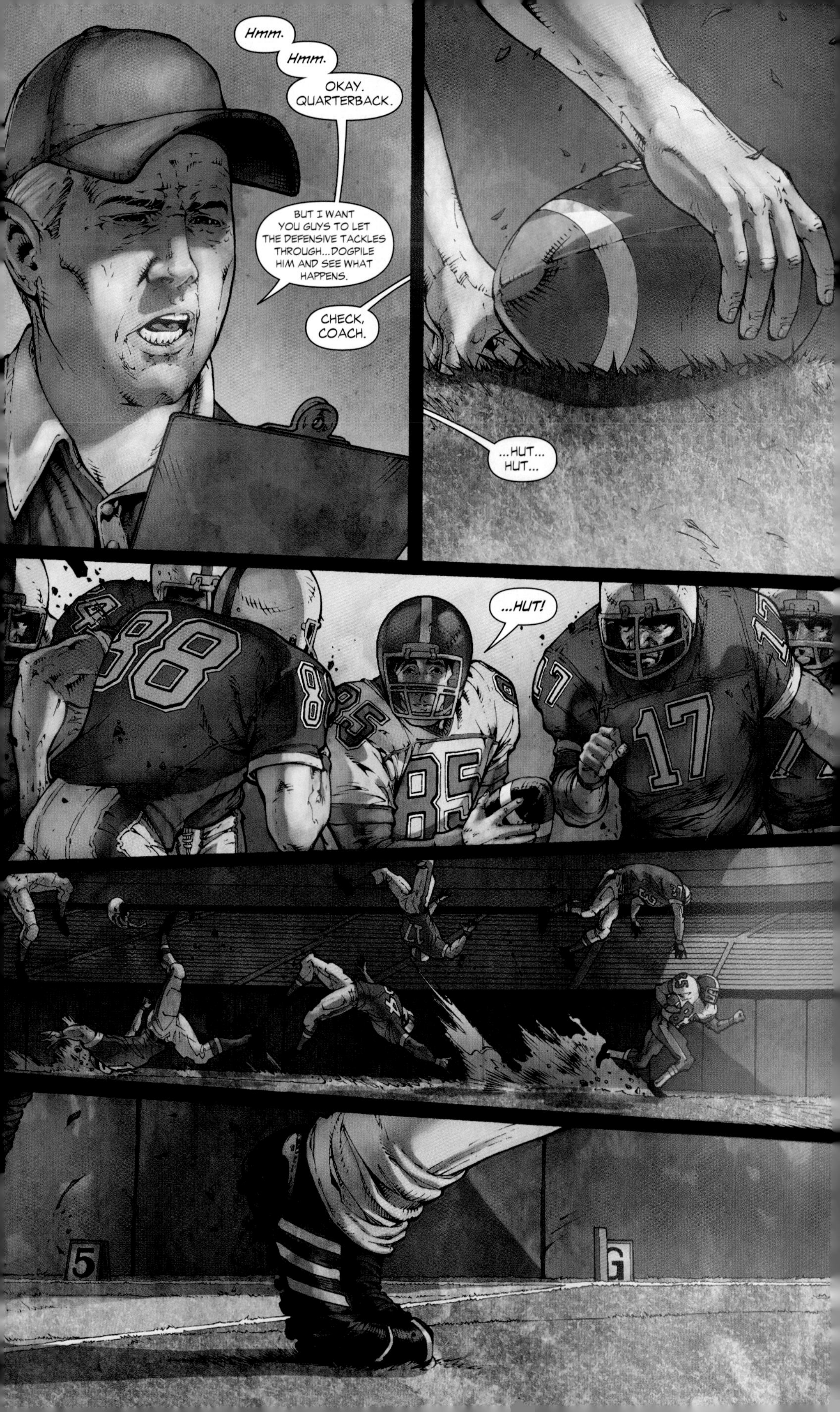

Hmm.
Hmm.
OKAY. QUARTERBACK.
BUT I WANT YOU GUYS TO LET THE DEFENSIVE TACKLES THROUGH...DOGPILE HIM AND SEE WHAT HAPPENS.
CHECK, COACH.
...HUT... HUT...
...HUT!

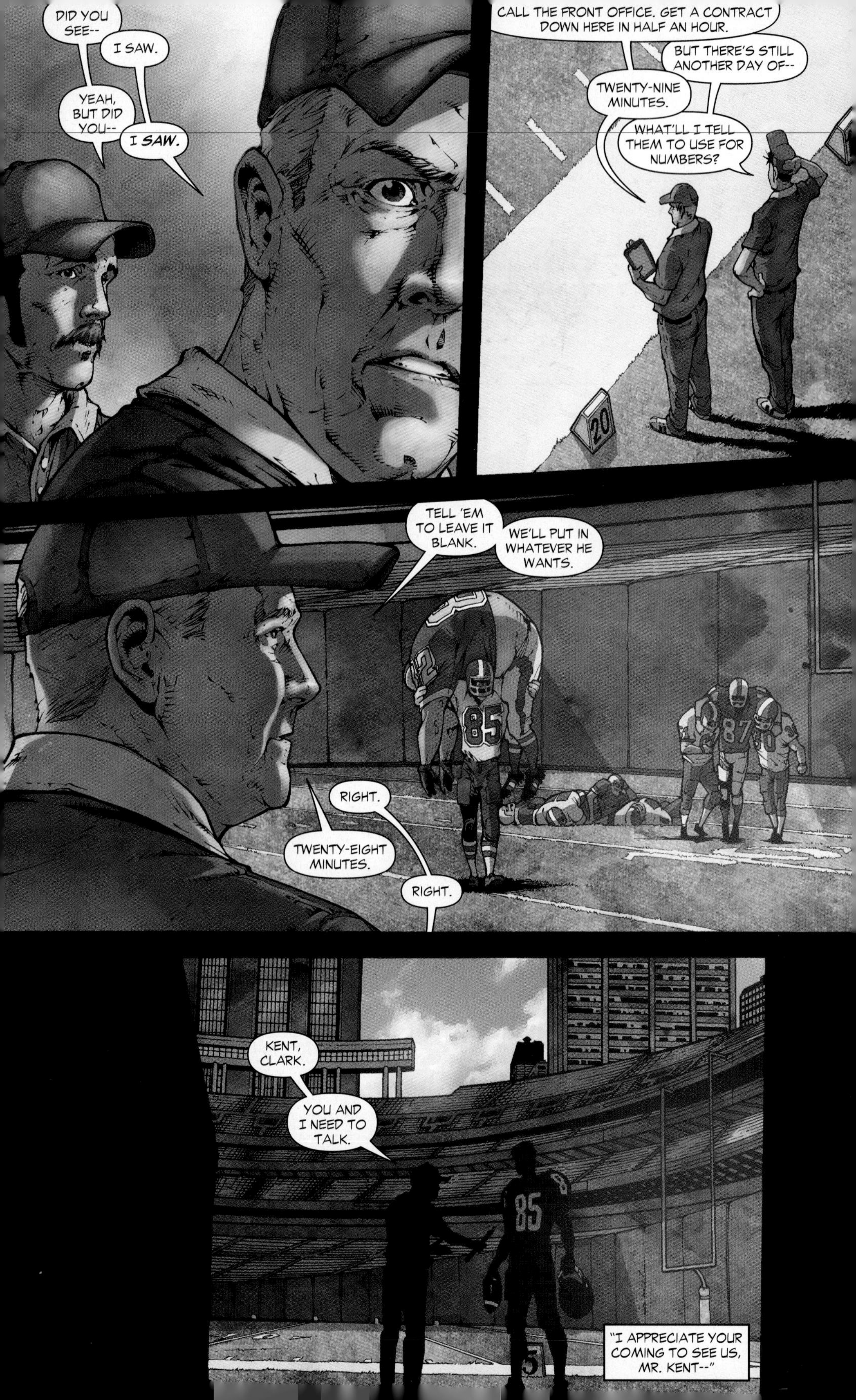
DID YOU SEE--
I SAW.
YEAH, BUT DID YOU--
I *SAW.*
CALL THE FRONT OFFICE. GET A CONTRACT DOWN HERE IN HALF AN HOUR.
BUT THERE'S STILL ANOTHER DAY OF--
TWENTY-NINE MINUTES.
WHAT'LL I TELL THEM TO USE FOR NUMBERS?
20
TELL 'EM TO LEAVE IT BLANK.
WE'LL PUT IN WHATEVER HE WANTS.
RIGHT.
TWENTY-EIGHT MINUTES.
RIGHT.
KENT, CLARK.
YOU AND I NEED TO TALK.
"I APPRECIATE YOUR COMING TO SEE US, MR. KENT--"

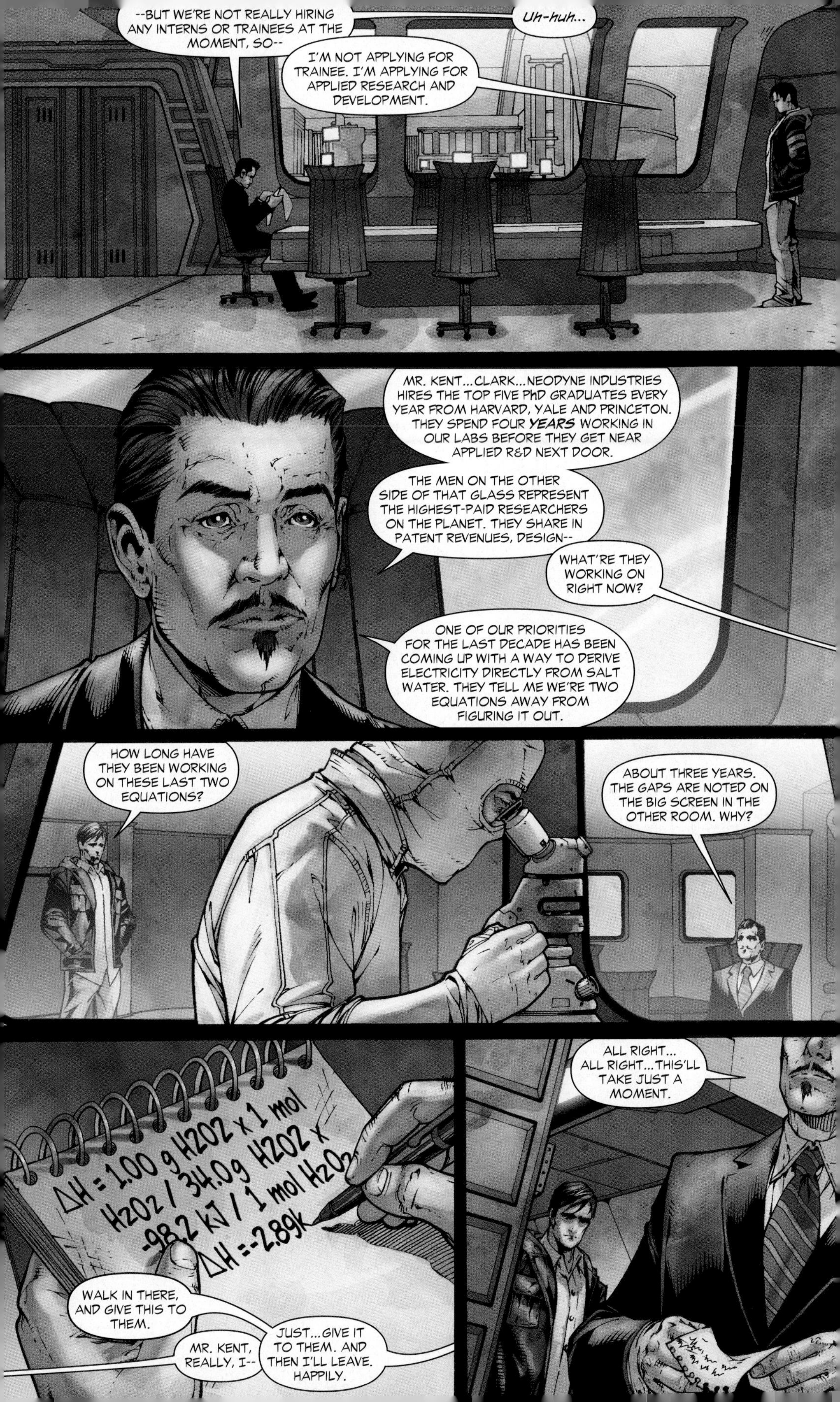
--BUT WE'RE NOT REALLY HIRING ANY INTERNS OR TRAINEES AT THE MOMENT, SO--
Uh-huh...
I'M NOT APPLYING FOR TRAINEE. I'M APPLYING FOR APPLIED RESEARCH AND DEVELOPMENT.
MR. KENT...CLARK...NEODYNE INDUSTRIES HIRES THE TOP FIVE PhD GRADUATES EVERY YEAR FROM HARVARD, YALE AND PRINCETON. THEY SPEND FOUR YEARS WORKING IN OUR LABS BEFORE THEY GET NEAR APPLIED R&D NEXT DOOR.
THE MEN ON THE OTHER SIDE OF THAT GLASS REPRESENT THE HIGHEST-PAID RESEARCHERS ON THE PLANET. THEY SHARE IN PATENT REVENUES, DESIGN--
WHAT'RE THEY WORKING ON RIGHT NOW?
ONE OF OUR PRIORITIES FOR THE LAST DECADE HAS BEEN COMING UP WITH A WAY TO DERIVE ELECTRICITY DIRECTLY FROM SALT WATER. THEY TELL ME WE'RE TWO EQUATIONS AWAY FROM FIGURING IT OUT.
HOW LONG HAVE THEY BEEN WORKING ON THESE LAST TWO EQUATIONS?
ABOUT THREE YEARS. THE GAPS ARE NOTED ON THE BIG SCREEN IN THE OTHER ROOM. WHY?
ΔH = 1.00 g H2O2 x 1 mol H2O2 / 34.0g H2O2 x -98.2 kJ / 1 mol H2O2
ΔH = -2.89k
WALK IN THERE, AND GIVE THIS TO THEM.
MR. KENT, REALLY, I--
JUST...GIVE IT TO THEM. AND THEN I'LL LEAVE. HAPPILY.
ALL RIGHT... ALL RIGHT...THIS'LL TAKE JUST A MOMENT.

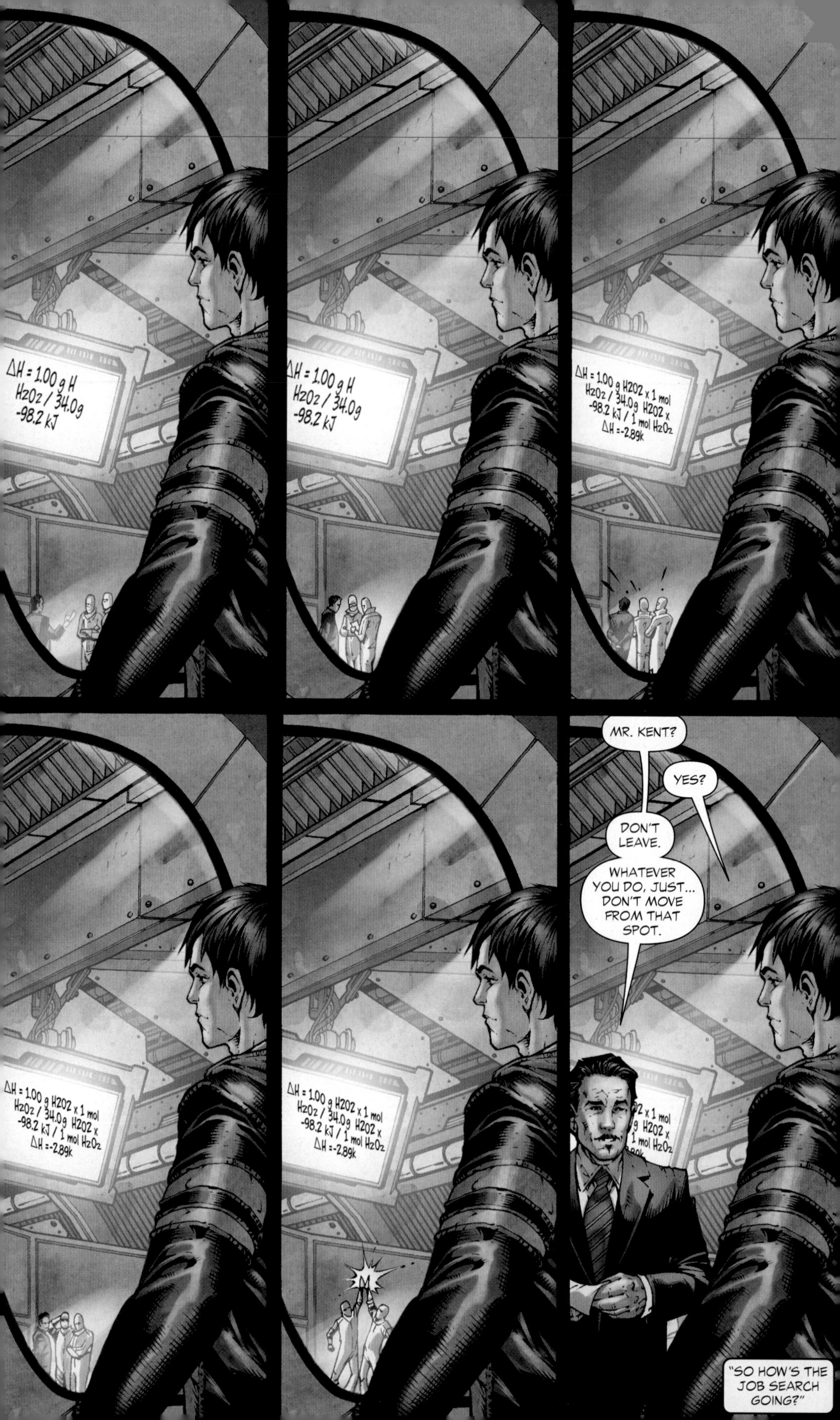
ΔH = 1.00 g H
H2O2 / 34.0g
-98.2 kJ
ΔH = 1.00 g H
H2O2 / 34.0g
-98.2 kJ
ΔH = 1.00 g H2O2 x 1 mol
H2O2 / 34.0g H2O2 x
-98.2 kJ / 1 mol H2O2
ΔH = -2.89k
ΔH = 1.00 g H2O2 x 1 mol
H2O2 / 34.0g H2O2 x
-98.2 kJ / 1 mol H2O2
ΔH = -2.89k
ΔH = 1.00 g H2O2 x 1 mol
H2O2 / 34.0g H2O2 x
-98.2 kJ / 1 mol H2O2
ΔH = -2.89k
MR. KENT?
YES?
DON'T LEAVE.
WHATEVER YOU DO, JUST... DON'T MOVE FROM THAT SPOT.
"SO HOW'S THE JOB SEARCH GOING?"

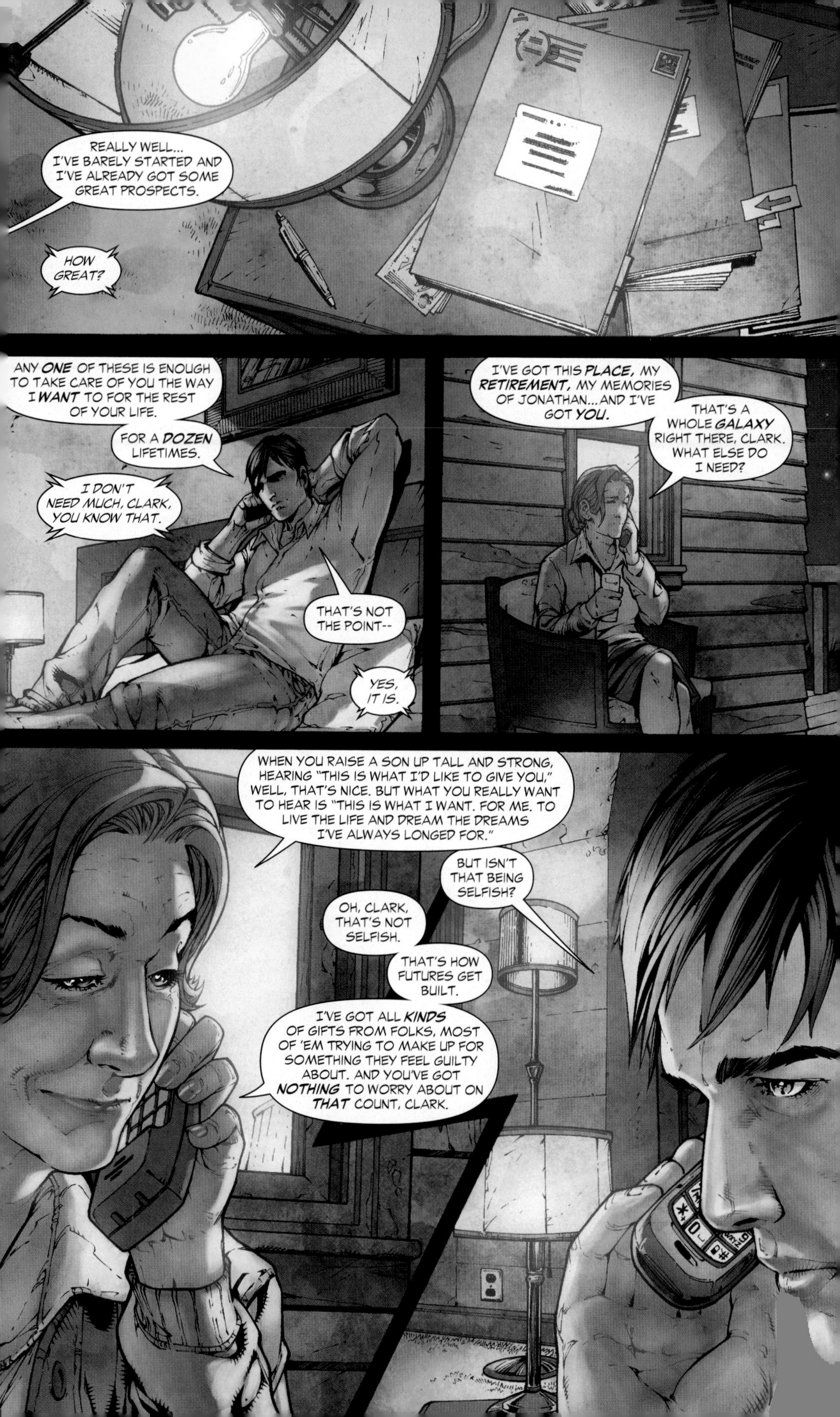

REALLY WELL... I'VE BARELY STARTED AND I'VE ALREADY GOT SOME GREAT PROSPECTS.
HOW GREAT?
ANY ONE OF THESE IS ENOUGH TO TAKE CARE OF YOU THE WAY I WANT TO FOR THE REST OF YOUR LIFE.
FOR A DOZEN LIFETIMES.
I DON'T NEED MUCH, CLARK, YOU KNOW THAT.
THAT'S NOT THE POINT--
YES, IT IS.
I'VE GOT THIS PLACE, MY RETIREMENT, MY MEMORIES OF JONATHAN... AND I'VE GOT YOU.
THAT'S A WHOLE GALAXY RIGHT THERE, CLARK. WHAT ELSE DO I NEED?
WHEN YOU RAISE A SON UP TALL AND STRONG, HEARING "THIS IS WHAT I'D LIKE TO GIVE YOU," WELL, THAT'S NICE. BUT WHAT YOU REALLY WANT TO HEAR IS "THIS IS WHAT I WANT. FOR ME. TO LIVE THE LIFE AND DREAM THE DREAMS I'VE ALWAYS LONGED FOR."
BUT ISN'T THAT BEING SELFISH?
OH, CLARK, THAT'S NOT SELFISH.
THAT'S HOW FUTURES GET BUILT.
I'VE GOT ALL KINDS OF GIFTS FROM FOLKS, MOST OF 'EM TRYING TO MAKE UP FOR SOMETHING THEY FEEL GUILTY ABOUT. AND YOU'VE GOT NOTHING TO WORRY ABOUT ON THAT COUNT, CLARK.

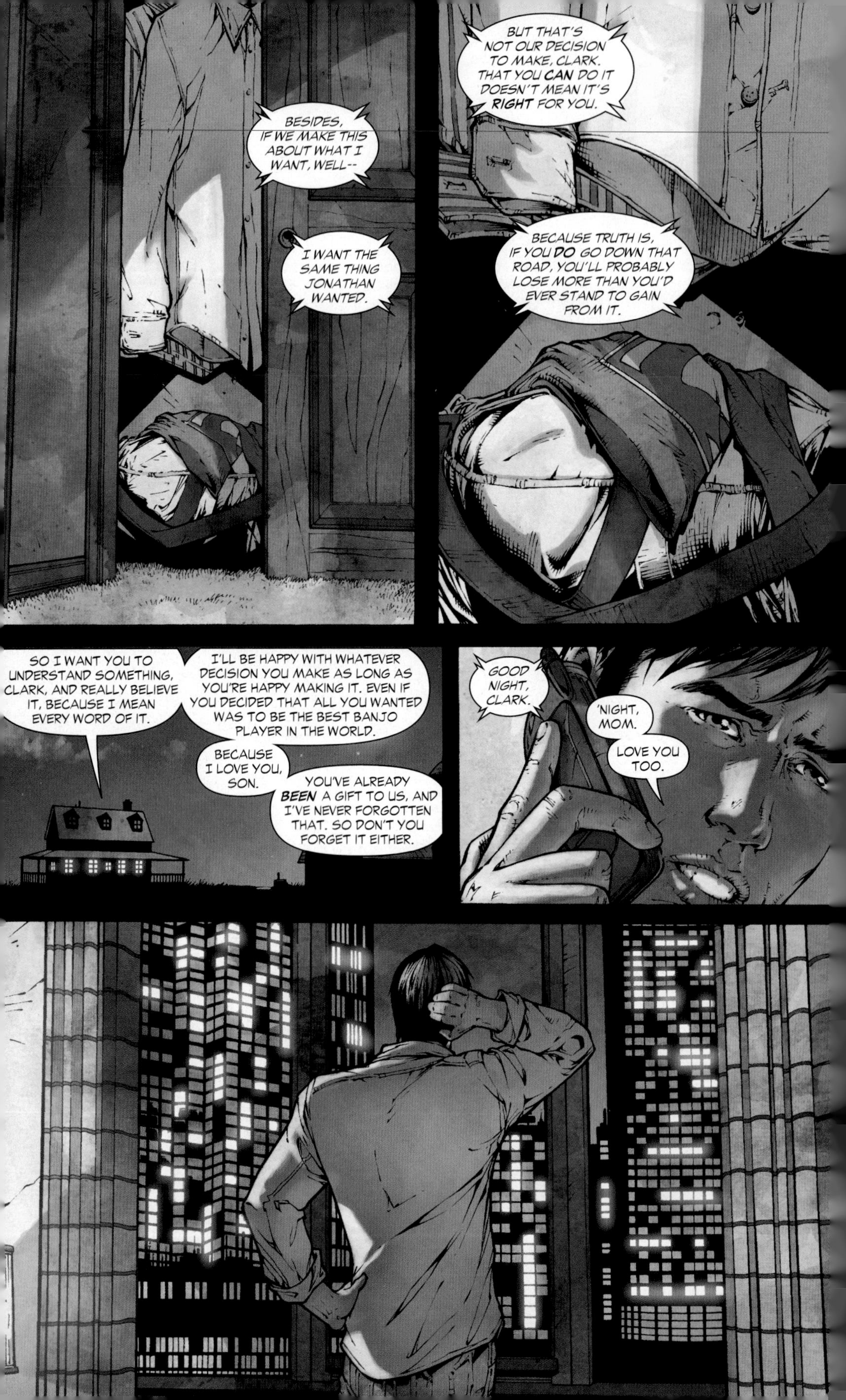
BESIDES, IF WE MAKE THIS ABOUT WHAT I WANT, WELL--
I WANT THE SAME THING JONATHAN WANTED.
BUT THAT'S NOT OUR DECISION TO MAKE, CLARK. THAT YOU CAN DO IT DOESN'T MEAN IT'S RIGHT FOR YOU.
BECAUSE TRUTH IS, IF YOU DO GO DOWN THAT ROAD, YOU'LL PROBABLY LOSE MORE THAN YOU'D EVER STAND TO GAIN FROM IT.
SO I WANT YOU TO UNDERSTAND SOMETHING, CLARK, AND REALLY BELIEVE IT, BECAUSE I MEAN EVERY WORD OF IT.
I'LL BE HAPPY WITH WHATEVER DECISION YOU MAKE AS LONG AS YOU'RE HAPPY MAKING IT. EVEN IF YOU DECIDED THAT ALL YOU WANTED WAS TO BE THE BEST BANJO PLAYER IN THE WORLD.
BECAUSE I LOVE YOU, SON.
YOU'VE ALREADY BEEN A GIFT TO US, AND I'VE NEVER FORGOTTEN THAT. SO DON'T YOU FORGET IT EITHER.
GOOD NIGHT, CLARK.
'NIGHT, MOM.
LOVE YOU TOO.

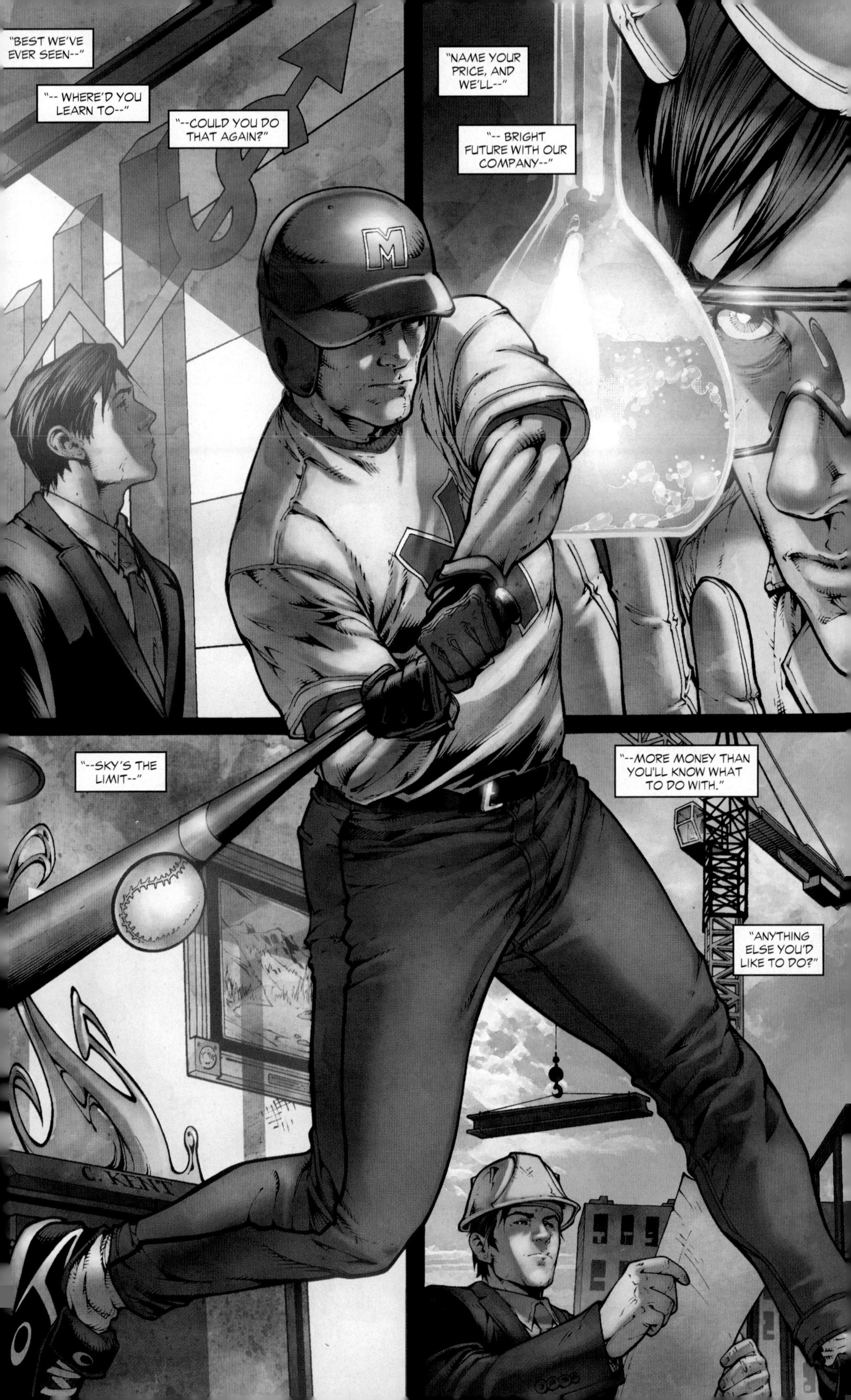
"BEST WE'VE EVER SEEN--"
"-- WHERE'D YOU LEARN TO--"
"--COULD YOU DO THAT AGAIN?"
"NAME YOUR PRICE, AND WE'LL--"
"-- BRIGHT FUTURE WITH OUR COMPANY--"
"--SKY'S THE LIMIT--"
"--MORE MONEY THAN YOU'LL KNOW WHAT TO DO WITH."
"ANYTHING ELSE YOU'D LIKE TO DO?"
C. KENT

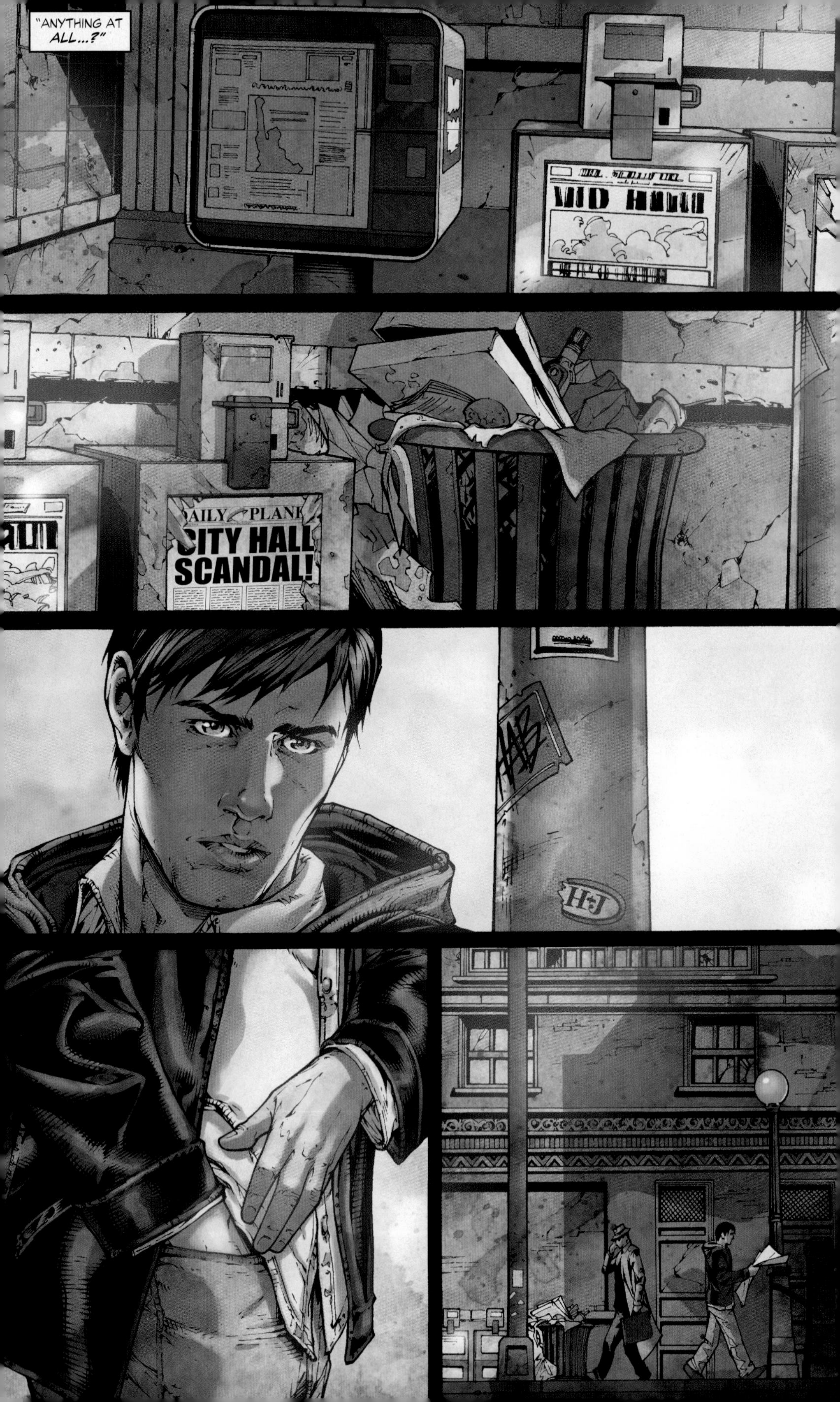

"ANYTHING AT ALL...?"
DAILY PLANET
CITY HALL SCANDAL!

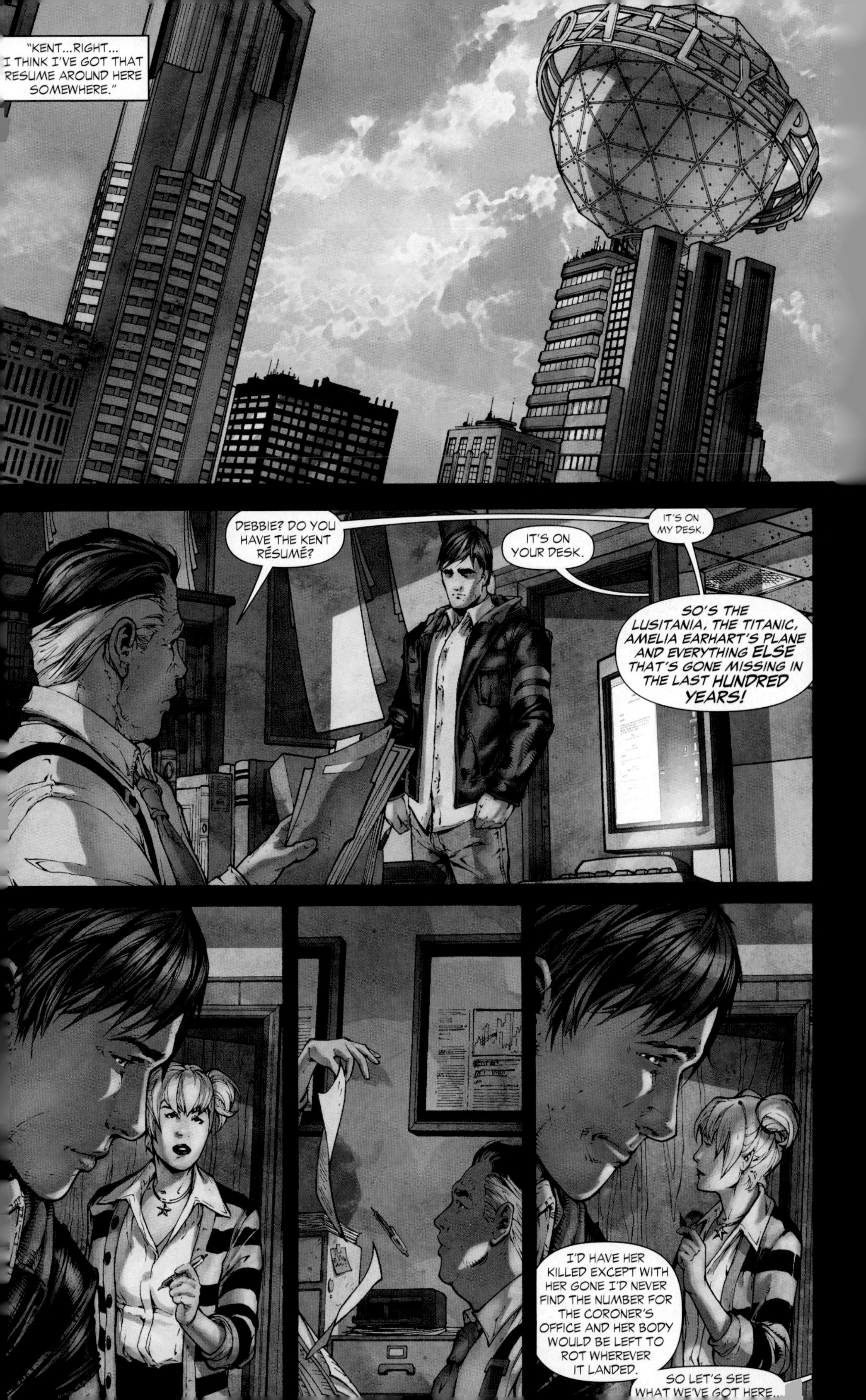

"KENT...RIGHT... I THINK I'VE GOT THAT RESUME AROUND HERE SOMEWHERE."
DEBBIE? DO YOU HAVE THE KENT RÉSUMÉ?
IT'S ON YOUR DESK.
IT'S ON MY DESK.
SO'S THE LUSITANIA, THE TITANIC, AMELIA EARHART'S PLANE AND EVERYTHING ELSE THAT'S GONE MISSING IN THE LAST HUNDRED YEARS!
I'D HAVE HER KILLED EXCEPT WITH HER GONE I'D NEVER FIND THE NUMBER FOR THE CORONER'S OFFICE AND HER BODY WOULD BE LEFT TO ROT WHEREVER IT LANDED.
SO LET'S SEE WHAT WE'VE GOT HERE...

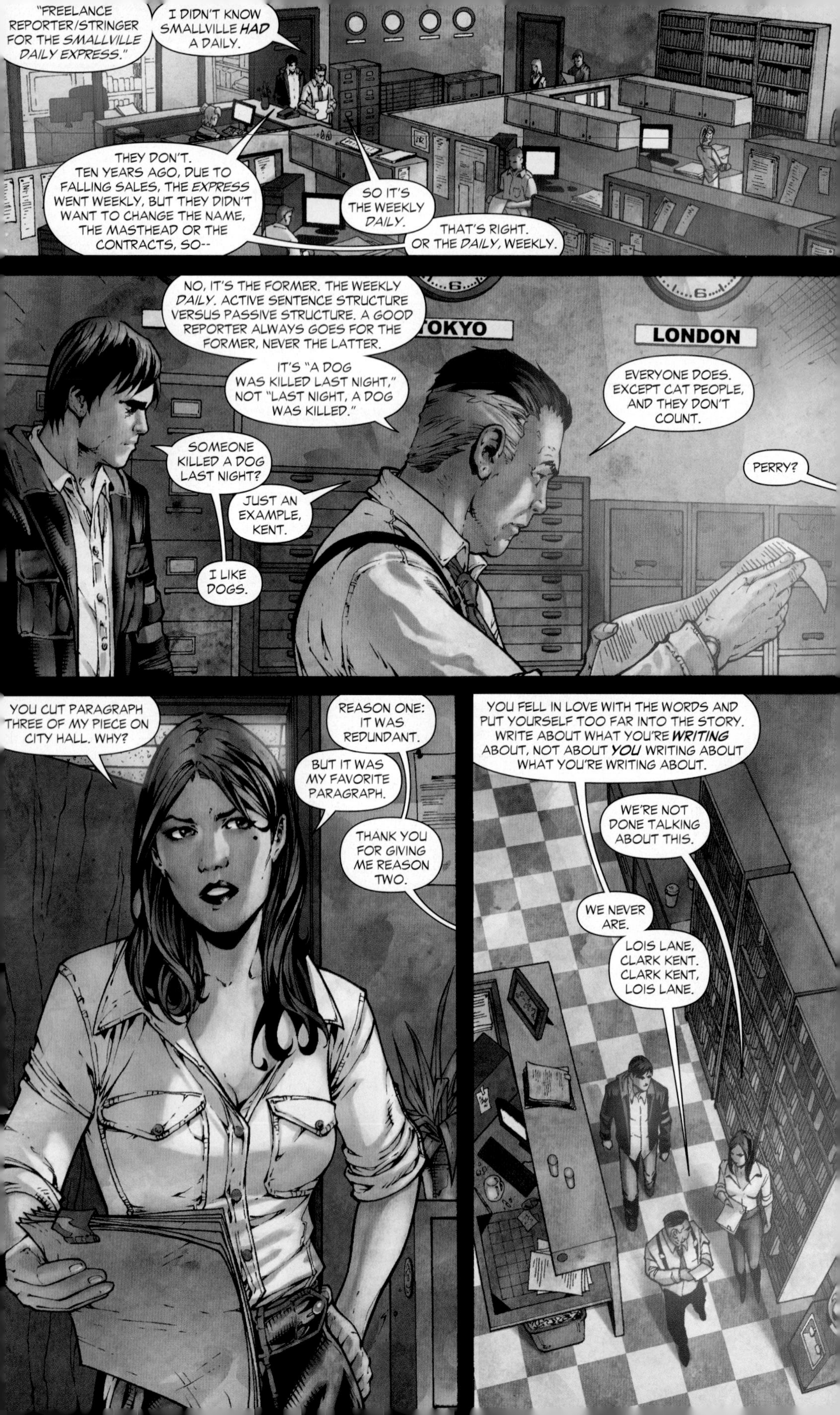

"FREELANCE REPORTER/STRINGER FOR THE SMALLVILLE DAILY EXPRESS."
I DIDN'T KNOW SMALLVILLE HAD A DAILY.
THEY DON'T. TEN YEARS AGO, DUE TO FALLING SALES, THE EXPRESS WENT WEEKLY, BUT THEY DIDN'T WANT TO CHANGE THE NAME, THE MASTHEAD OR THE CONTRACTS, SO--
SO IT'S THE WEEKLY DAILY.
THAT'S RIGHT. OR THE DAILY, WEEKLY.
NO, IT'S THE FORMER. THE WEEKLY DAILY. ACTIVE SENTENCE STRUCTURE VERSUS PASSIVE STRUCTURE. A GOOD REPORTER ALWAYS GOES FOR THE FORMER, NEVER THE LATTER.
TOKYO
LONDON
IT'S "A DOG WAS KILLED LAST NIGHT," NOT "LAST NIGHT, A DOG WAS KILLED."
SOMEONE KILLED A DOG LAST NIGHT?
JUST AN EXAMPLE, KENT.
I LIKE DOGS.
EVERYONE DOES. EXCEPT CAT PEOPLE, AND THEY DON'T COUNT.
PERRY?
YOU CUT PARAGRAPH THREE OF MY PIECE ON CITY HALL. WHY?
REASON ONE: IT WAS REDUNDANT.
BUT IT WAS MY FAVORITE PARAGRAPH.
THANK YOU FOR GIVING ME REASON TWO.
YOU FELL IN LOVE WITH THE WORDS AND PUT YOURSELF TOO FAR INTO THE STORY. WRITE ABOUT WHAT YOU'RE WRITING ABOUT, NOT ABOUT YOU WRITING ABOUT WHAT YOU'RE WRITING ABOUT.
WE'RE NOT DONE TALKING ABOUT THIS.
WE NEVER ARE.
LOIS LANE, CLARK KENT. CLARK KENT, LOIS LANE.

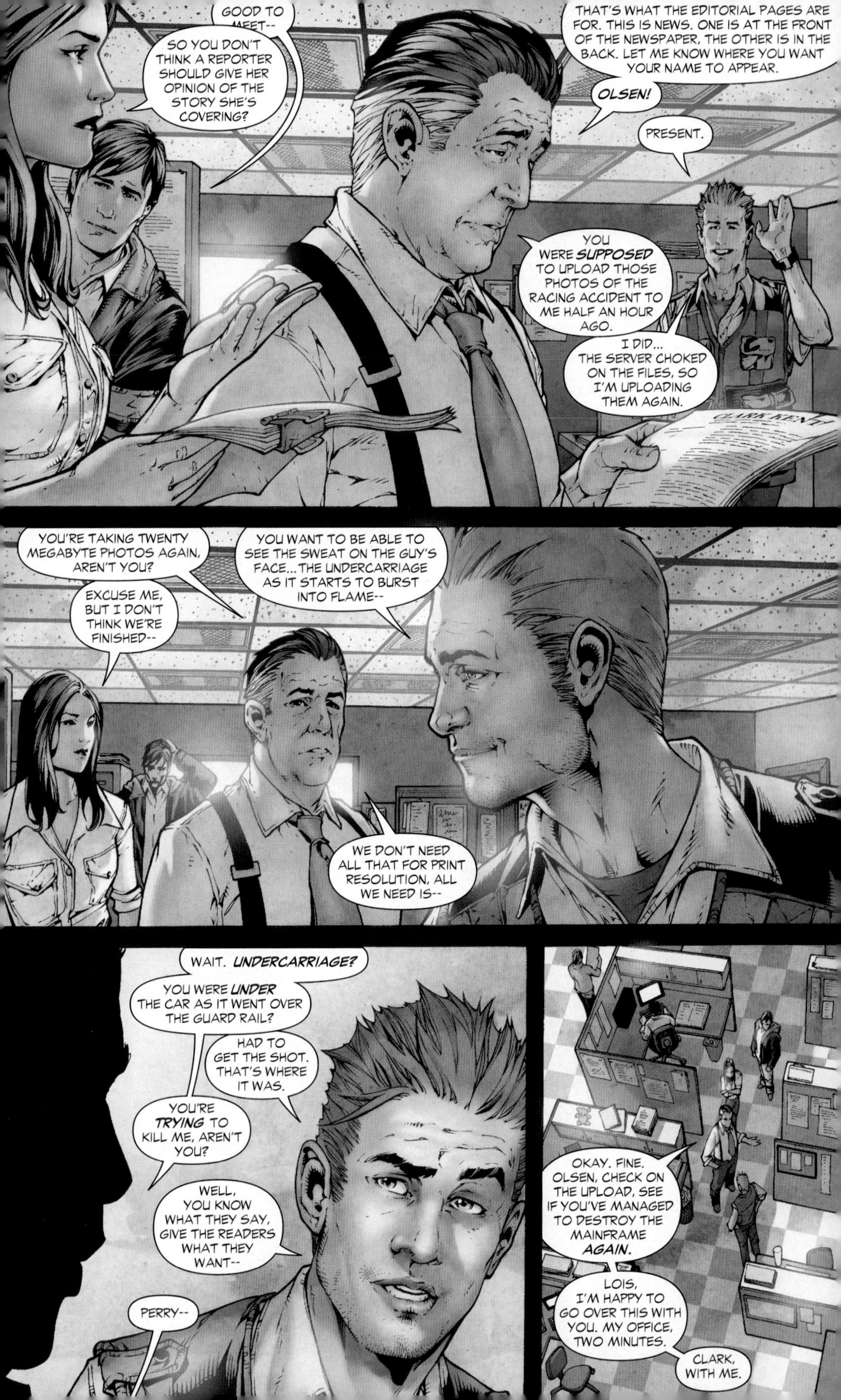

GOOD TO MEET--
SO YOU DON'T THINK A REPORTER SHOULD GIVE HER OPINION OF THE STORY SHE'S COVERING?
THAT'S WHAT THE EDITORIAL PAGES ARE FOR. THIS IS NEWS. ONE IS AT THE FRONT OF THE NEWSPAPER, THE OTHER IS IN THE BACK. LET ME KNOW WHERE YOU WANT YOUR NAME TO APPEAR.
OLSEN!
PRESENT.
YOU WERE *SUPPOSED* TO UPLOAD THOSE PHOTOS OF THE RACING ACCIDENT TO ME HALF AN HOUR AGO.
I DID... THE SERVER CHOKED ON THE FILES, SO I'M UPLOADING THEM AGAIN.
CLARK KENT
YOU'RE TAKING TWENTY MEGABYTE PHOTOS AGAIN, AREN'T YOU?
EXCUSE ME, BUT I DON'T THINK WE'RE FINISHED--
YOU WANT TO BE ABLE TO SEE THE SWEAT ON THE GUY'S FACE... THE UNDERCARRIAGE AS IT STARTS TO BURST INTO FLAME--
WE DON'T NEED ALL THAT FOR PRINT RESOLUTION, ALL WE NEED IS--
WAIT. *UNDERCARRIAGE?*
YOU WERE *UNDER* THE CAR AS IT WENT OVER THE GUARD RAIL?
HAD TO GET THE SHOT. THAT'S WHERE IT WAS.
YOU'RE *TRYING* TO KILL ME, AREN'T YOU?
WELL, YOU KNOW WHAT THEY SAY, GIVE THE READERS WHAT THEY WANT--
PERRY--
OKAY. FINE. OLSEN, CHECK ON THE UPLOAD, SEE IF YOU'VE MANAGED TO DESTROY THE MAINFRAME *AGAIN.*
LOIS, I'M HAPPY TO GO OVER THIS WITH YOU. MY OFFICE, TWO MINUTES.
CLARK, WITH ME.

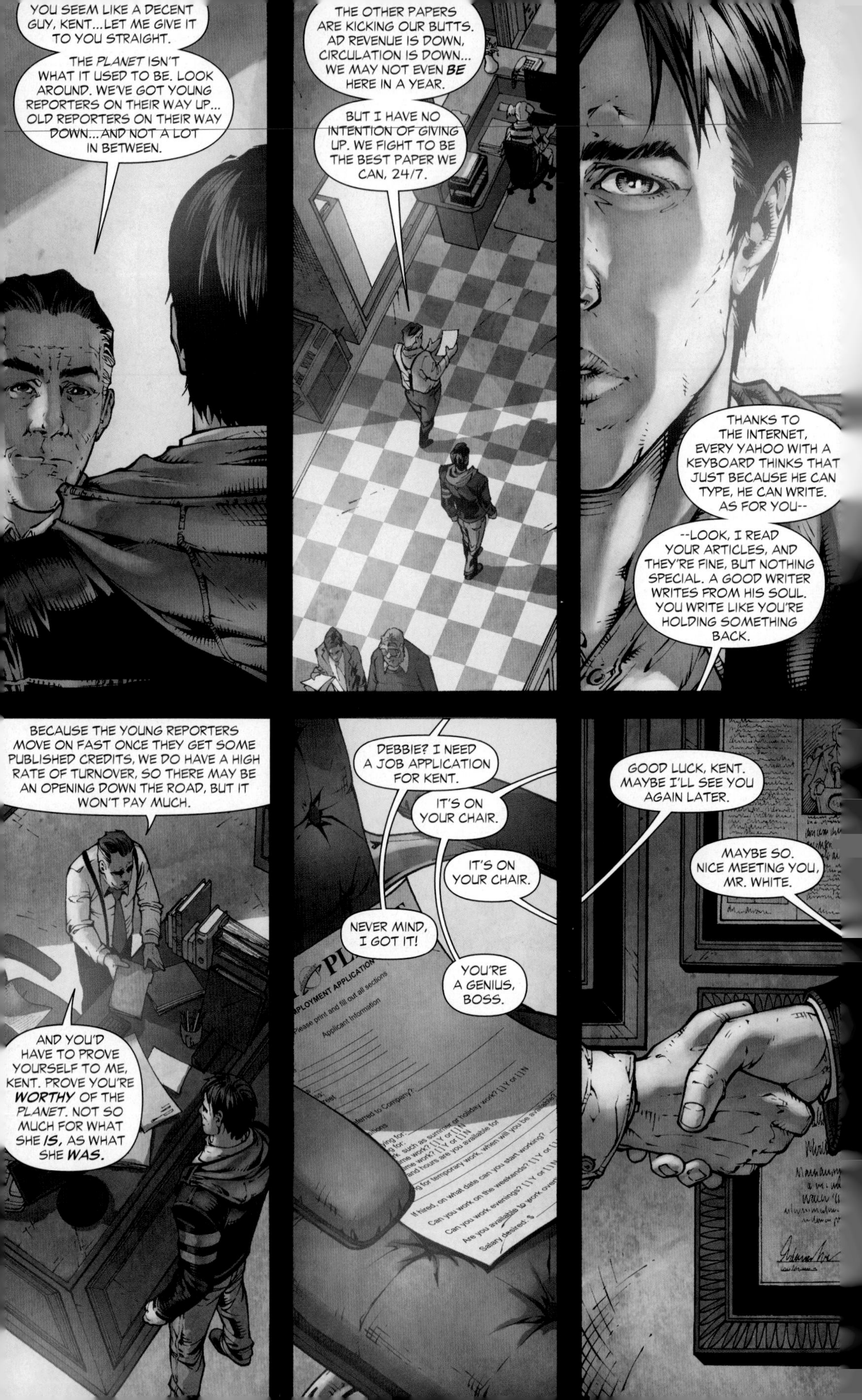
YOU SEEM LIKE A DECENT GUY, KENT...LET ME GIVE IT TO YOU STRAIGHT.
THE *PLANET* ISN'T WHAT IT USED TO BE. LOOK AROUND. WE'VE GOT YOUNG REPORTERS ON THEIR WAY UP... OLD REPORTERS ON THEIR WAY DOWN...AND NOT A LOT IN BETWEEN.
THE OTHER PAPERS ARE KICKING OUR BUTTS. AD REVENUE IS DOWN, CIRCULATION IS DOWN... WE MAY NOT EVEN ***BE*** HERE IN A YEAR.
BUT I HAVE NO INTENTION OF GIVING UP. WE FIGHT TO BE THE BEST PAPER WE CAN, 24/7.
THANKS TO THE INTERNET, EVERY YAHOO WITH A KEYBOARD THINKS THAT JUST BECAUSE HE CAN TYPE, HE CAN WRITE. AS FOR YOU--
--LOOK, I READ YOUR ARTICLES, AND THEY'RE FINE, BUT NOTHING SPECIAL. A GOOD WRITER WRITES FROM HIS SOUL. YOU WRITE LIKE YOU'RE HOLDING SOMETHING BACK.
BECAUSE THE YOUNG REPORTERS MOVE ON FAST ONCE THEY GET SOME PUBLISHED CREDITS, WE DO HAVE A HIGH RATE OF TURNOVER, SO THERE MAY BE AN OPENING DOWN THE ROAD, BUT IT WON'T PAY MUCH.
AND YOU'D HAVE TO PROVE YOURSELF TO ME, KENT. PROVE YOU'RE ***WORTHY*** OF THE *PLANET*. NOT SO MUCH FOR WHAT SHE ***IS***, AS WHAT SHE ***WAS***.
DEBBIE? I NEED A JOB APPLICATION FOR KENT.
IT'S ON YOUR CHAIR.
IT'S ON YOUR CHAIR.
NEVER MIND, I GOT IT!
YOU'RE A GENIUS, BOSS.
PLANET
EMPLOYMENT APPLICATION
Please print and fill out all sections
Applicant Information
If hired, on what date can you start working?
Can you work on the weekends? [ ] Y or [ ] N
Can you work evenings? [ ] Y or [ ] N
Salary desired: $
GOOD LUCK, KENT. MAYBE I'LL SEE YOU AGAIN LATER.
MAYBE SO. NICE MEETING YOU, MR. WHITE.

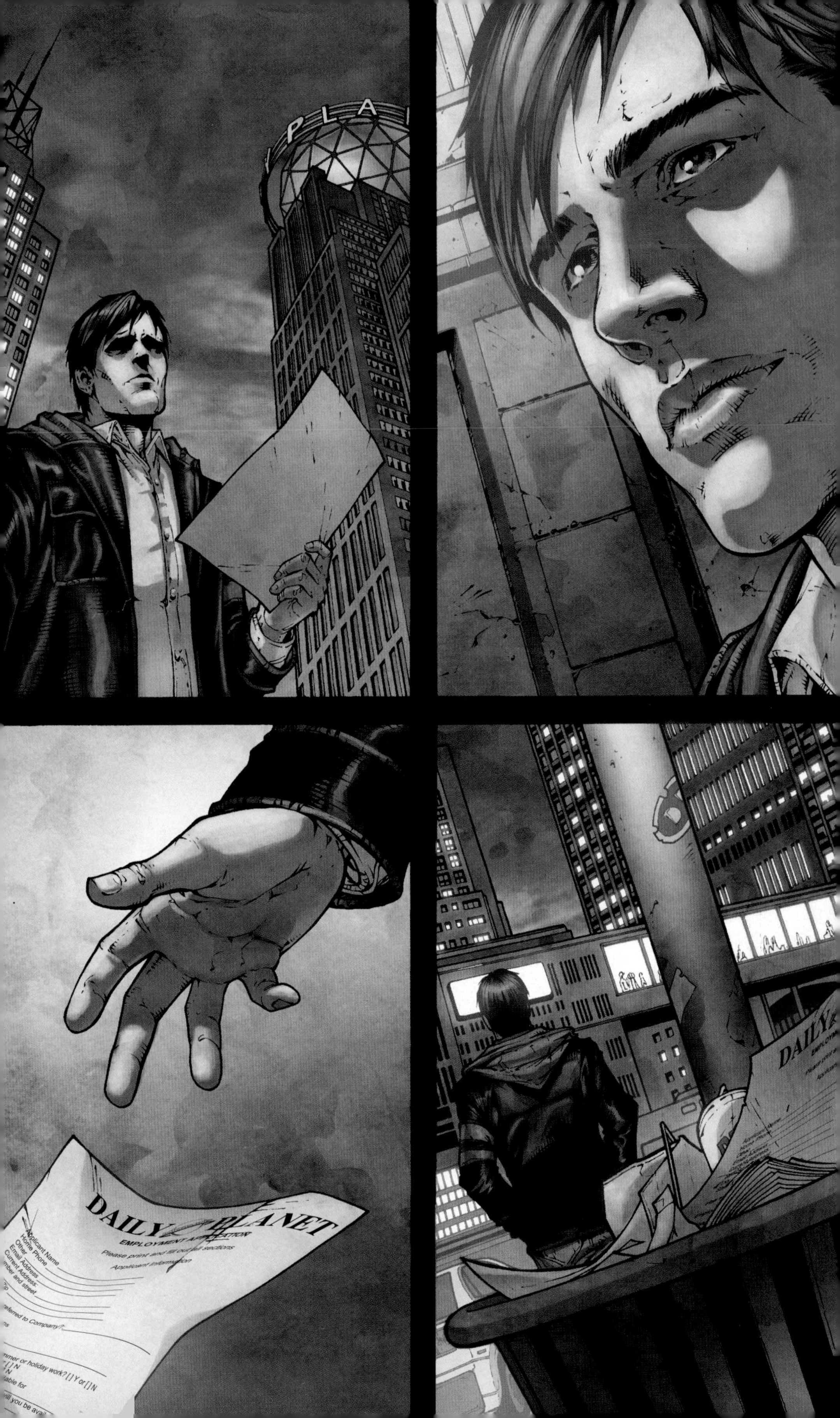
DAILY PLANET
Applicant Name
Home Phone
Other Phone
Email Address:
Current Address:

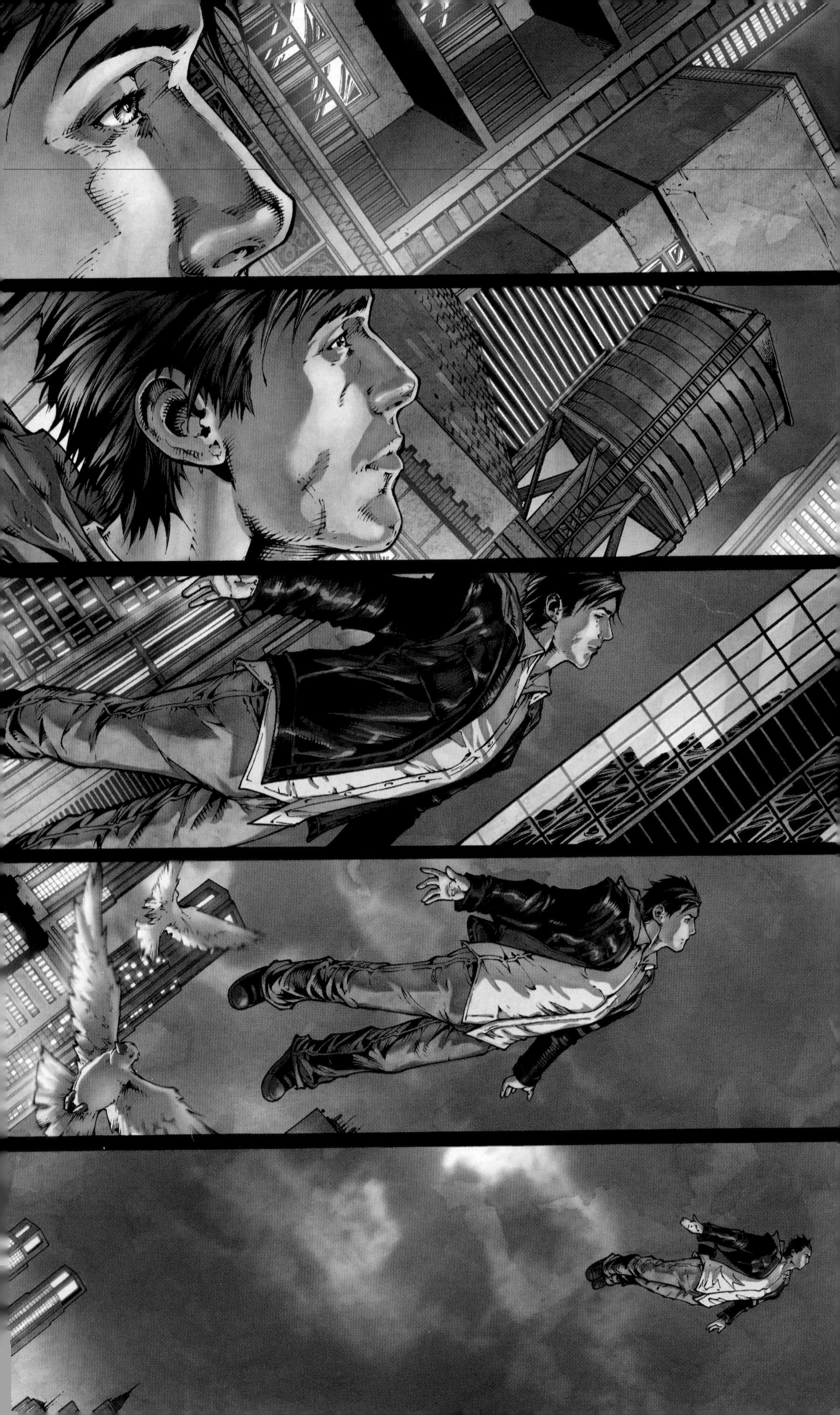

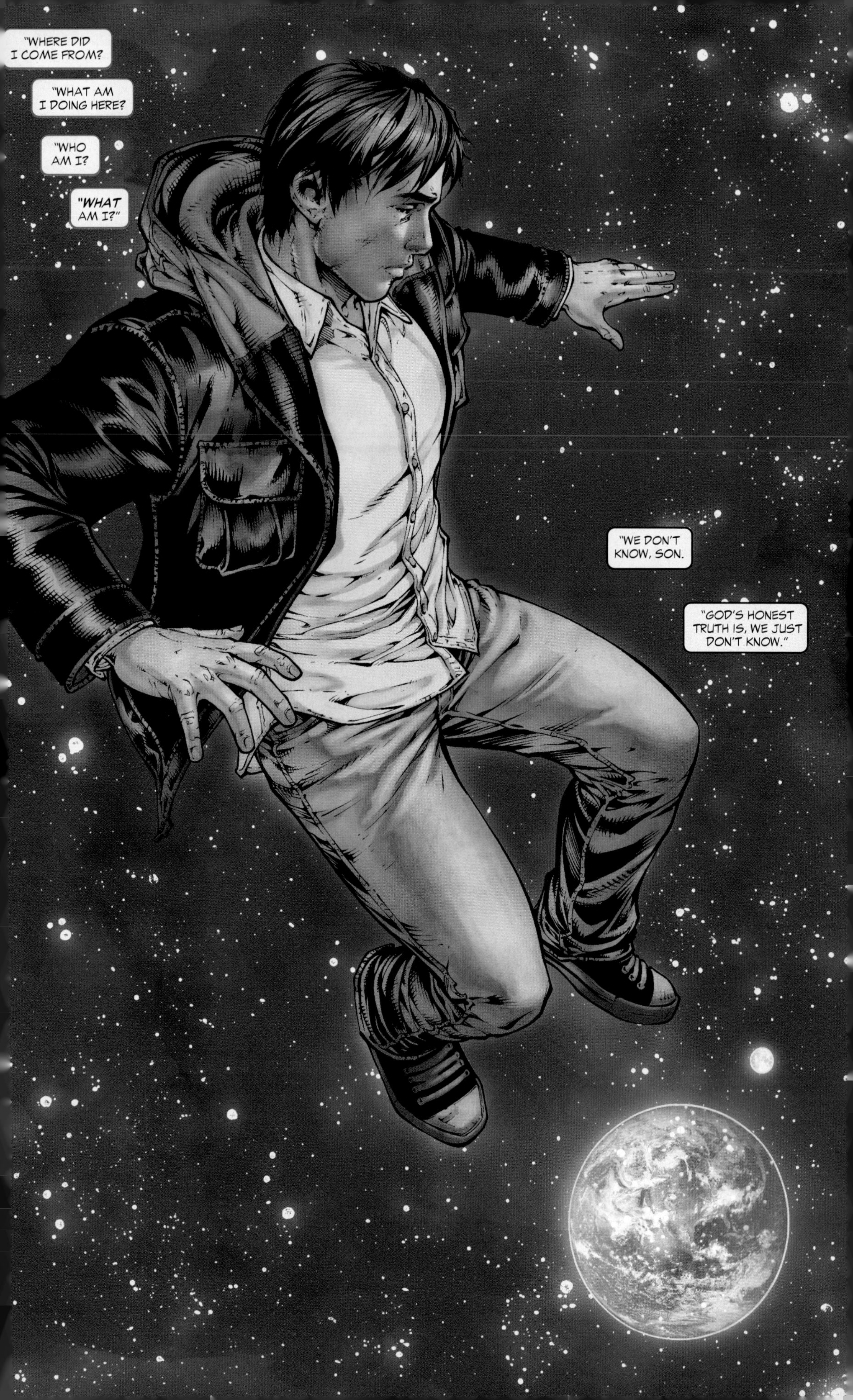
"WHERE DID I COME FROM?
"WHAT AM I DOING HERE?
"WHO AM I?
"WHAT AM I?"
"WE DON'T KNOW, SON.
"GOD'S HONEST TRUTH IS, WE JUST DON'T KNOW."

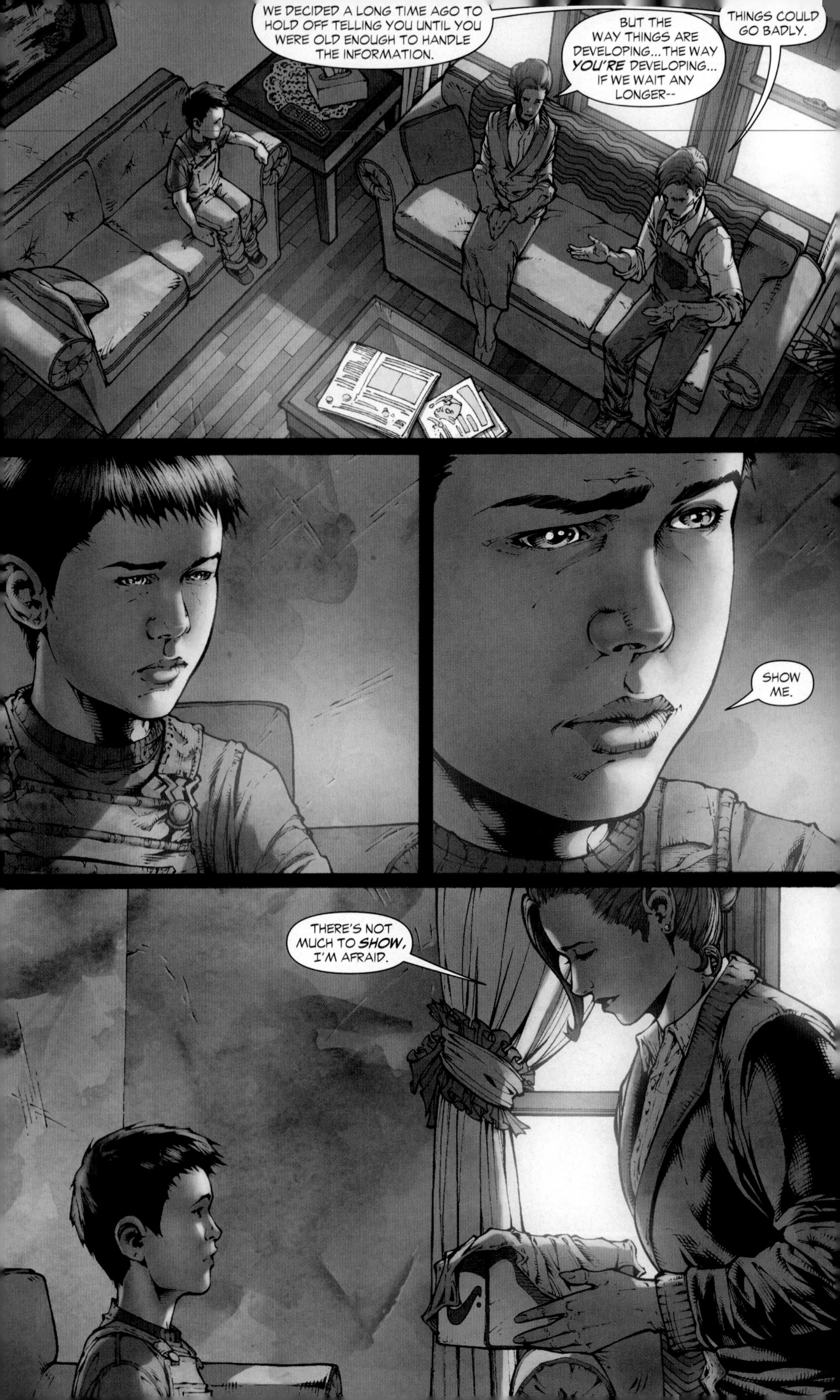
WE DECIDED A LONG TIME AGO TO HOLD OFF TELLING YOU UNTIL YOU WERE OLD ENOUGH TO HANDLE THE INFORMATION.
BUT THE WAY THINGS ARE DEVELOPING...THE WAY *YOU'RE* DEVELOPING... IF WE WAIT ANY LONGER--
THINGS COULD GO BADLY.
SHOW ME.
THERE'S NOT MUCH TO *SHOW*, I'M AFRAID.

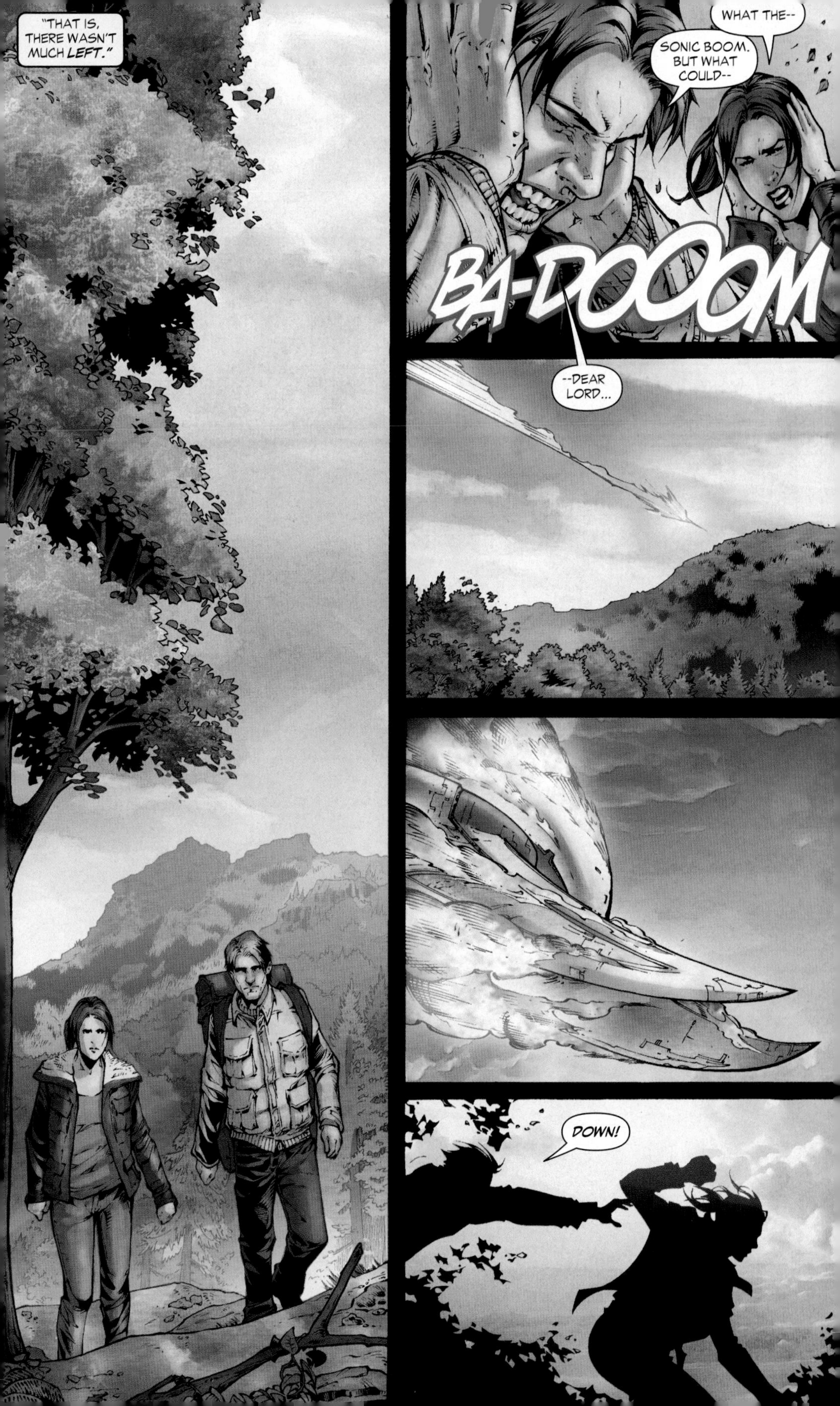
"THAT IS, THERE WASN'T MUCH *LEFT.*"
WHAT THE--
SONIC BOOM. BUT WHAT COULD--
BA-DOOOOM
--DEAR LORD...
DOWN!

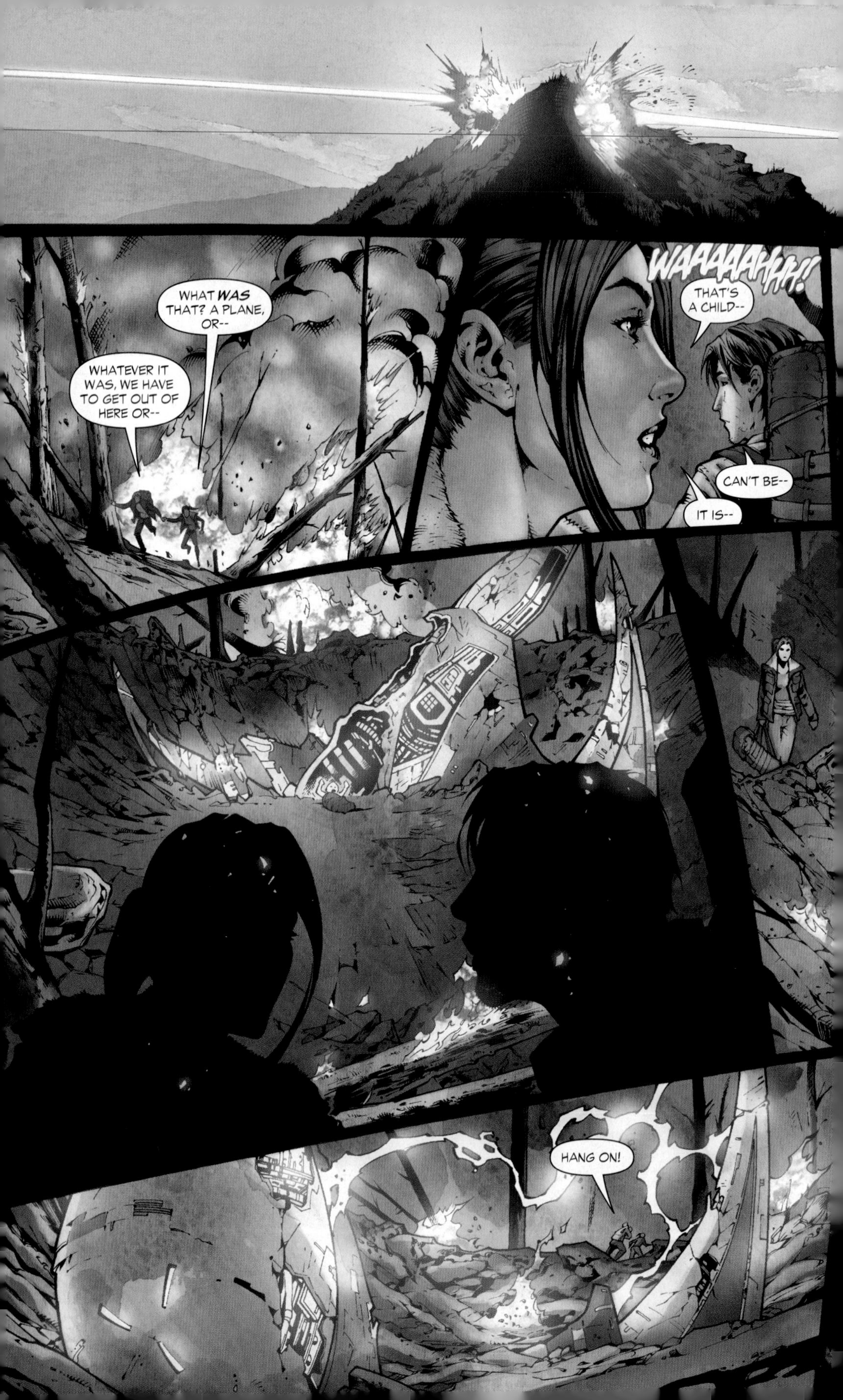
WHAT WAS THAT? A PLANE, OR--
WHATEVER IT WAS, WE HAVE TO GET OUT OF HERE OR--
WAAAAAHHH!!
THAT'S A CHILD--
CAN'T BE--
IT IS--
HANG ON!

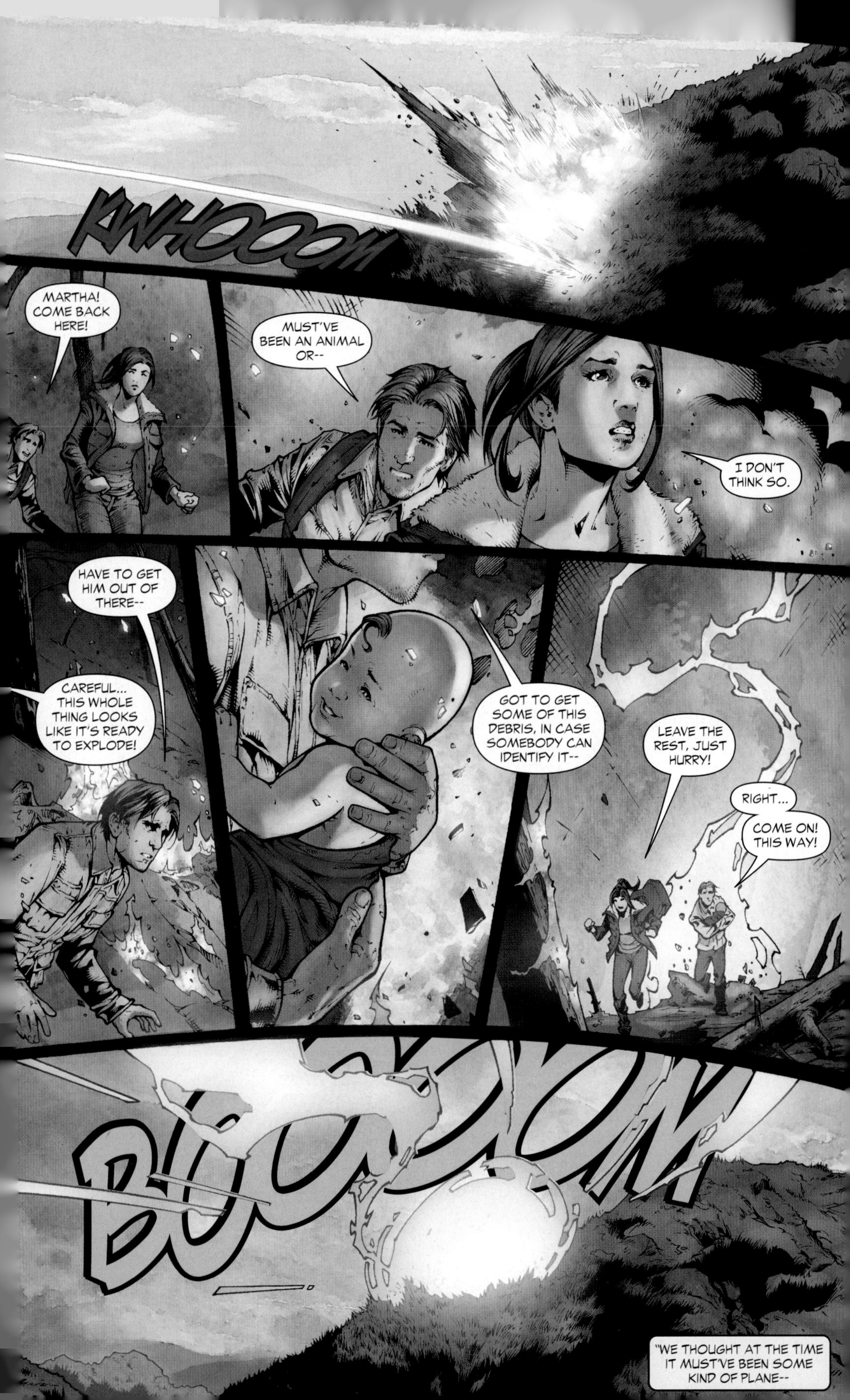
KWHOOOOM
MARTHA! COME BACK HERE!
MUST'VE BEEN AN ANIMAL OR--
I DON'T THINK SO.
HAVE TO GET HIM OUT OF THERE--
CAREFUL... THIS WHOLE THING LOOKS LIKE IT'S READY TO EXPLODE!
GOT TO GET SOME OF THIS DEBRIS, IN CASE SOMEBODY CAN IDENTIFY IT--
LEAVE THE REST, JUST HURRY!
RIGHT...
COME ON! THIS WAY!
BOOOOM
"WE THOUGHT AT THE TIME IT MUST'VE BEEN SOME KIND OF PLANE--

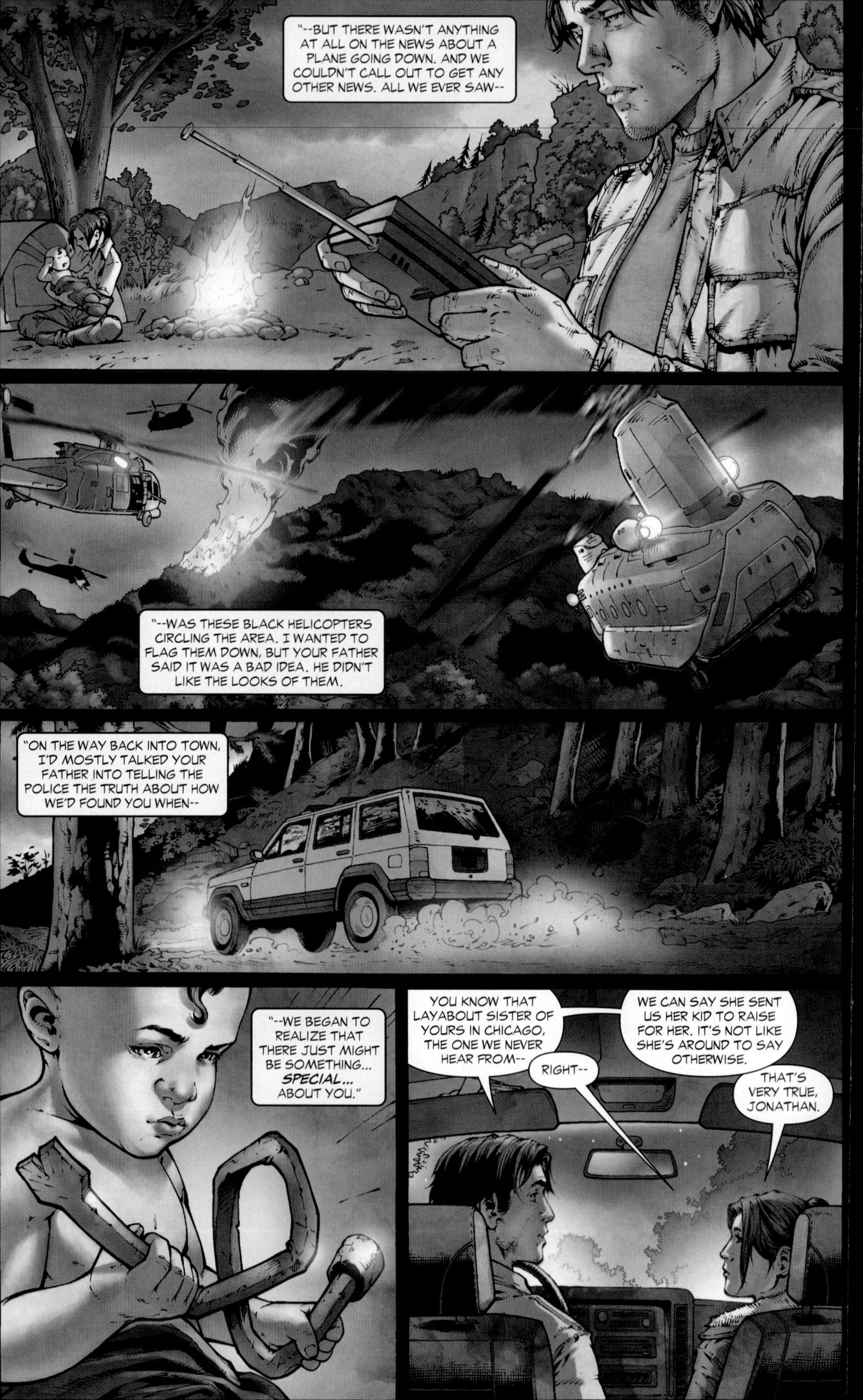
"--BUT THERE WASN'T ANYTHING AT ALL ON THE NEWS ABOUT A PLANE GOING DOWN. AND WE COULDN'T CALL OUT TO GET ANY OTHER NEWS. ALL WE EVER SAW--
"--WAS THESE BLACK HELICOPTERS CIRCLING THE AREA. I WANTED TO FLAG THEM DOWN, BUT YOUR FATHER SAID IT WAS A BAD IDEA. HE DIDN'T LIKE THE LOOKS OF THEM.
"ON THE WAY BACK INTO TOWN, I'D MOSTLY TALKED YOUR FATHER INTO TELLING THE POLICE THE TRUTH ABOUT HOW WE'D FOUND YOU WHEN--
"--WE BEGAN TO REALIZE THAT THERE JUST MIGHT BE SOMETHING... *SPECIAL*... ABOUT YOU."
YOU KNOW THAT LAYABOUT SISTER OF YOURS IN CHICAGO, THE ONE WE NEVER HEAR FROM--
RIGHT--
WE CAN SAY SHE SENT US HER KID TO RAISE FOR HER. IT'S NOT LIKE SHE'S AROUND TO SAY OTHERWISE.
THAT'S VERY TRUE, JONATHAN.

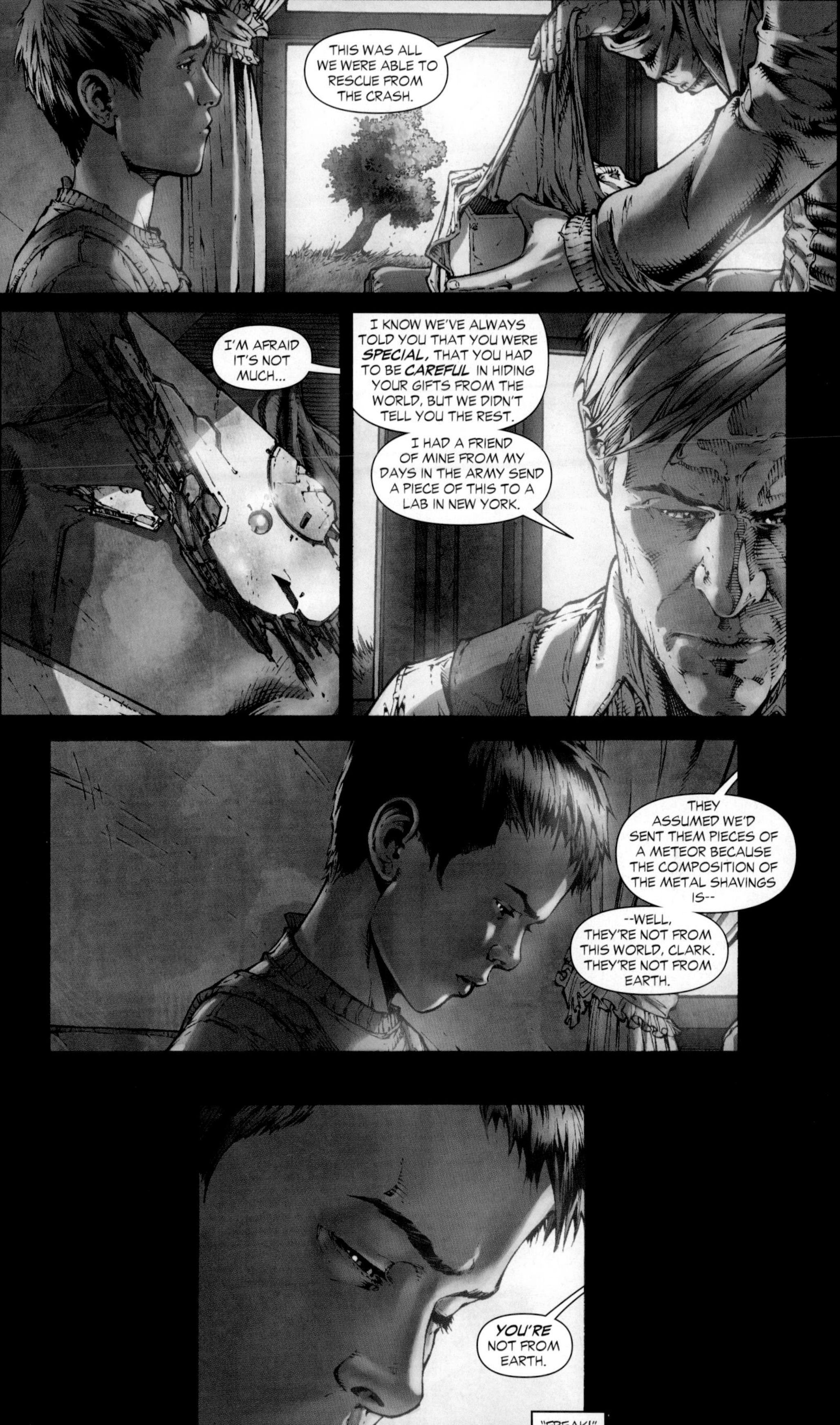
THIS WAS ALL WE WERE ABLE TO RESCUE FROM THE CRASH.
I'M AFRAID IT'S NOT MUCH...
I KNOW WE'VE ALWAYS TOLD YOU THAT YOU WERE *SPECIAL*, THAT YOU HAD TO BE *CAREFUL* IN HIDING YOUR GIFTS FROM THE WORLD, BUT WE DIDN'T TELL YOU THE REST.
I HAD A FRIEND OF MINE FROM MY DAYS IN THE ARMY SEND A PIECE OF THIS TO A LAB IN NEW YORK.
THEY ASSUMED WE'D SENT THEM PIECES OF A METEOR BECAUSE THE COMPOSITION OF THE METAL SHAVINGS IS--
--WELL, THEY'RE NOT FROM THIS WORLD, CLARK. THEY'RE NOT FROM EARTH.
YOU'RE NOT FROM EARTH.
"FREAK!"

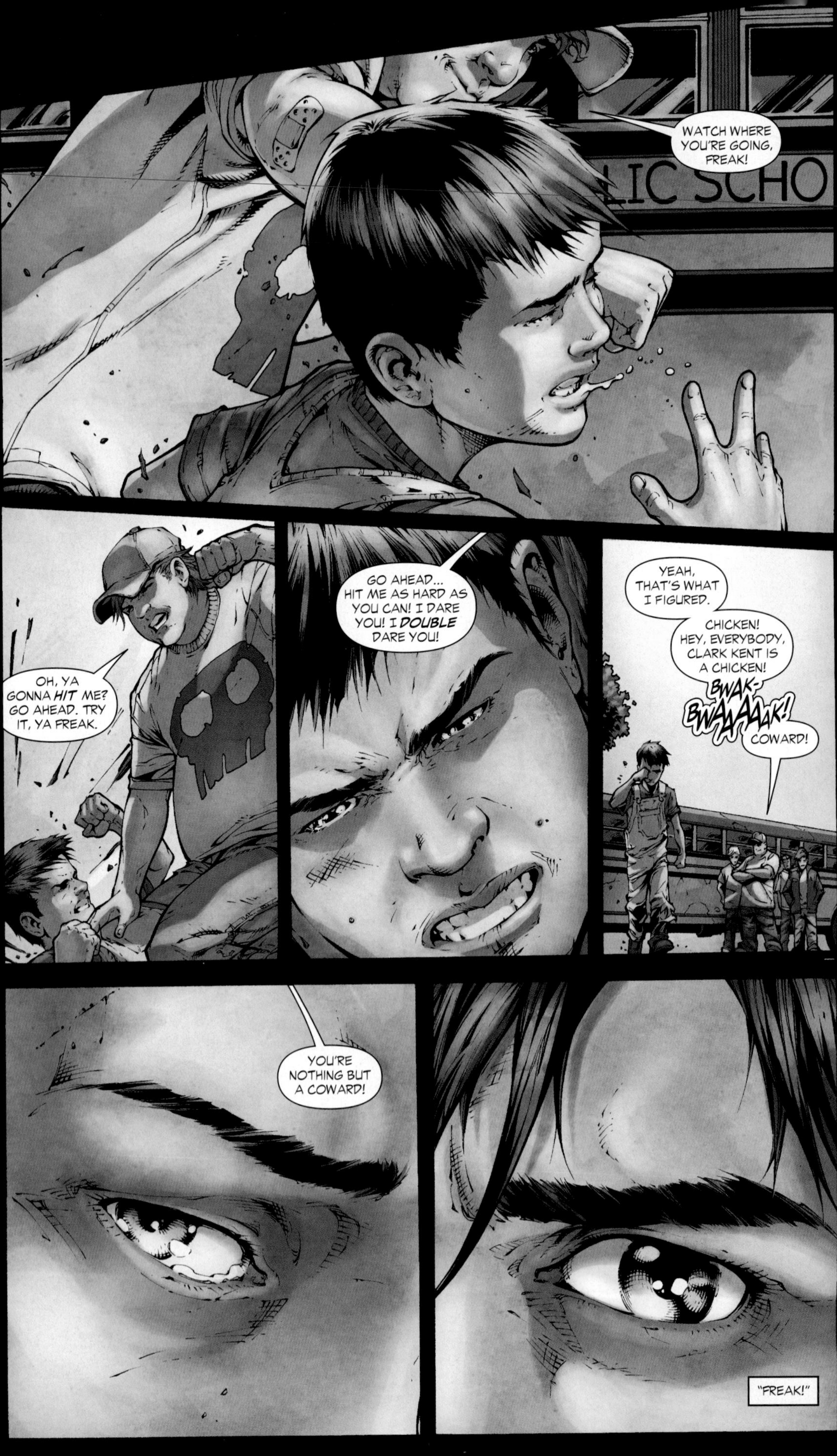
WATCH WHERE YOU'RE GOING, FREAK!
LIC SCHO
OH, YA GONNA HIT ME? GO AHEAD. TRY IT, YA FREAK.
GO AHEAD... HIT ME AS HARD AS YOU CAN! I DARE YOU! I DOUBLE DARE YOU!
YEAH, THAT'S WHAT I FIGURED.
CHICKEN! HEY, EVERYBODY, CLARK KENT IS A CHICKEN!
BWAK-BWAAAAAK!
COWARD!
YOU'RE NOTHING BUT A COWARD!
"FREAK!"

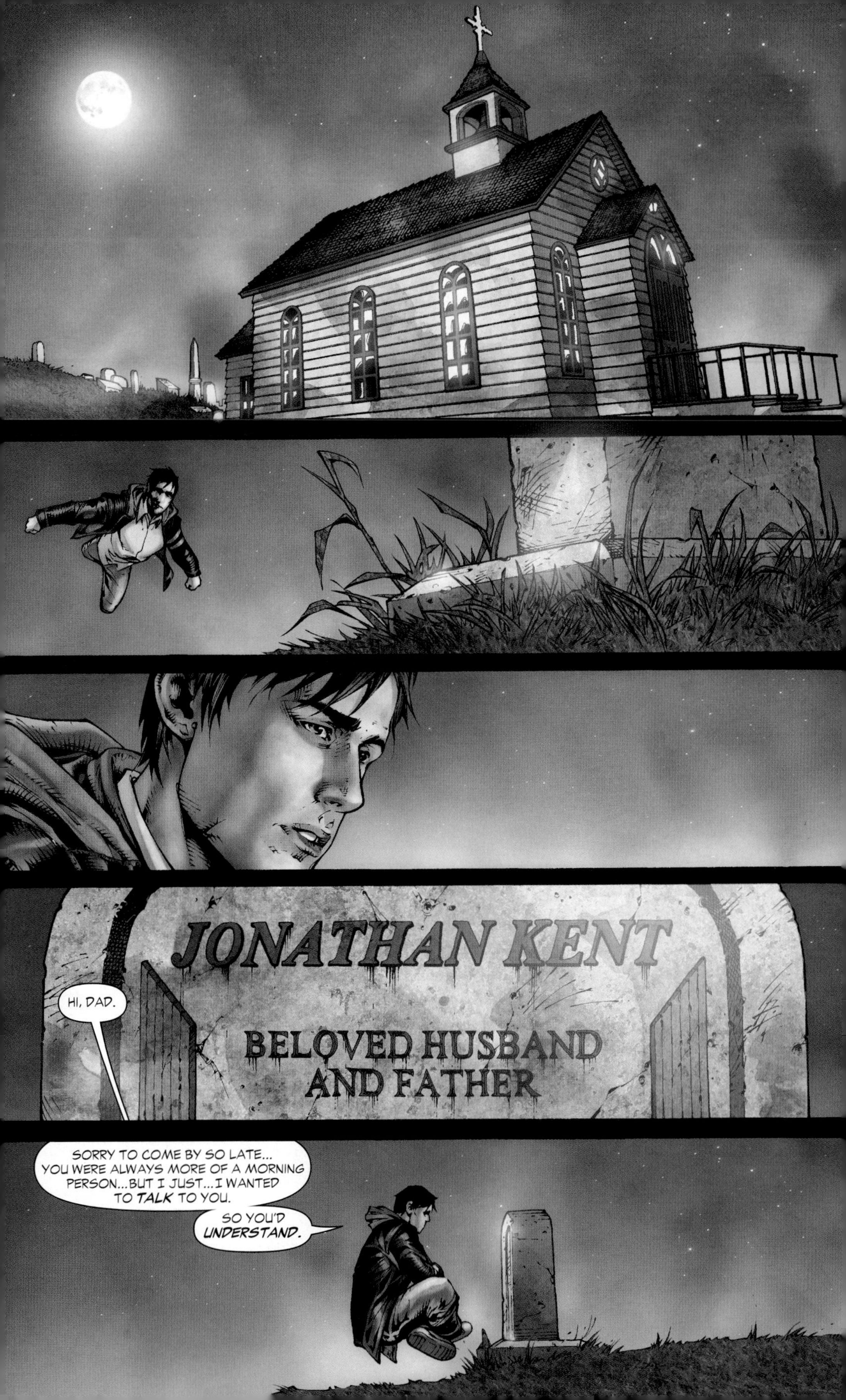
JONATHAN KENT
BELOVED HUSBAND AND FATHER
HI, DAD.
SORRY TO COME BY SO LATE... YOU WERE ALWAYS MORE OF A MORNING PERSON...BUT I JUST...I WANTED TO TALK TO YOU.
SO YOU'D UNDERSTAND.

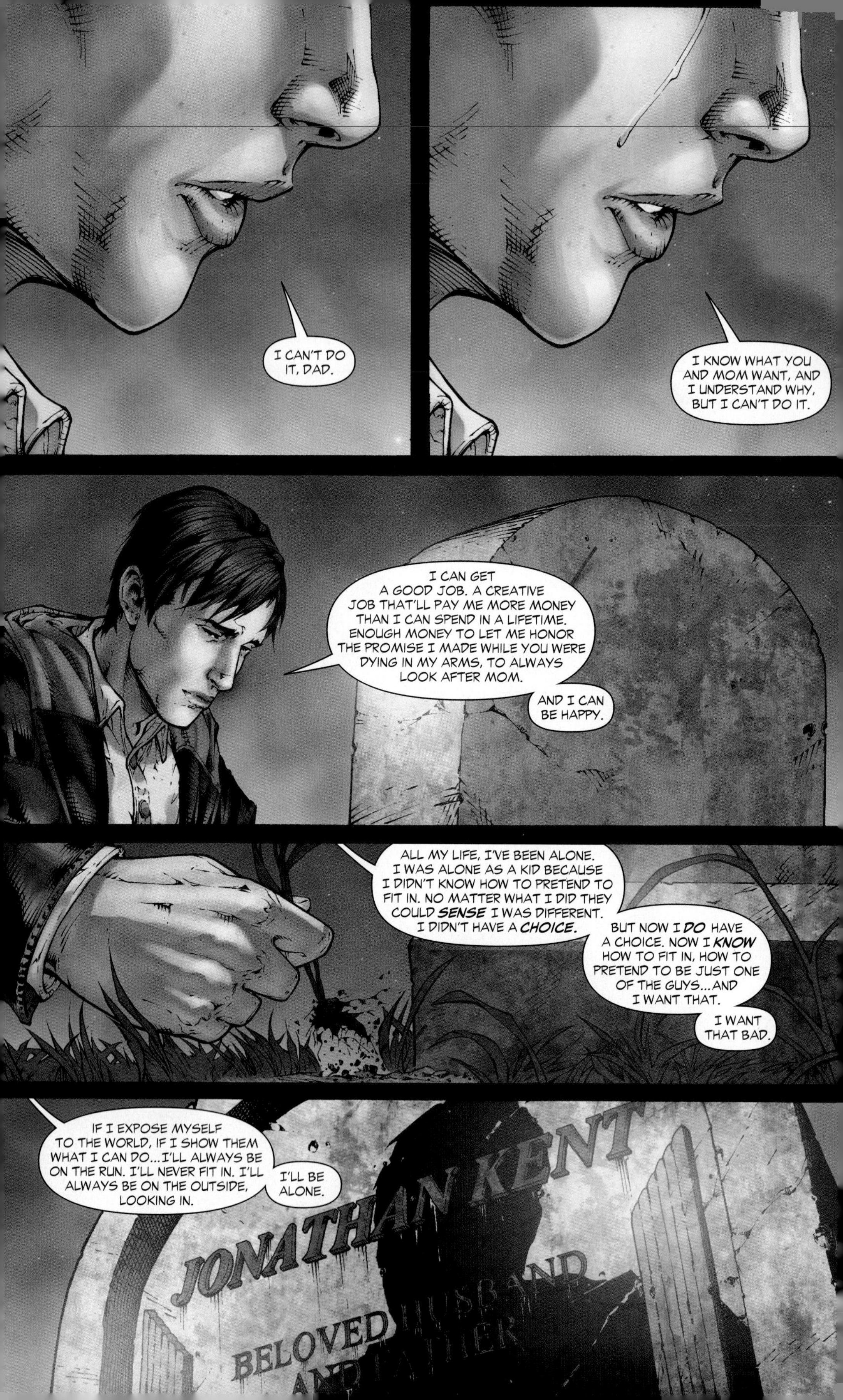

I CAN'T DO IT, DAD.
I KNOW WHAT YOU AND MOM WANT, AND I UNDERSTAND WHY, BUT I CAN'T DO IT.
I CAN GET A GOOD JOB. A CREATIVE JOB THAT'LL PAY ME MORE MONEY THAN I CAN SPEND IN A LIFETIME. ENOUGH MONEY TO LET ME HONOR THE PROMISE I MADE WHILE YOU WERE DYING IN MY ARMS, TO ALWAYS LOOK AFTER MOM.
AND I CAN BE HAPPY.
ALL MY LIFE, I'VE BEEN ALONE. I WAS ALONE AS A KID BECAUSE I DIDN'T KNOW HOW TO PRETEND TO FIT IN. NO MATTER WHAT I DID THEY COULD *SENSE* I WAS DIFFERENT. I DIDN'T HAVE A *CHOICE.*
BUT NOW I *DO* HAVE A CHOICE. NOW I *KNOW* HOW TO FIT IN, HOW TO PRETEND TO BE JUST ONE OF THE GUYS...AND I WANT THAT.
I WANT THAT BAD.
IF I EXPOSE MYSELF TO THE WORLD, IF I SHOW THEM WHAT I CAN DO...I'LL ALWAYS BE ON THE RUN. I'LL NEVER FIT IN. I'LL ALWAYS BE ON THE OUTSIDE, LOOKING IN.
I'LL BE ALONE.
JONATHAN KENT
BELOVED HUSBAND AND FATHER

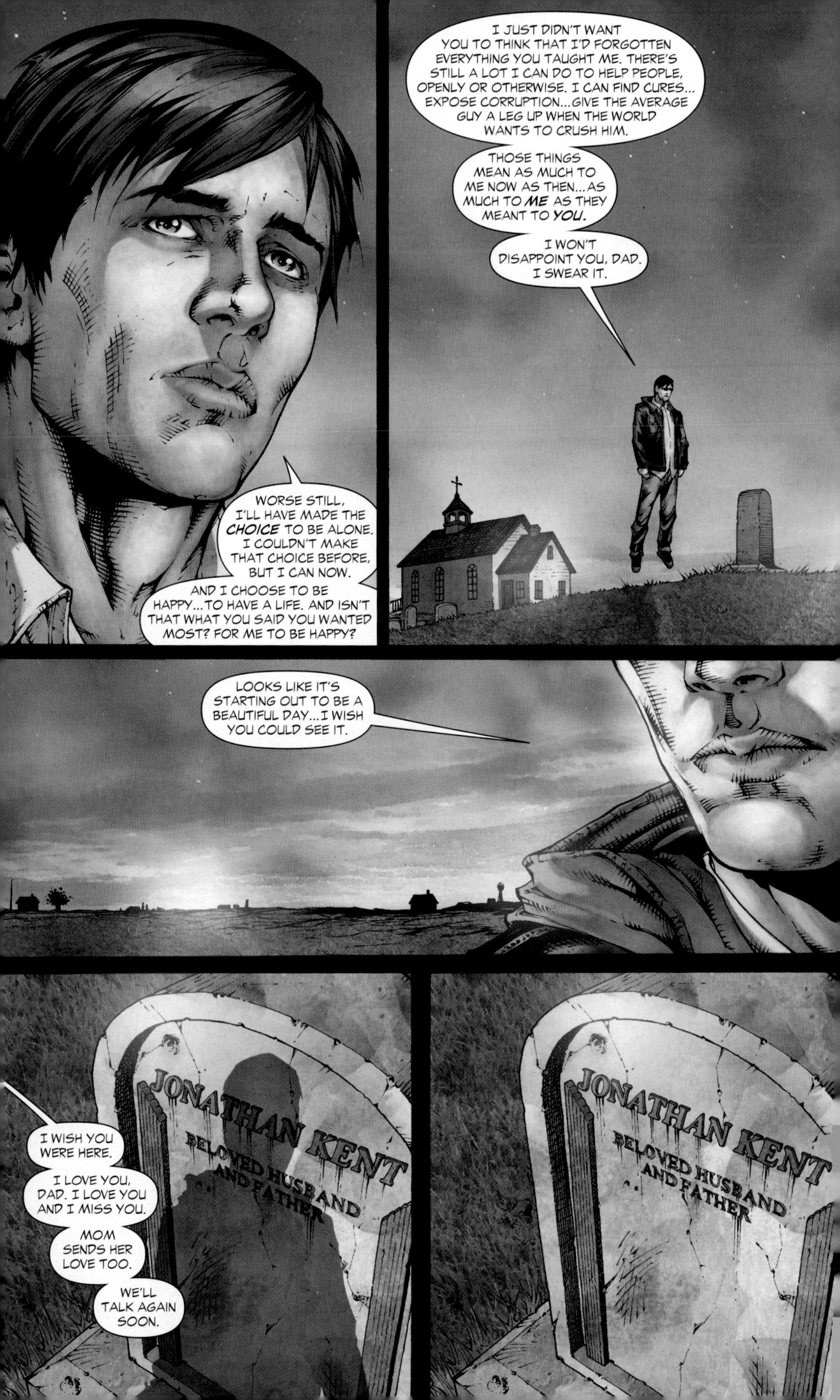
I JUST DIDN'T WANT YOU TO THINK THAT I'D FORGOTTEN EVERYTHING YOU TAUGHT ME. THERE'S STILL A LOT I CAN DO TO HELP PEOPLE, OPENLY OR OTHERWISE. I CAN FIND CURES... EXPOSE CORRUPTION...GIVE THE AVERAGE GUY A LEG UP WHEN THE WORLD WANTS TO CRUSH HIM.
THOSE THINGS MEAN AS MUCH TO ME NOW AS THEN...AS MUCH TO ME AS THEY MEANT TO YOU.
I WON'T DISAPPOINT YOU, DAD. I SWEAR IT.
WORSE STILL, I'LL HAVE MADE THE CHOICE TO BE ALONE. I COULDN'T MAKE THAT CHOICE BEFORE, BUT I CAN NOW.
AND I CHOOSE TO BE HAPPY...TO HAVE A LIFE. AND ISN'T THAT WHAT YOU SAID YOU WANTED MOST? FOR ME TO BE HAPPY?
LOOKS LIKE IT'S STARTING OUT TO BE A BEAUTIFUL DAY...I WISH YOU COULD SEE IT.
JONATHAN KENT
BELOVED HUSBAND AND FATHER
I WISH YOU WERE HERE.
I LOVE YOU, DAD. I LOVE YOU AND I MISS YOU.
MOM SENDS HER LOVE TOO.
WE'LL TALK AGAIN SOON.
JONATHAN KENT
BELOVED HUSBAND AND FATHER

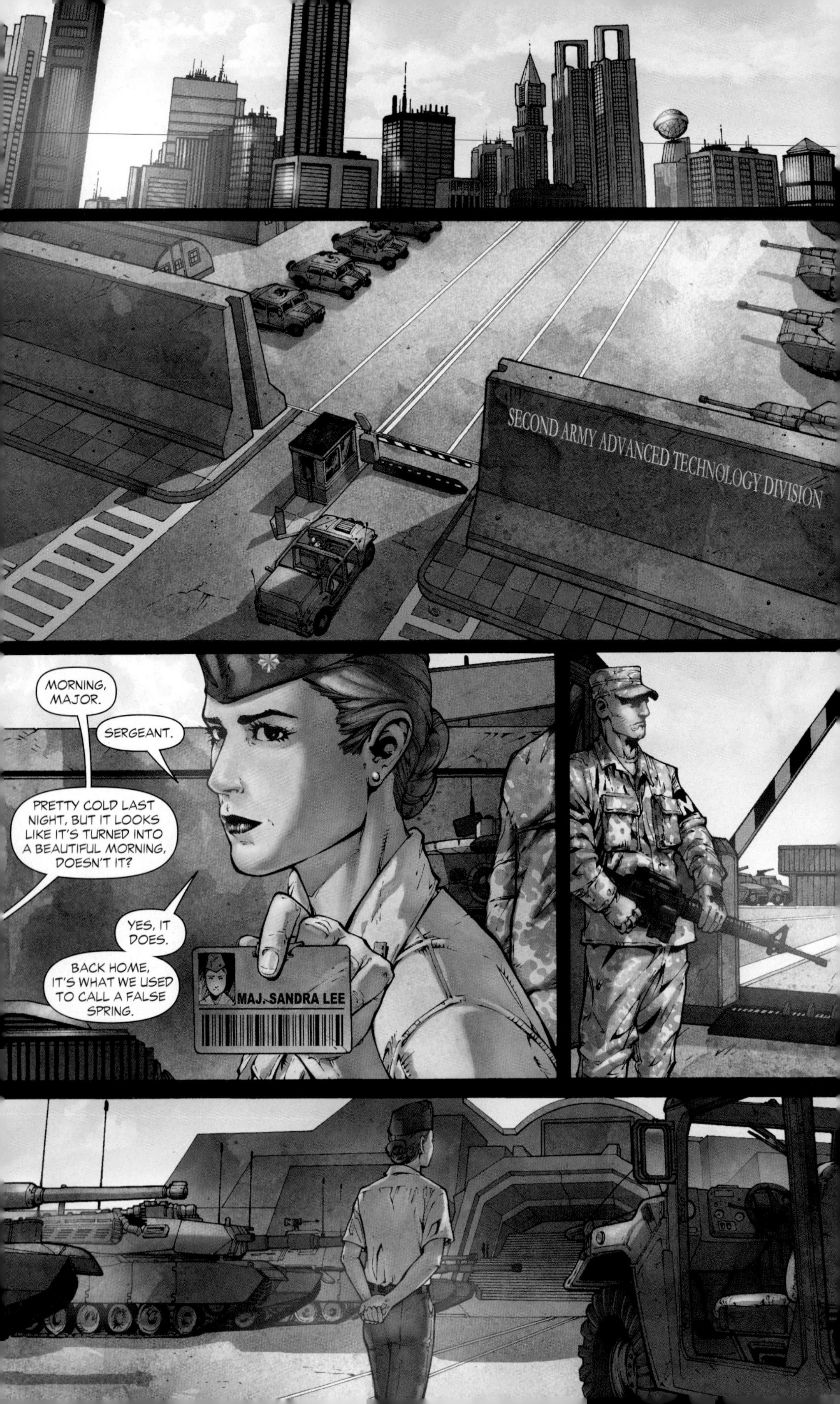
SECOND ARMY ADVANCED TECHNOLOGY DIVISION
MORNING, MAJOR.
SERGEANT.
PRETTY COLD LAST NIGHT, BUT IT LOOKS LIKE IT'S TURNED INTO A BEAUTIFUL MORNING, DOESN'T IT?
YES, IT DOES.
BACK HOME, IT'S WHAT WE USED TO CALL A FALSE SPRING.
MAJ. SANDRA LEE

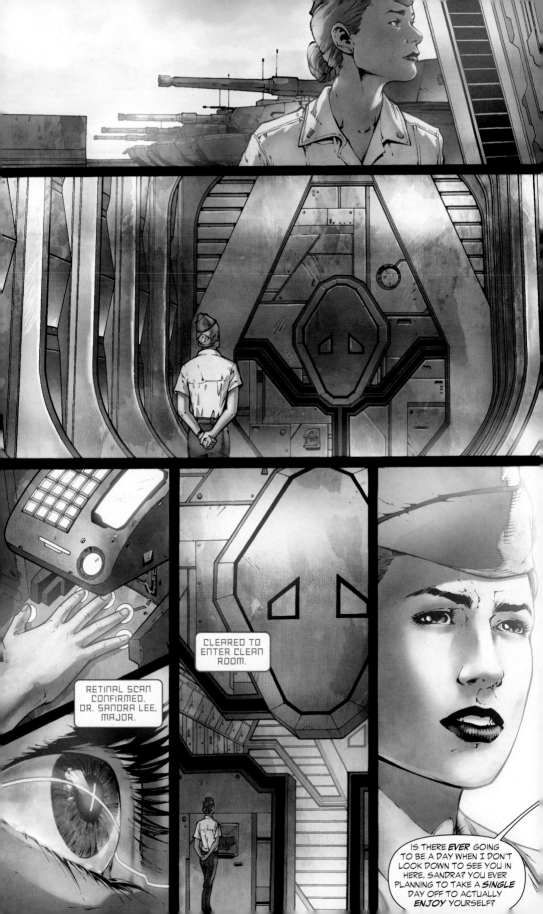

CLEARED TO ENTER CLEAN ROOM.

RETINAL SCAN CONFIRMED. DR. SANDRA LEE, MAJOR.

IS THERE *EVER* GOING TO BE A DAY WHEN I DON'T LOOK DOWN TO SEE YOU IN HERE, SANDRA? YOU EVER PLANNING TO TAKE A *SINGLE* DAY OFF TO ACTUALLY *ENJOY* YOURSELF?

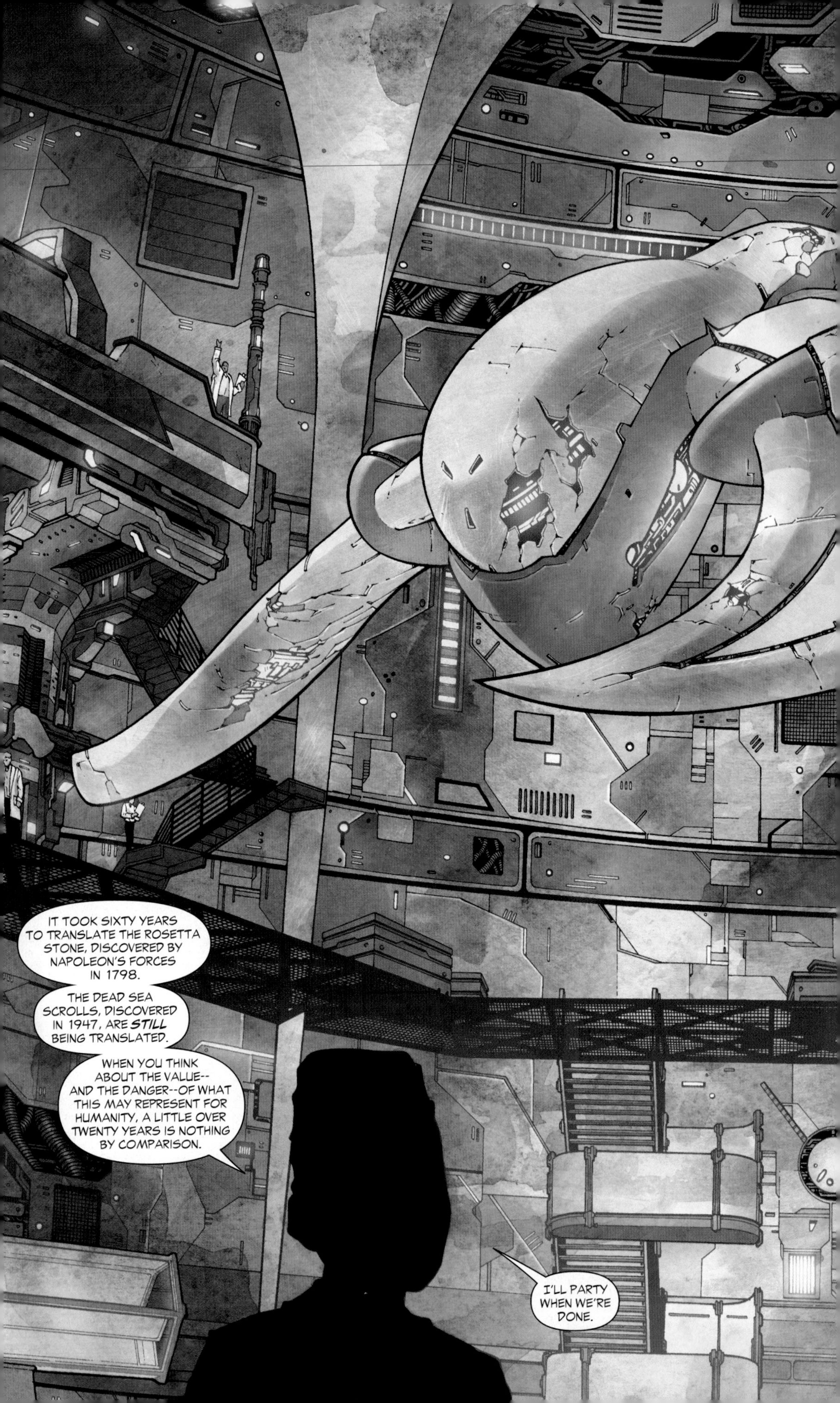

IT TOOK SIXTY YEARS TO TRANSLATE THE ROSETTA STONE, DISCOVERED BY NAPOLEON'S FORCES IN 1798.
THE DEAD SEA SCROLLS, DISCOVERED IN 1947, ARE *STILL* BEING TRANSLATED.
WHEN YOU THINK ABOUT THE VALUE-- AND THE DANGER--OF WHAT THIS MAY REPRESENT FOR HUMANITY, A LITTLE OVER TWENTY YEARS IS NOTHING BY COMPARISON.
I'LL PARTY WHEN WE'RE DONE.

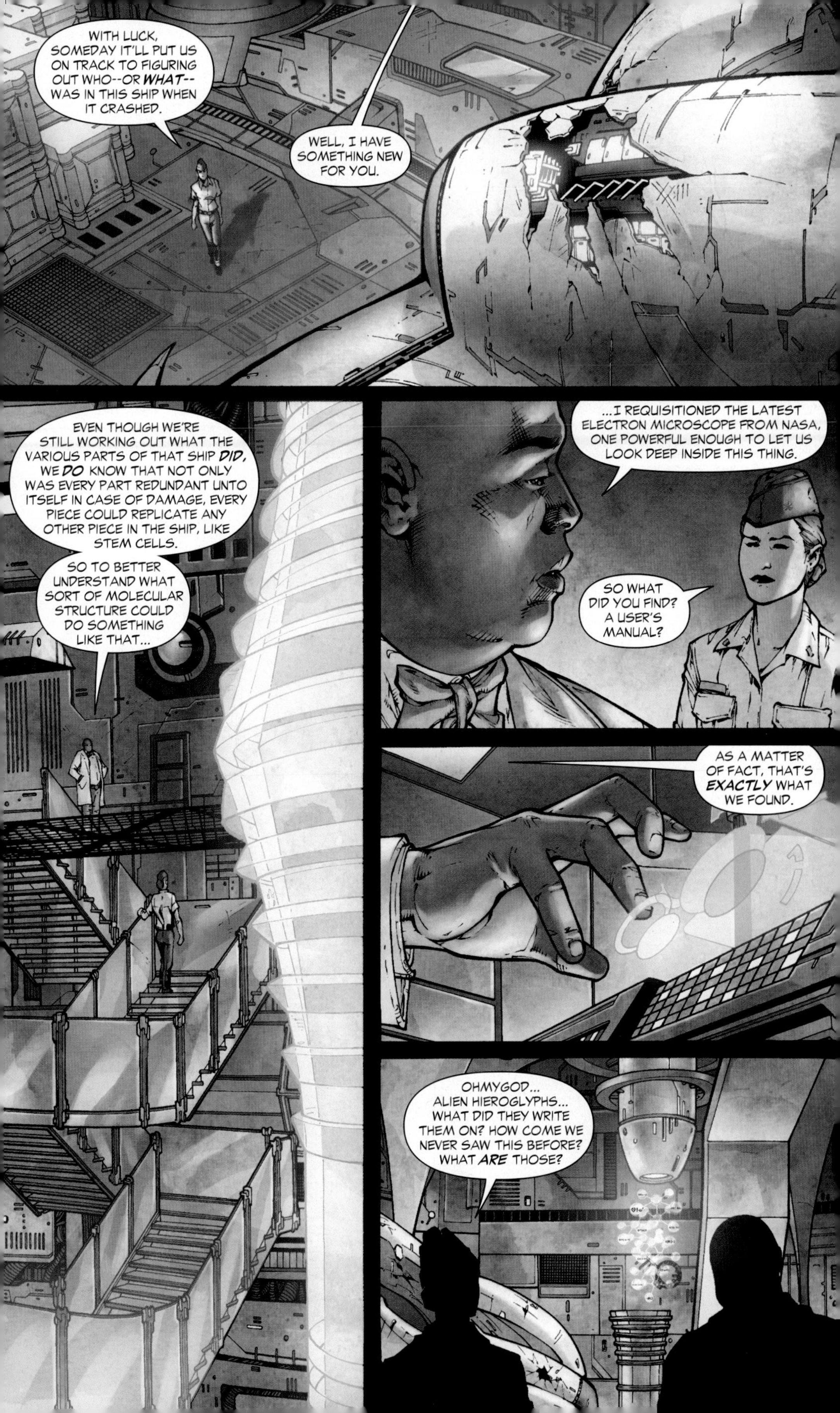
WITH LUCK, SOMEDAY IT'LL PUT US ON TRACK TO FIGURING OUT WHO--OR *WHAT*--WAS IN THIS SHIP WHEN IT CRASHED.
WELL, I HAVE SOMETHING NEW FOR YOU.
EVEN THOUGH WE'RE STILL WORKING OUT WHAT THE VARIOUS PARTS OF THAT SHIP *DID*, WE *DO* KNOW THAT NOT ONLY WAS EVERY PART REDUNDANT UNTO ITSELF IN CASE OF DAMAGE, EVERY PIECE COULD REPLICATE ANY OTHER PIECE IN THE SHIP, LIKE STEM CELLS.
SO TO BETTER UNDERSTAND WHAT SORT OF MOLECULAR STRUCTURE COULD DO SOMETHING LIKE THAT...
...I REQUISITIONED THE LATEST ELECTRON MICROSCOPE FROM NASA, ONE POWERFUL ENOUGH TO LET US LOOK DEEP INSIDE THIS THING.
SO WHAT DID YOU FIND? A USER'S MANUAL?
AS A MATTER OF FACT, THAT'S *EXACTLY* WHAT WE FOUND.
OHMYGOD... ALIEN HIEROGLYPHS... WHAT DID THEY WRITE THEM ON? HOW COME WE NEVER SAW THIS BEFORE? WHAT *ARE* THOSE?

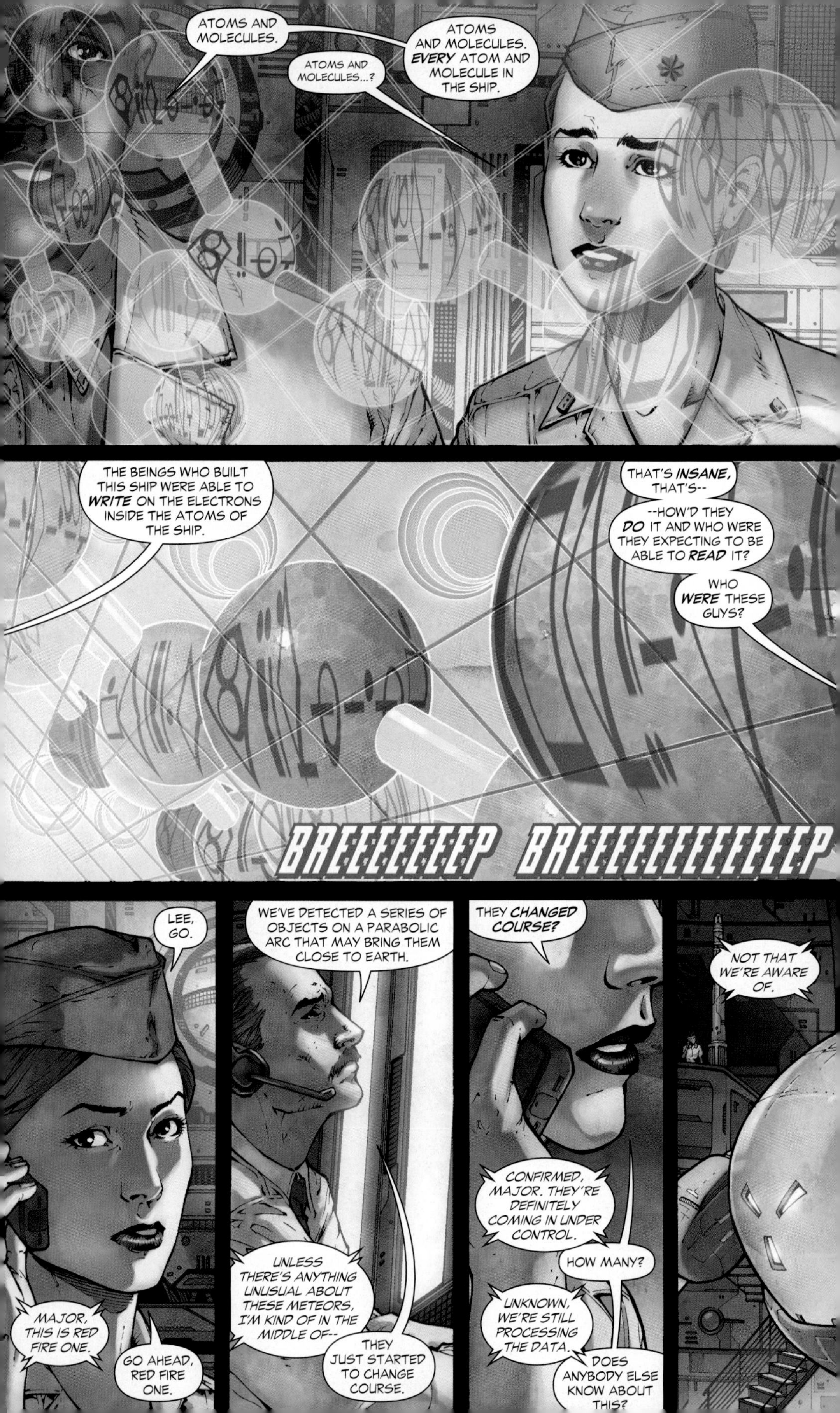
ATOMS AND MOLECULES.
ATOMS AND MOLECULES...?
ATOMS AND MOLECULES. EVERY ATOM AND MOLECULE IN THE SHIP.
THE BEINGS WHO BUILT THIS SHIP WERE ABLE TO WRITE ON THE ELECTRONS INSIDE THE ATOMS OF THE SHIP.
THAT'S INSANE, THAT'S--
--HOW'D THEY DO IT AND WHO WERE THEY EXPECTING TO BE ABLE TO READ IT?
WHO WERE THESE GUYS?
BREEEEEEEEP BREEEEEEEEEEEEEP
LEE, GO.
MAJOR, THIS IS RED FIRE ONE.
GO AHEAD, RED FIRE ONE.
WE'VE DETECTED A SERIES OF OBJECTS ON A PARABOLIC ARC THAT MAY BRING THEM CLOSE TO EARTH.
UNLESS THERE'S ANYTHING UNUSUAL ABOUT THESE METEORS, I'M KIND OF IN THE MIDDLE OF--
THEY JUST STARTED TO CHANGE COURSE.
THEY CHANGED COURSE?
CONFIRMED, MAJOR. THEY'RE DEFINITELY COMING IN UNDER CONTROL.
HOW MANY?
UNKNOWN, WE'RE STILL PROCESSING THE DATA.
DOES ANYBODY ELSE KNOW ABOUT THIS?
NOT THAT WE'RE AWARE OF.

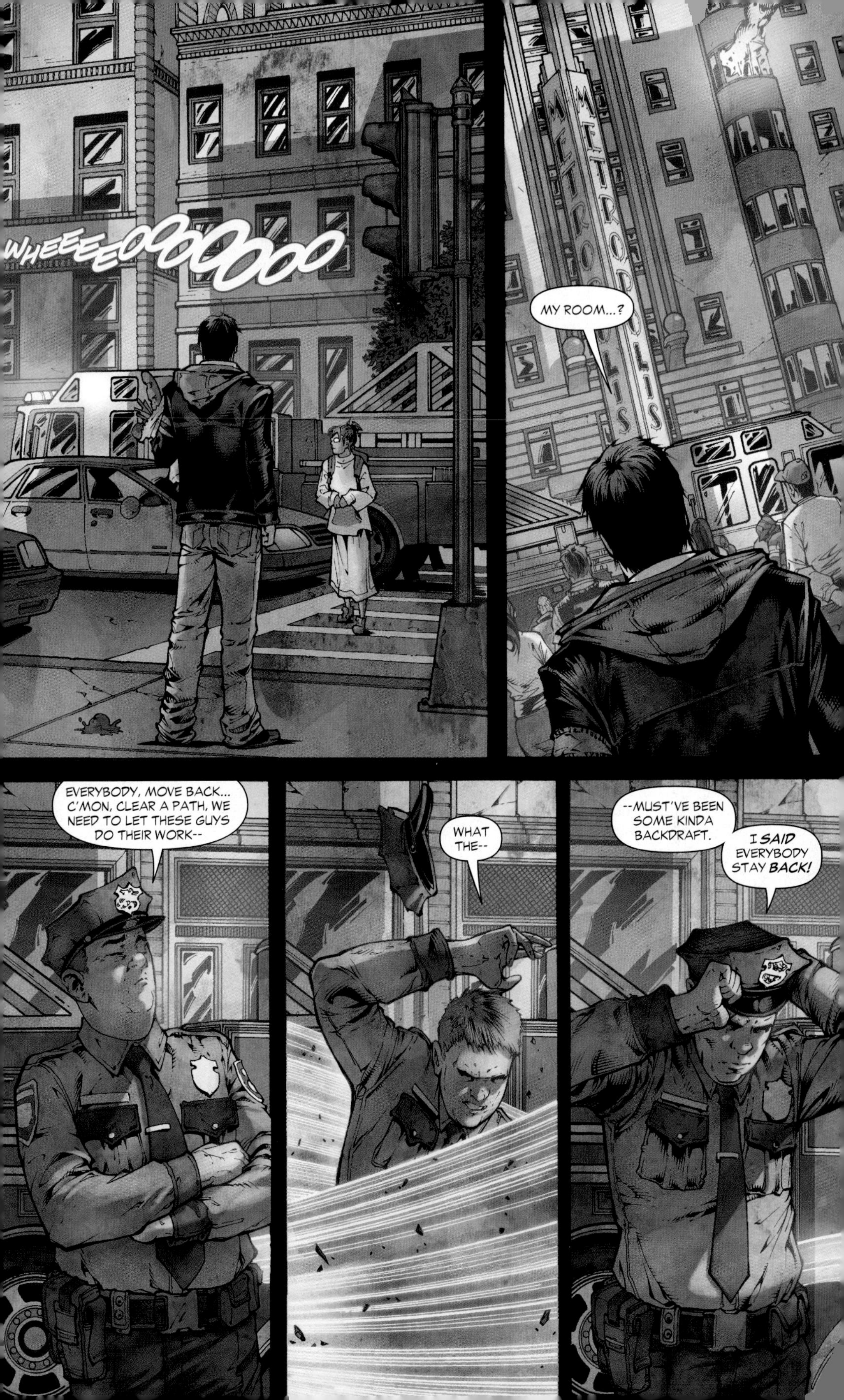
WHEEEEEOOOOOOOOOO
METROPOLIS
MY ROOM...?
EVERYBODY, MOVE BACK... C'MON, CLEAR A PATH, WE NEED TO LET THESE GUYS DO THEIR WORK--
WHAT THE--
--MUST'VE BEEN SOME KINDA BACKDRAFT.
I *SAID* EVERYBODY STAY ***BACK!***

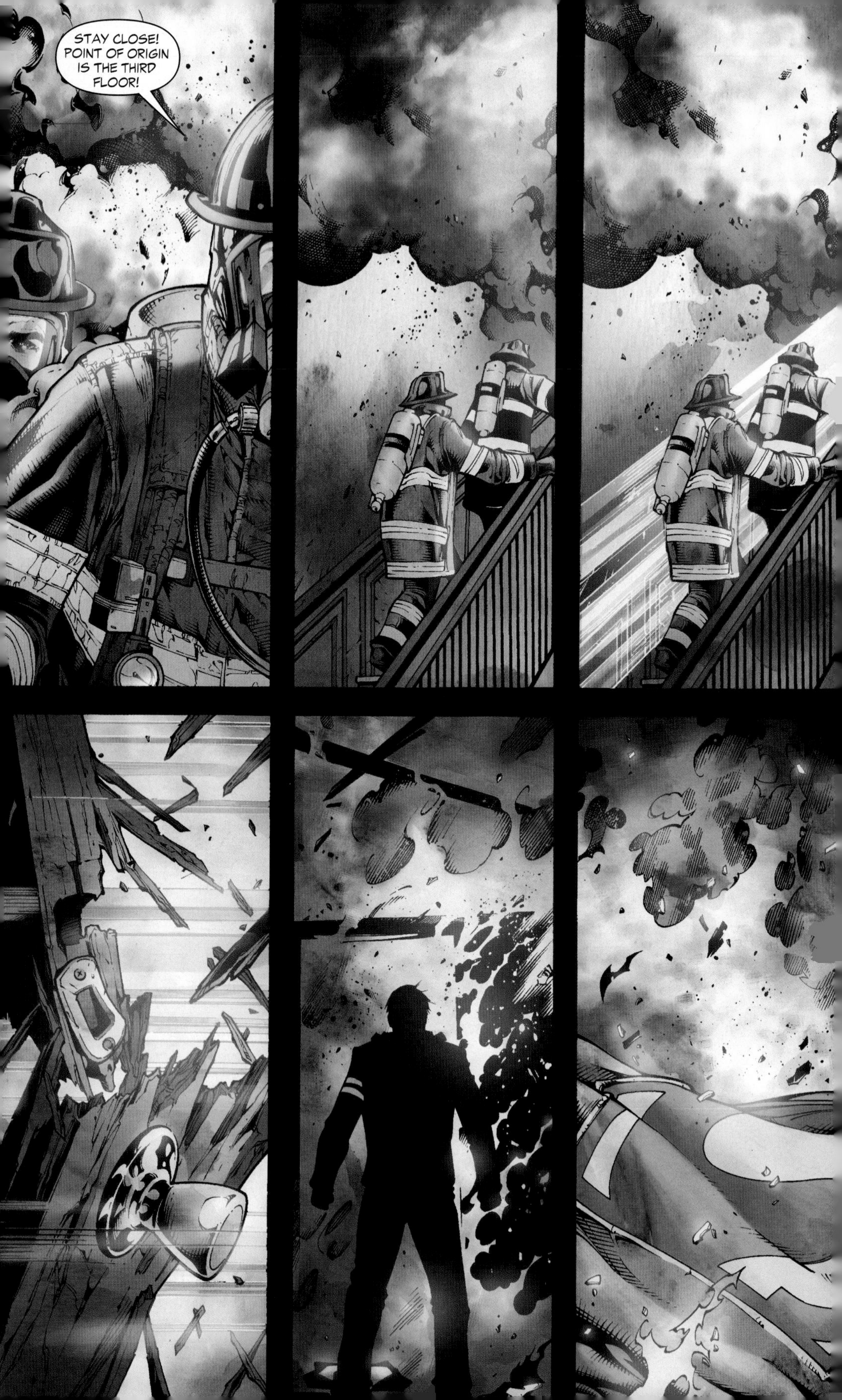
STAY CLOSE! POINT OF ORIGIN IS THE THIRD FLOOR!

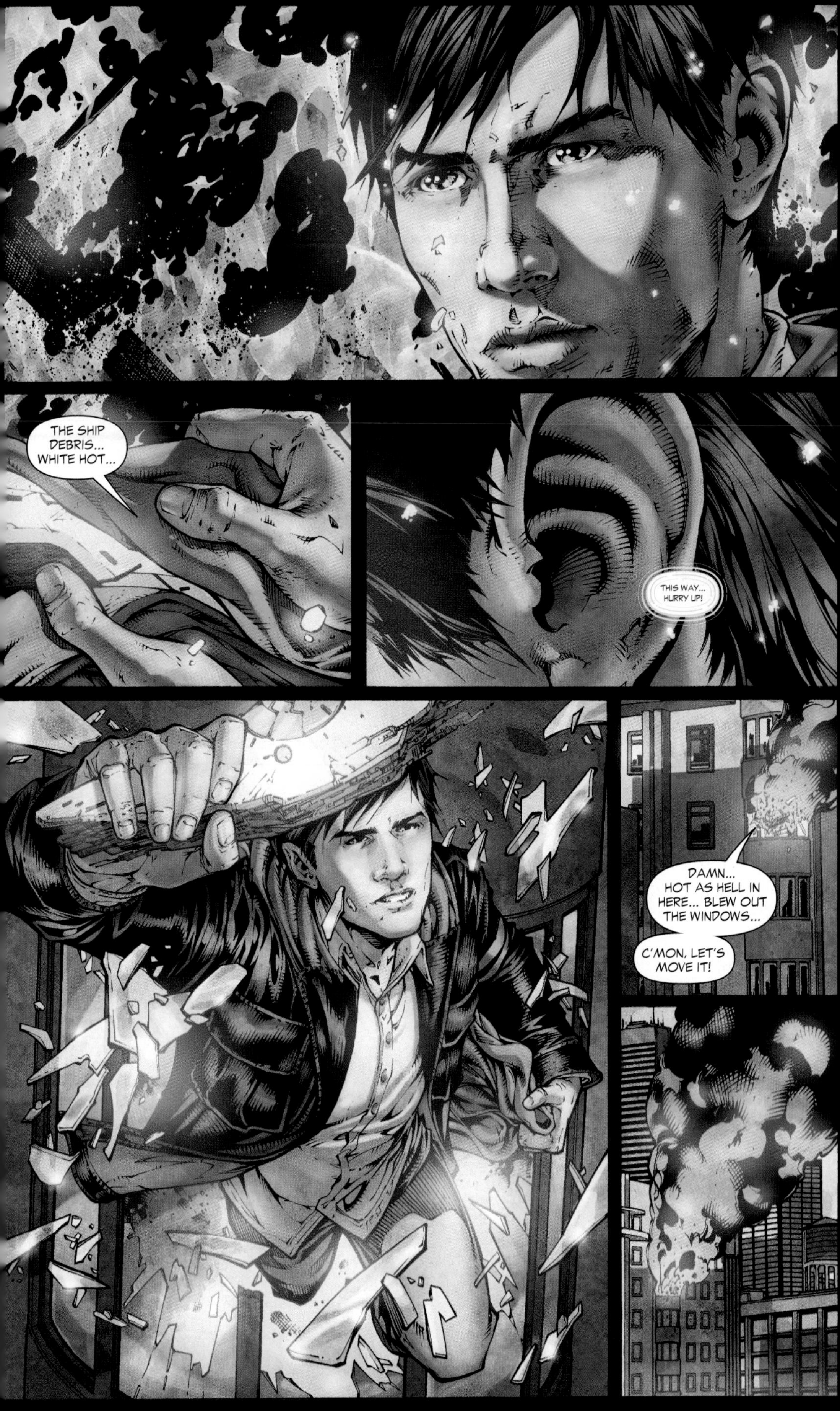
THE SHIP DEBRIS... WHITE HOT...
THIS WAY... HURRY UP!
DAMN... HOT AS HELL IN HERE... BLEW OUT THE WINDOWS...
C'MON, LET'S MOVE IT!

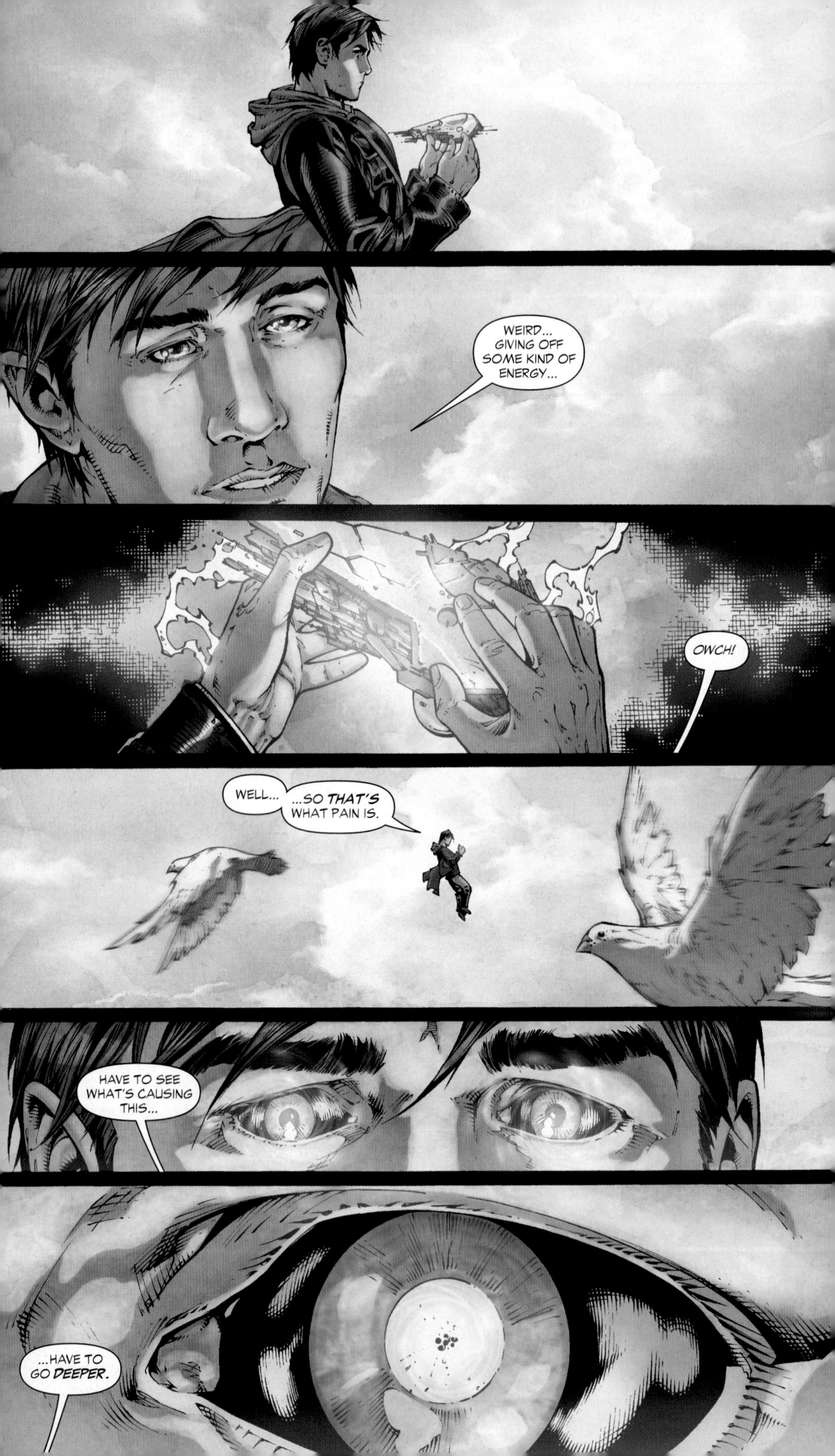
WEIRD... GIVING OFF SOME KIND OF ENERGY...
OWCH!
WELL...
...SO THAT'S WHAT PAIN IS.
HAVE TO SEE WHAT'S CAUSING THIS...
...HAVE TO GO DEEPER.

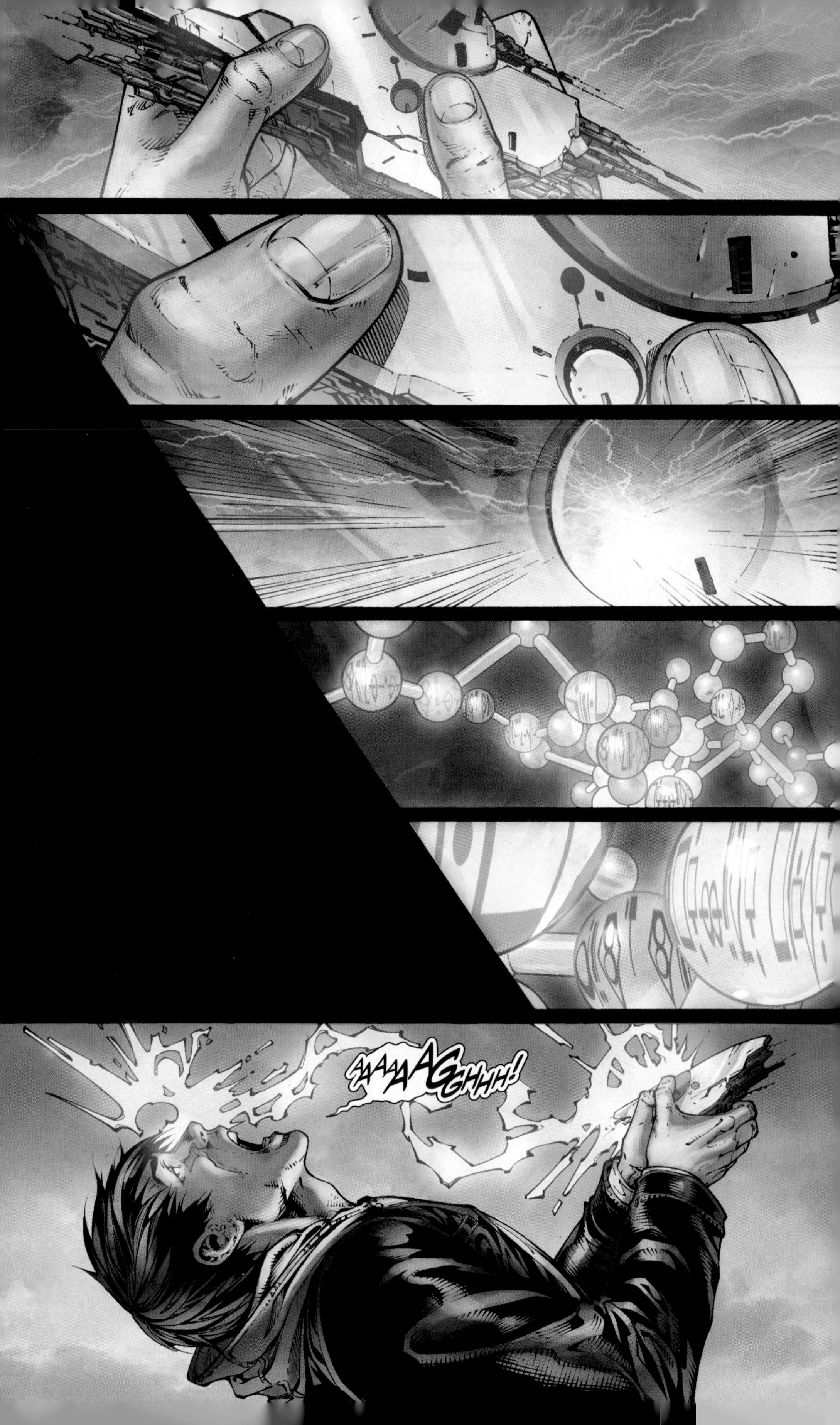
AAAAAAGHHH!

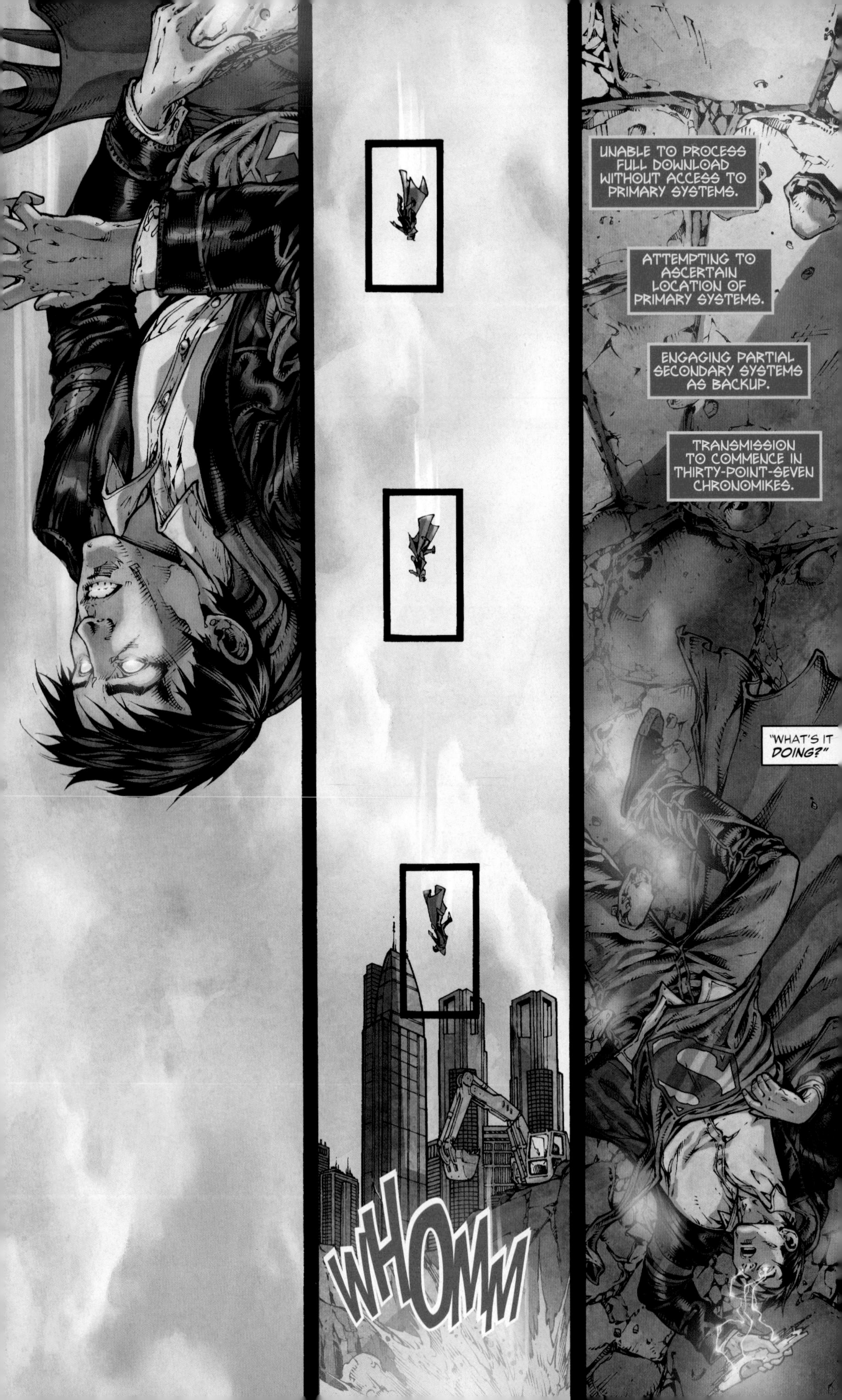
WHOMM
UNABLE TO PROCESS FULL DOWNLOAD WITHOUT ACCESS TO PRIMARY SYSTEMS.
ATTEMPTING TO ASCERTAIN LOCATION OF PRIMARY SYSTEMS.
ENGAGING PARTIAL SECONDARY SYSTEMS AS BACKUP.
TRANSMISSION TO COMMENCE IN THIRTY-POINT-SEVEN CHRONOMIKES.
"WHAT'S IT DOING?"

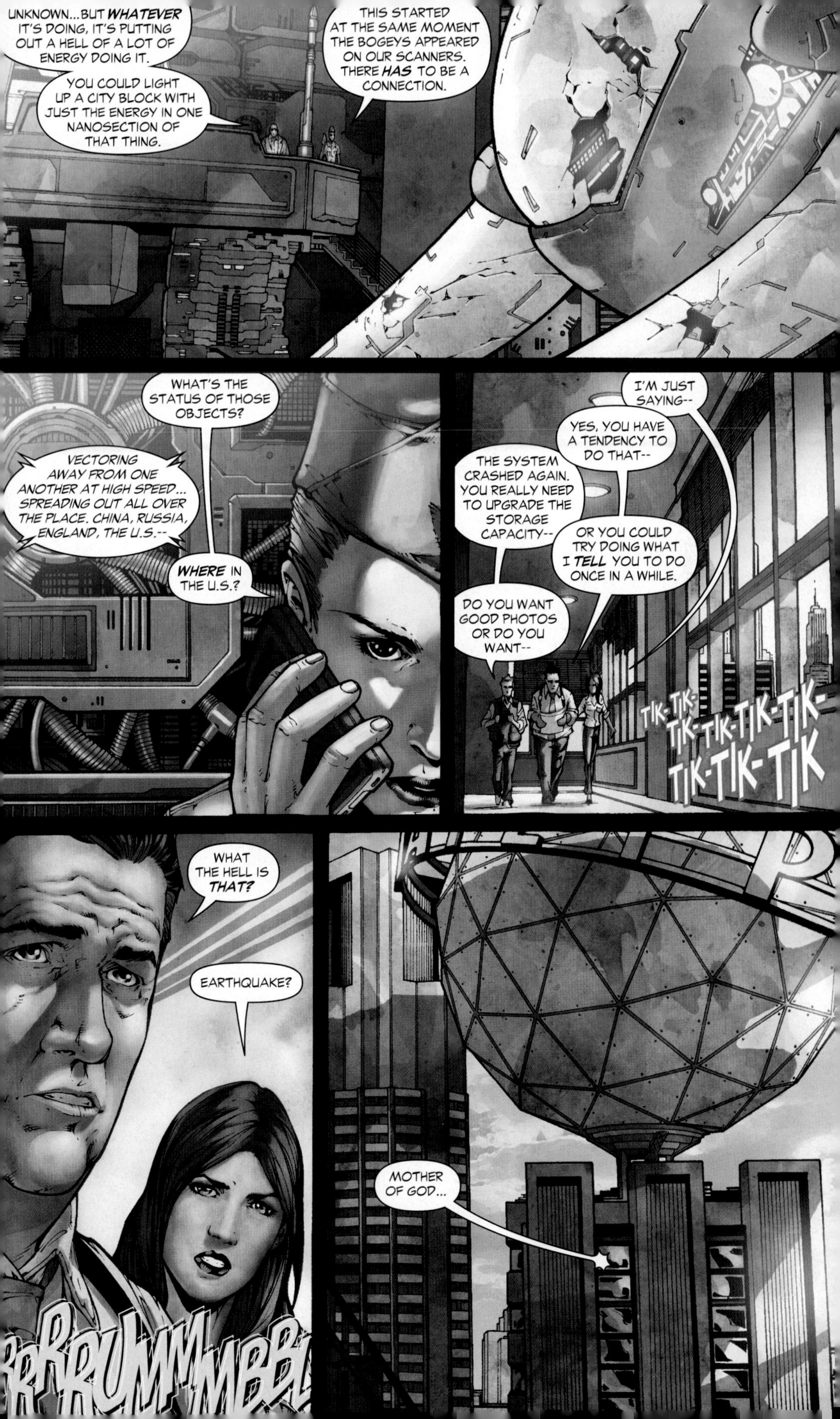

UNKNOWN...BUT WHATEVER IT'S DOING, IT'S PUTTING OUT A HELL OF A LOT OF ENERGY DOING IT.
YOU COULD LIGHT UP A CITY BLOCK WITH JUST THE ENERGY IN ONE NANOSECTION OF THAT THING.
THIS STARTED AT THE SAME MOMENT THE BOGEYS APPEARED ON OUR SCANNERS. THERE HAS TO BE A CONNECTION.
WHAT'S THE STATUS OF THOSE OBJECTS?
VECTORING AWAY FROM ONE ANOTHER AT HIGH SPEED... SPREADING OUT ALL OVER THE PLACE. CHINA, RUSSIA, ENGLAND, THE U.S.--
WHERE IN THE U.S.?
I'M JUST SAYING--
YES, YOU HAVE A TENDENCY TO DO THAT--
THE SYSTEM CRASHED AGAIN. YOU REALLY NEED TO UPGRADE THE STORAGE CAPACITY--
OR YOU COULD TRY DOING WHAT I TELL YOU TO DO ONCE IN A WHILE.
DO YOU WANT GOOD PHOTOS OR DO YOU WANT--
TIK-TIK-TIK-TIK-TIK-TIK-TIK-TIK-TIK-TIK
WHAT THE HELL IS THAT?
EARTHQUAKE?
RRRUMMMBBL
MOTHER OF GOD...

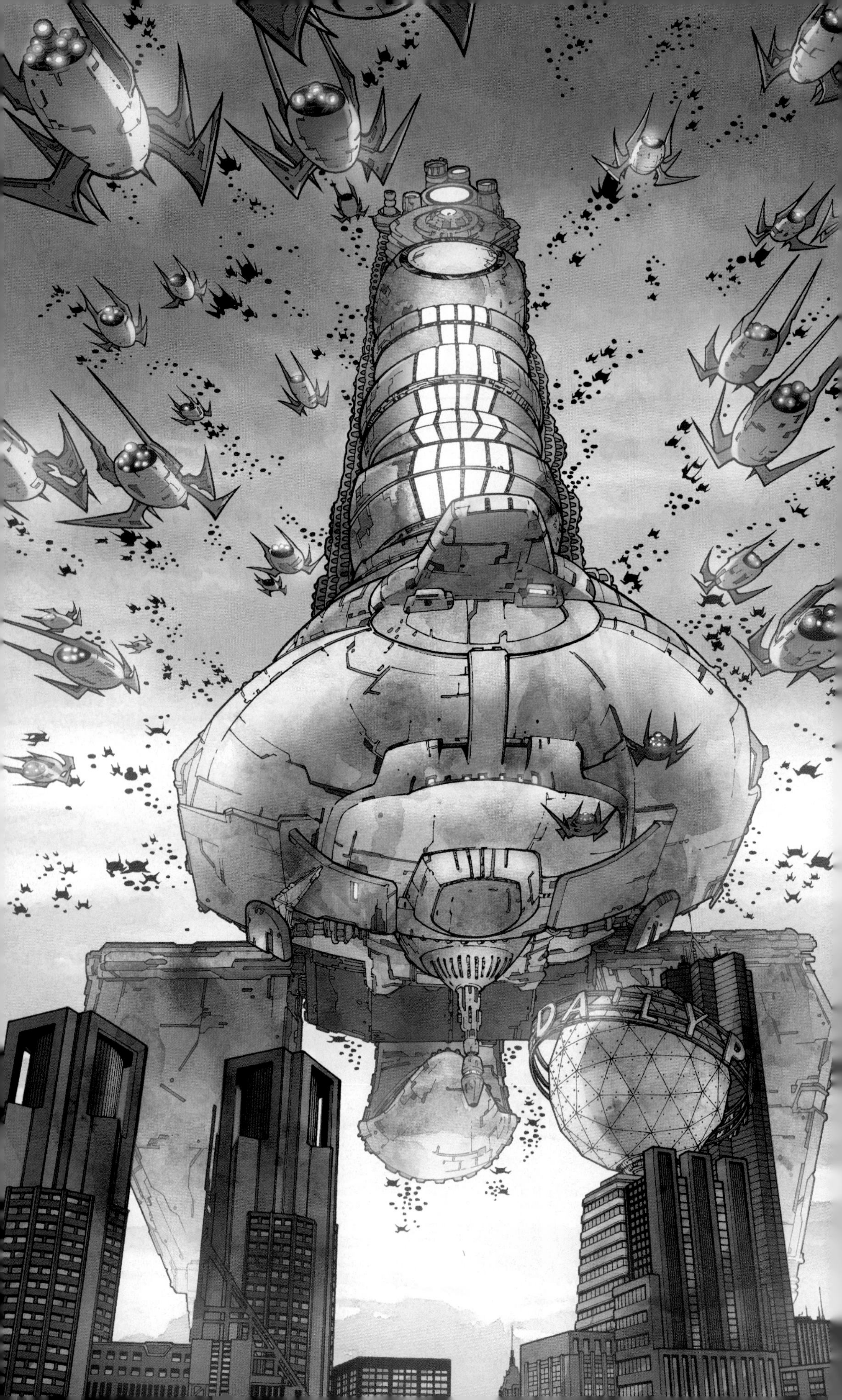
DA LY P

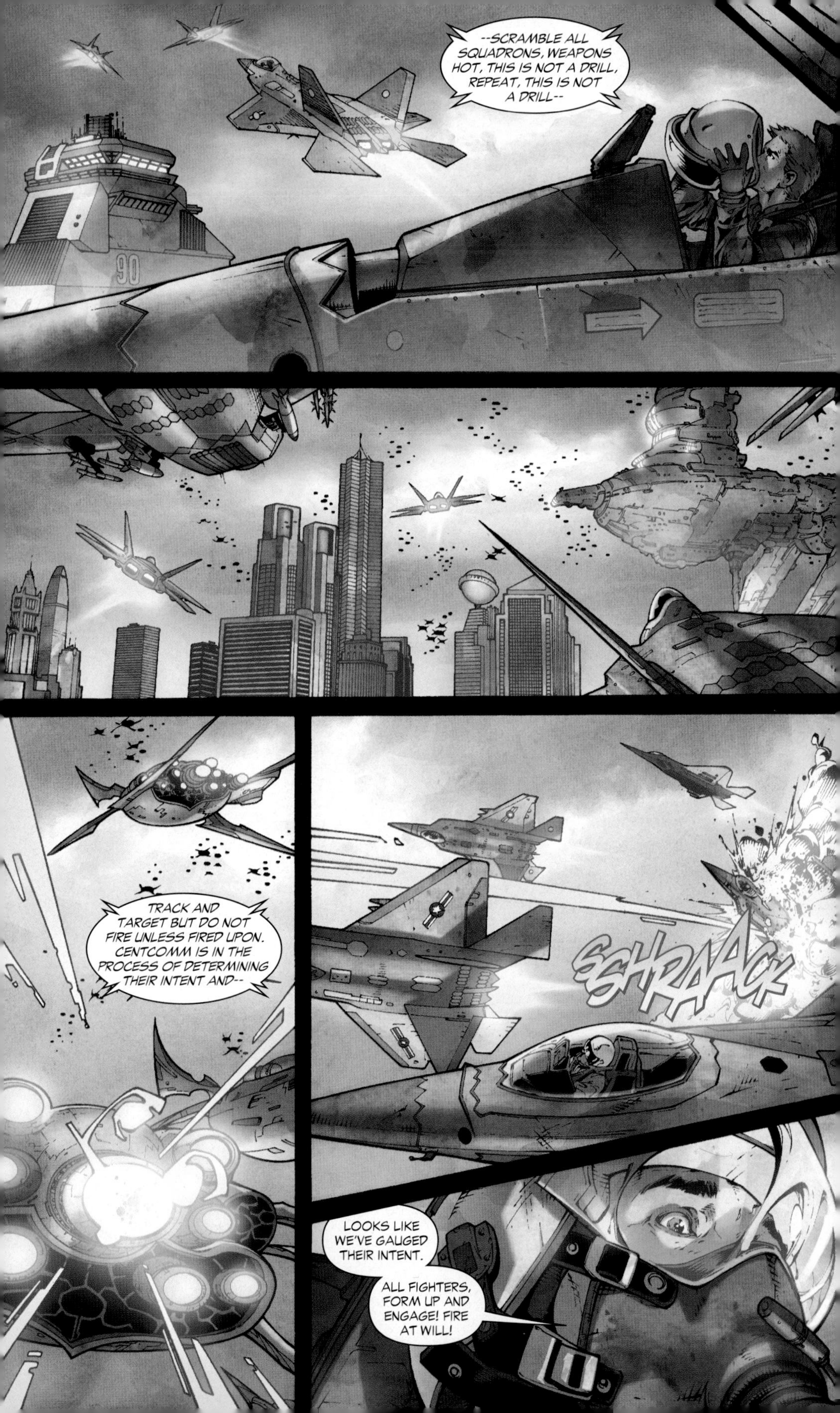
--SCRAMBLE ALL SQUADRONS, WEAPONS HOT, THIS IS NOT A DRILL, REPEAT, THIS IS NOT A DRILL--
90
TRACK AND TARGET BUT DO NOT FIRE UNLESS FIRED UPON. CENTCOMM IS IN THE PROCESS OF DETERMINING THEIR INTENT AND--
SCHRAACK
LOOKS LIKE WE'VE GAUGED THEIR INTENT.
ALL FIGHTERS, FORM UP AND ENGAGE! FIRE AT WILL!

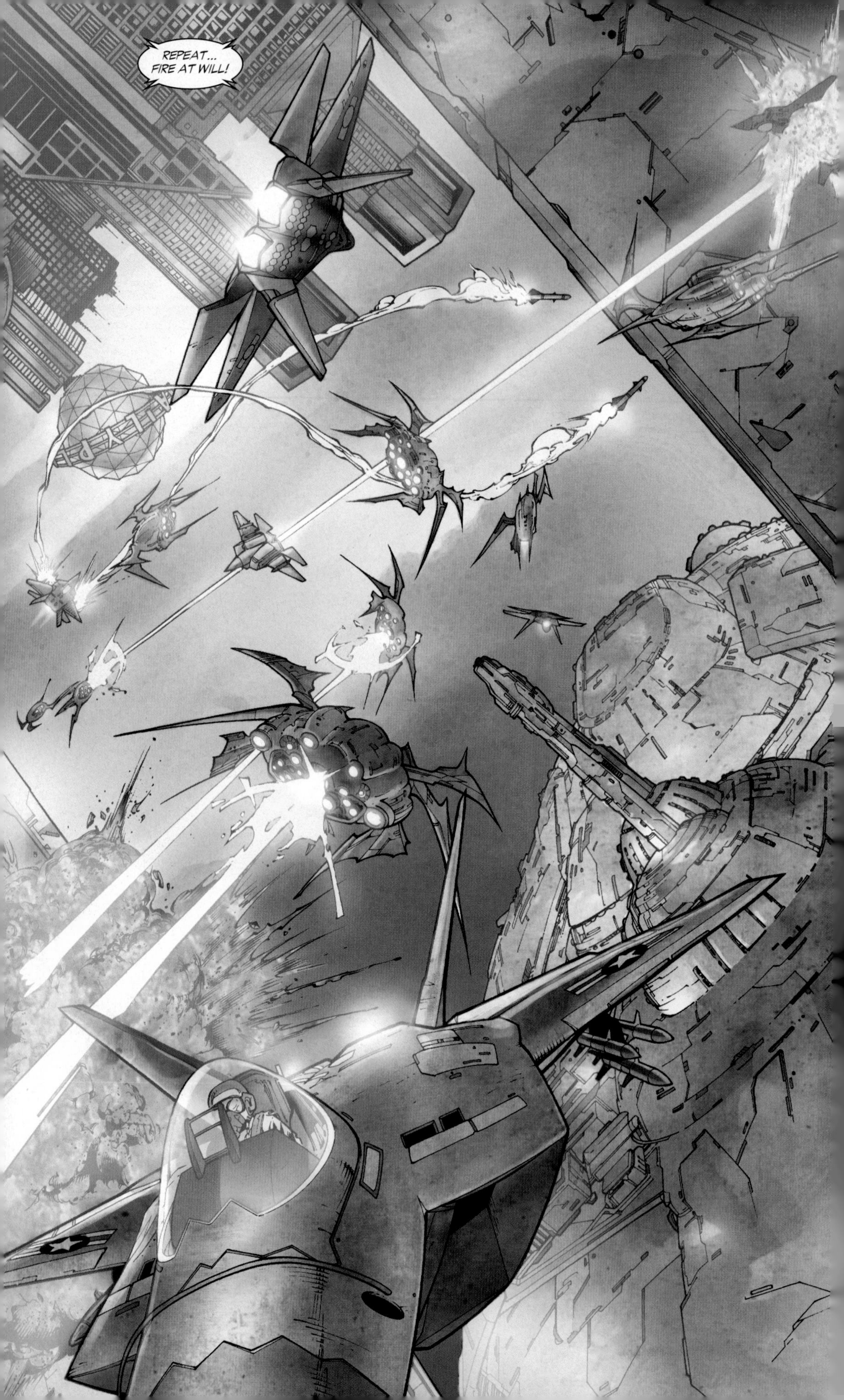
REPEAT...
FIRE AT WILL!

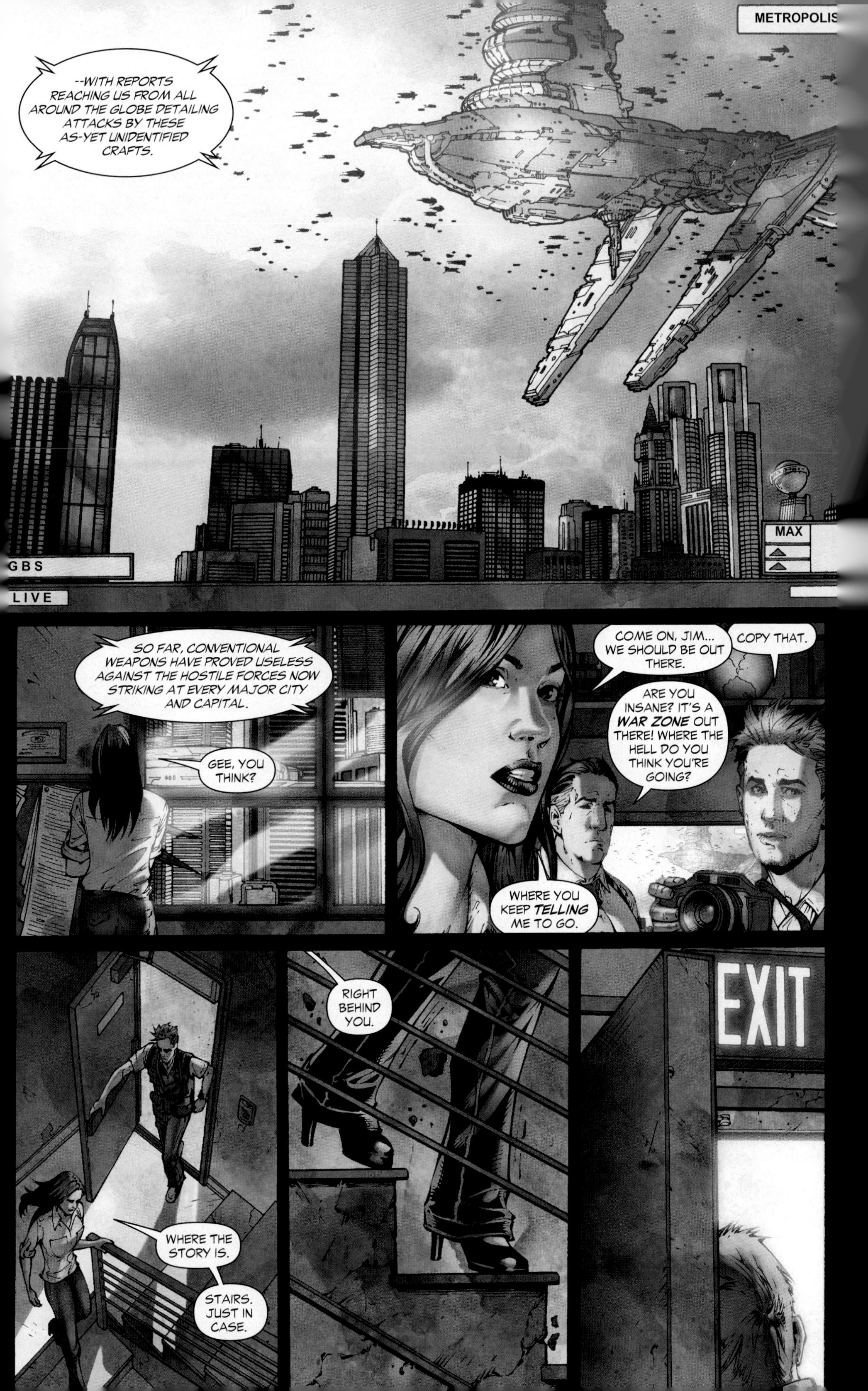
METROPOLIS
--WITH REPORTS REACHING US FROM ALL AROUND THE GLOBE DETAILING ATTACKS BY THESE AS-YET UNIDENTIFIED CRAFTS.
GBS
LIVE
MAX
SO FAR, CONVENTIONAL WEAPONS HAVE PROVED USELESS AGAINST THE HOSTILE FORCES NOW STRIKING AT EVERY MAJOR CITY AND CAPITAL.
GEE, YOU THINK?
COME ON, JIM... WE SHOULD BE OUT THERE.
COPY THAT.
ARE YOU INSANE? IT'S A WAR ZONE OUT THERE! WHERE THE HELL DO YOU THINK YOU'RE GOING?
WHERE YOU KEEP TELLING ME TO GO.
WHERE THE STORY IS.
STAIRS. JUST IN CASE.
RIGHT BEHIND YOU.
EXIT

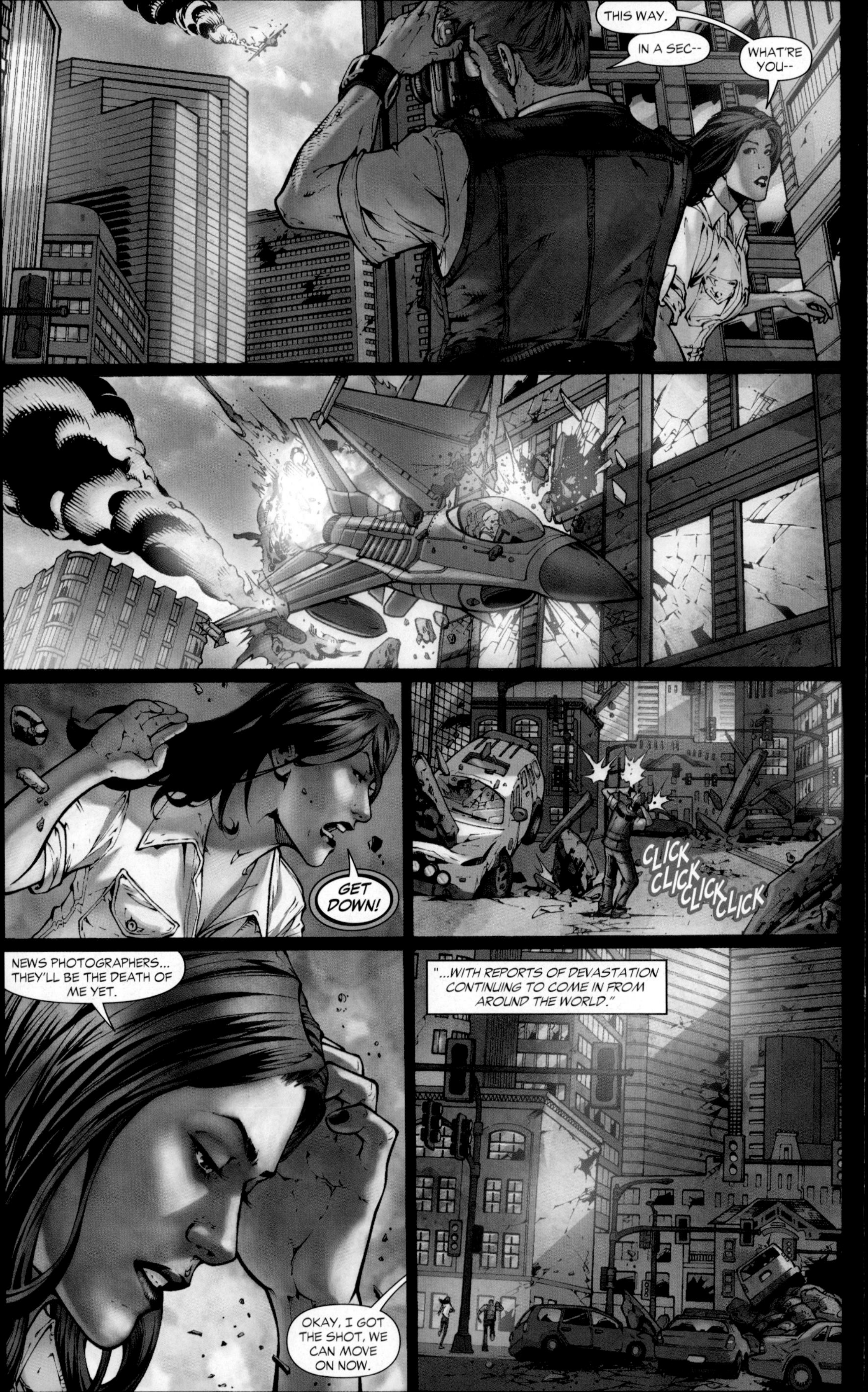
THIS WAY.
IN A SEC--
WHAT'RE YOU--
GET DOWN!
CLICK CLICK CLICK CLICK
NEWS PHOTOGRAPHERS... THEY'LL BE THE DEATH OF ME YET.
OKAY, I GOT THE SHOT, WE CAN MOVE ON NOW.
"...WITH REPORTS OF DEVASTATION CONTINUING TO COME IN FROM AROUND THE WORLD."

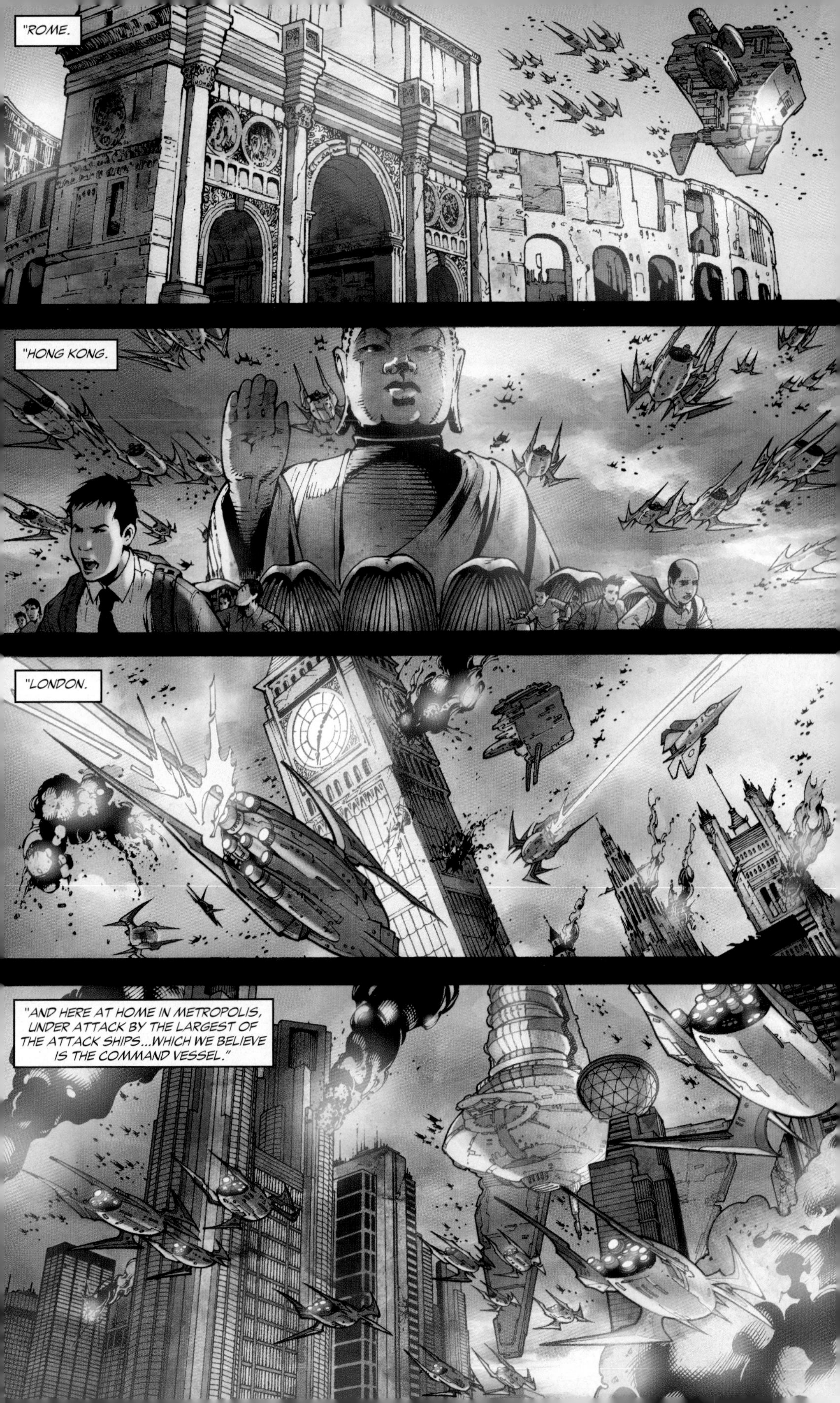
"ROME.
"HONG KONG.
"LONDON.
"AND HERE AT HOME IN METROPOLIS, UNDER ATTACK BY THE LARGEST OF THE ATTACK SHIPS...WHICH WE BELIEVE IS THE COMMAND VESSEL."

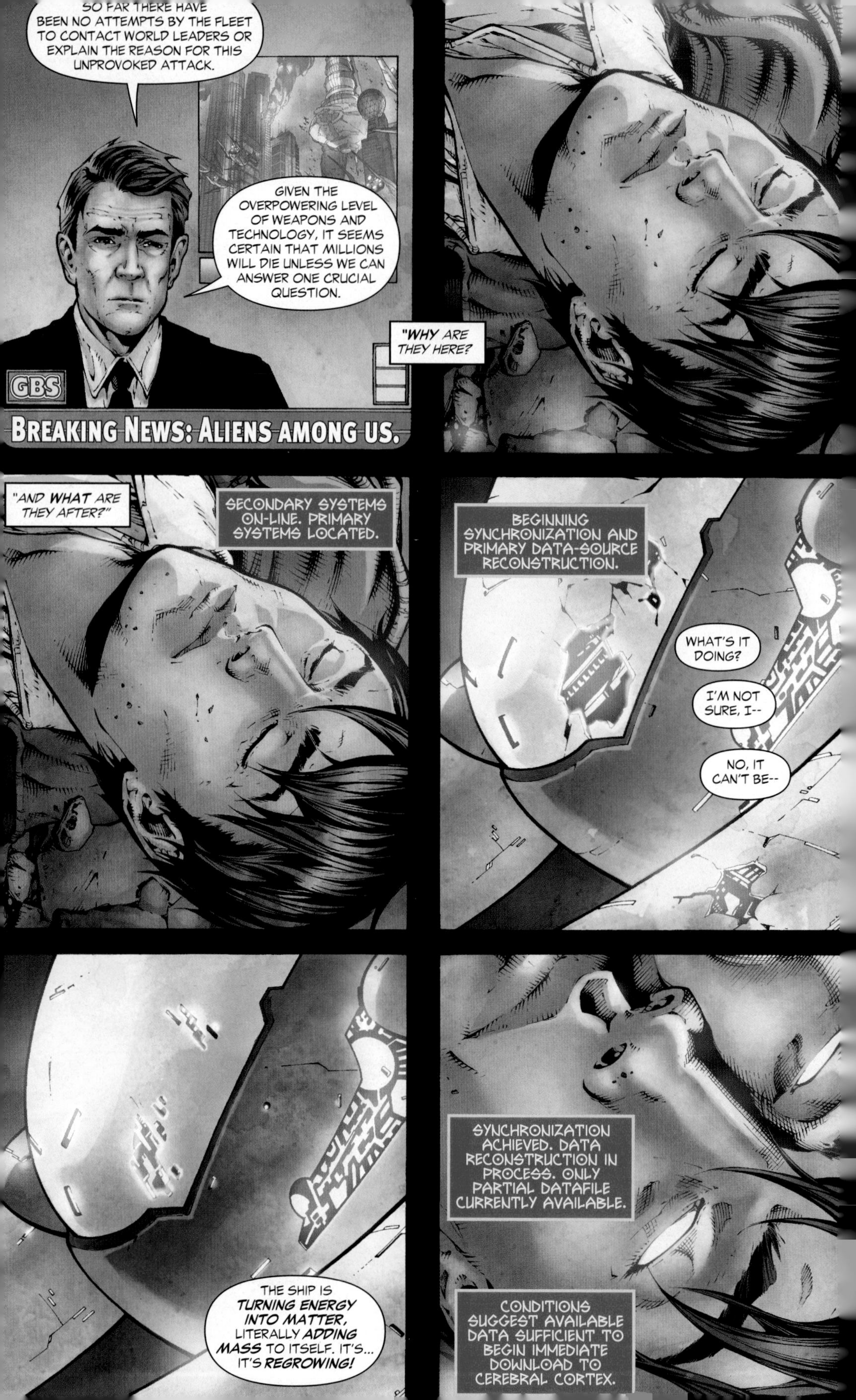
SO FAR THERE HAVE BEEN NO ATTEMPTS BY THE FLEET TO CONTACT WORLD LEADERS OR EXPLAIN THE REASON FOR THIS UNPROVOKED ATTACK.
GIVEN THE OVERPOWERING LEVEL OF WEAPONS AND TECHNOLOGY, IT SEEMS CERTAIN THAT MILLIONS WILL DIE UNLESS WE CAN ANSWER ONE CRUCIAL QUESTION.
GBS
BREAKING NEWS: ALIENS AMONG US.
"WHY ARE THEY HERE?
"AND WHAT ARE THEY AFTER?"
SECONDARY SYSTEMS ON-LINE. PRIMARY SYSTEMS LOCATED.
BEGINNING SYNCHRONIZATION AND PRIMARY DATA-SOURCE RECONSTRUCTION.
WHAT'S IT DOING?
I'M NOT SURE, I--
NO, IT CAN'T BE--
THE SHIP IS TURNING ENERGY INTO MATTER, LITERALLY ADDING MASS TO ITSELF. IT'S... IT'S REGROWING!
SYNCHRONIZATION ACHIEVED. DATA RECONSTRUCTION IN PROCESS. ONLY PARTIAL DATAFILE CURRENTLY AVAILABLE.
CONDITIONS SUGGEST AVAILABLE DATA SUFFICIENT TO BEGIN IMMEDIATE DOWNLOAD TO CEREBRAL CORTEX.

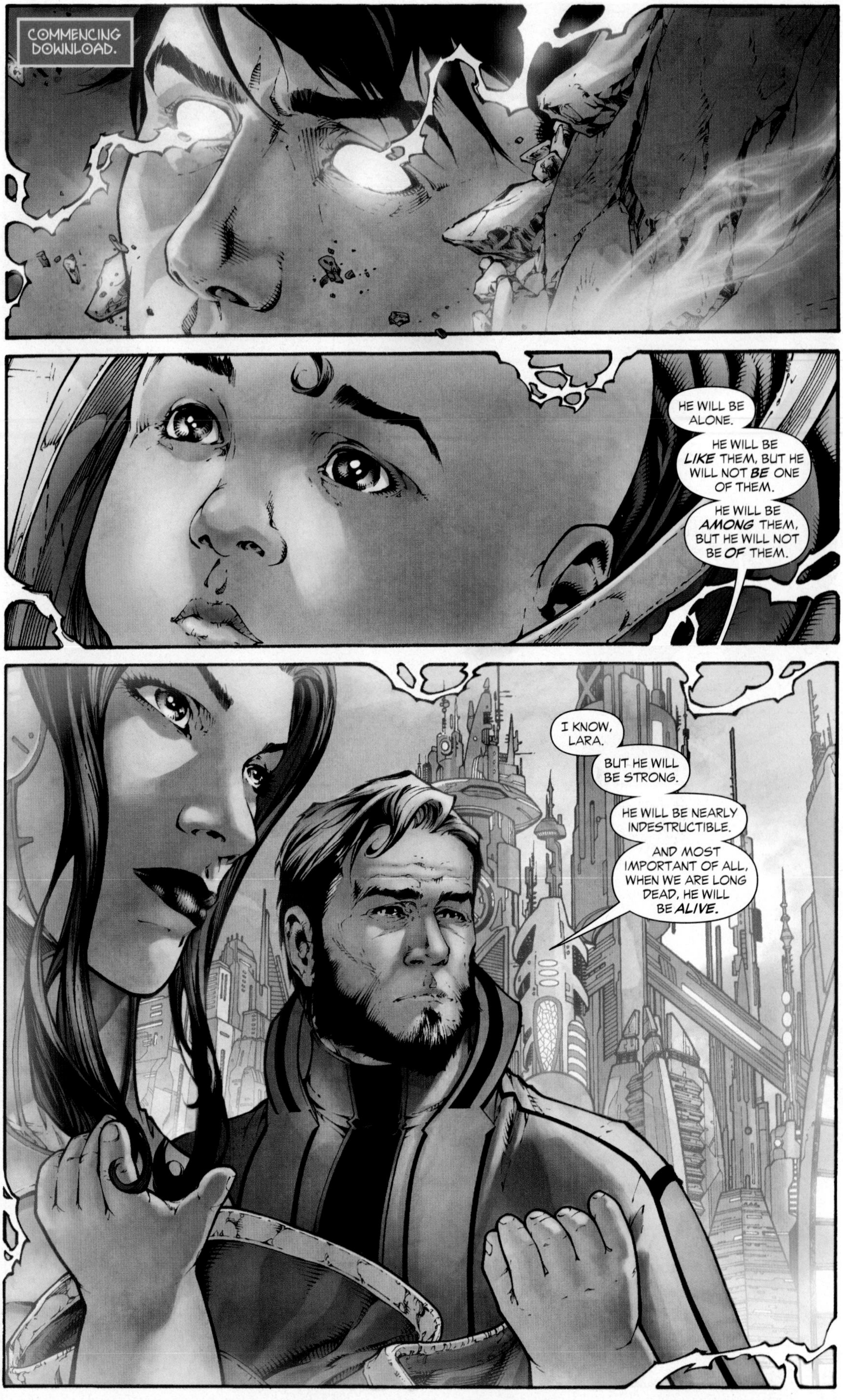
COMMENCING DOWNLOAD.
HE WILL BE ALONE.
HE WILL BE LIKE THEM, BUT HE WILL NOT BE ONE OF THEM.
HE WILL BE AMONG THEM, BUT HE WILL NOT BE OF THEM.
I KNOW, LARA.
BUT HE WILL BE STRONG.
HE WILL BE NEARLY INDESTRUCTIBLE.
AND MOST IMPORTANT OF ALL, WHEN WE ARE LONG DEAD, HE WILL BE ALIVE.

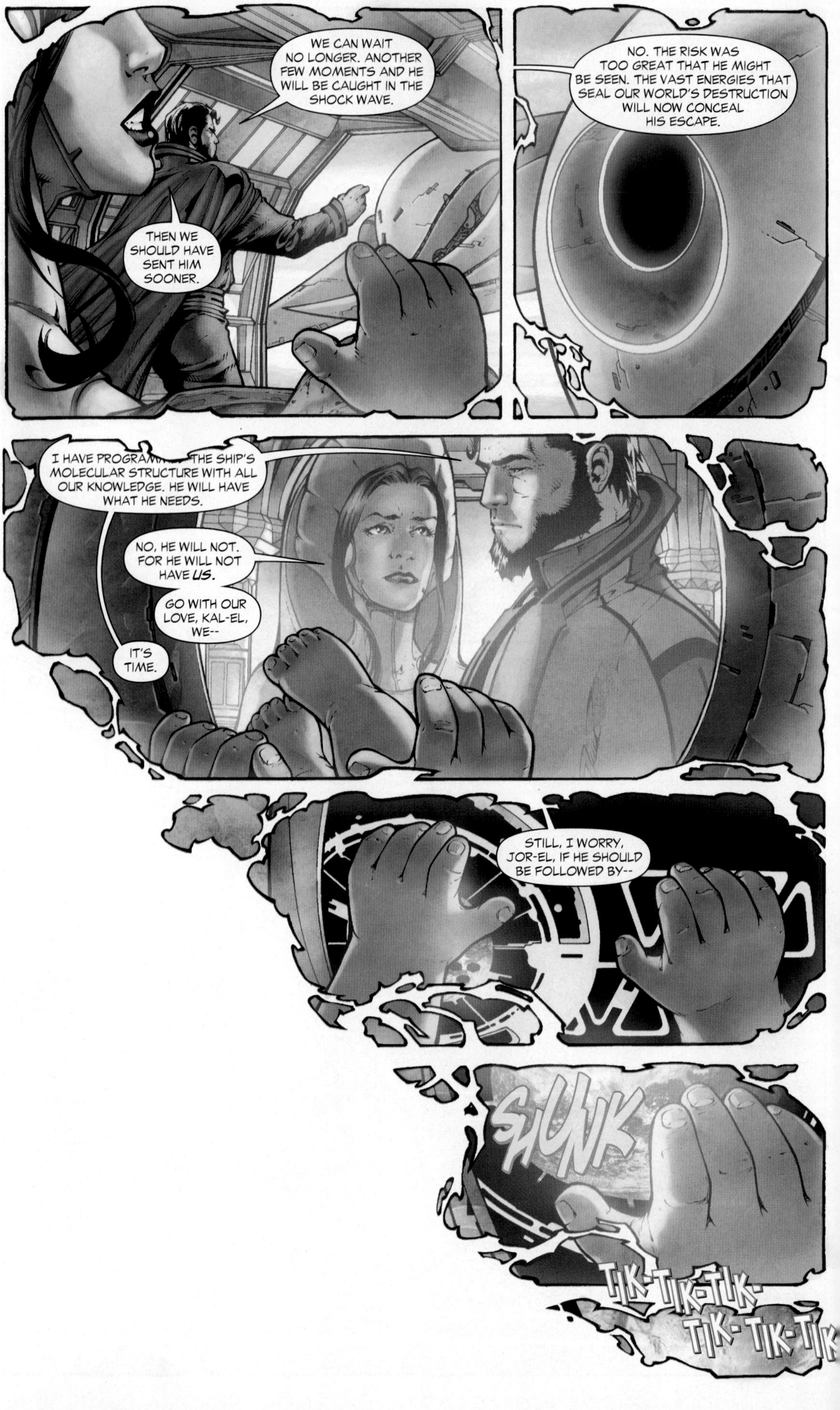

WE CAN WAIT NO LONGER. ANOTHER FEW MOMENTS AND HE WILL BE CAUGHT IN THE SHOCK WAVE.
THEN WE SHOULD HAVE SENT HIM SOONER.
NO. THE RISK WAS TOO GREAT THAT HE MIGHT BE SEEN. THE VAST ENERGIES THAT SEAL OUR WORLD'S DESTRUCTION WILL NOW CONCEAL HIS ESCAPE.
I HAVE PROGRAMMED THE SHIP'S MOLECULAR STRUCTURE WITH ALL OUR KNOWLEDGE. HE WILL HAVE WHAT HE NEEDS.
NO, HE WILL NOT. FOR HE WILL NOT HAVE *US.*
GO WITH OUR LOVE, KAL-EL, WE--
IT'S TIME.
STILL, I WORRY, JOR-EL, IF HE SHOULD BE FOLLOWED BY--
SHUNK
TIK-TIK-TIK-
TIK-TIK-TIK

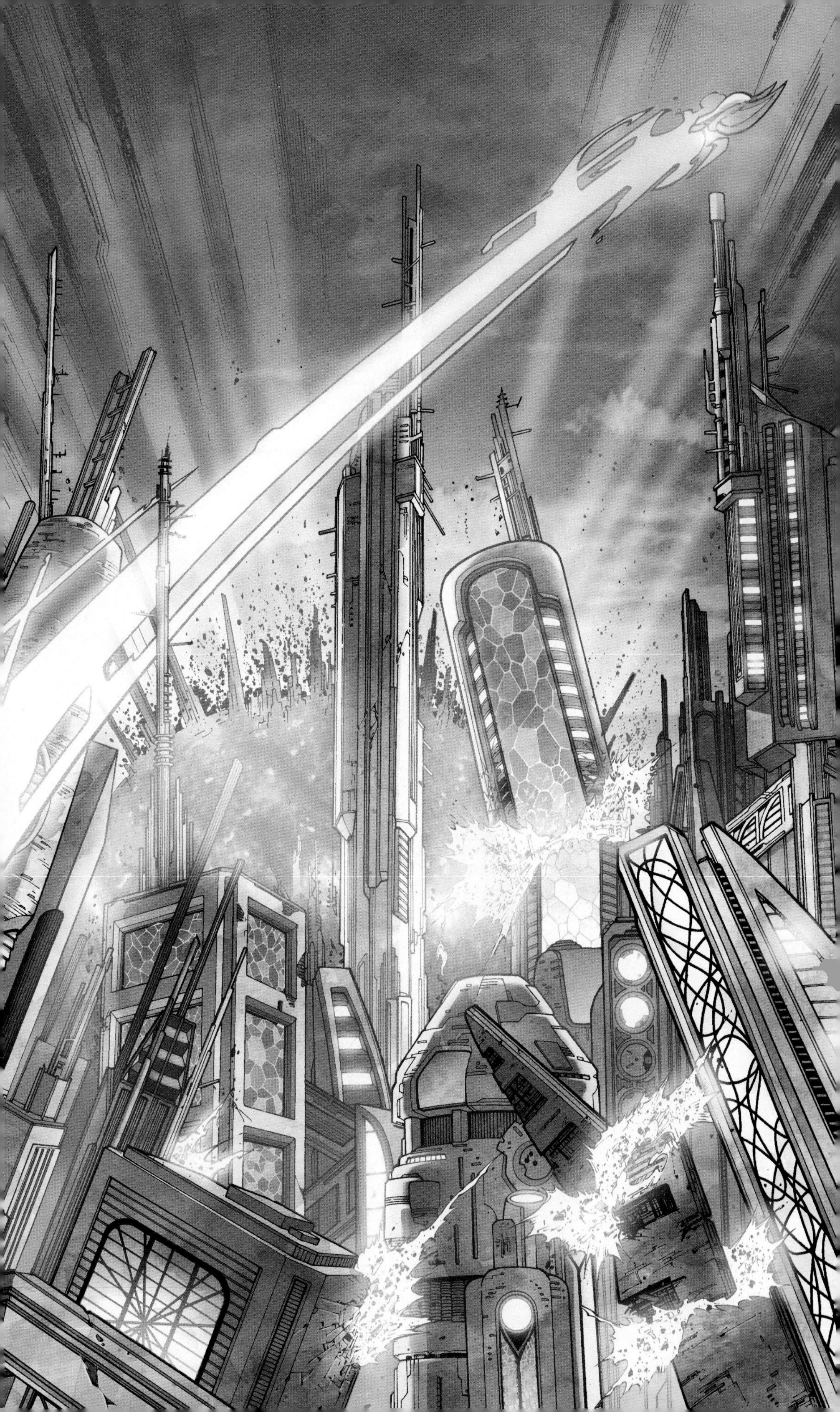

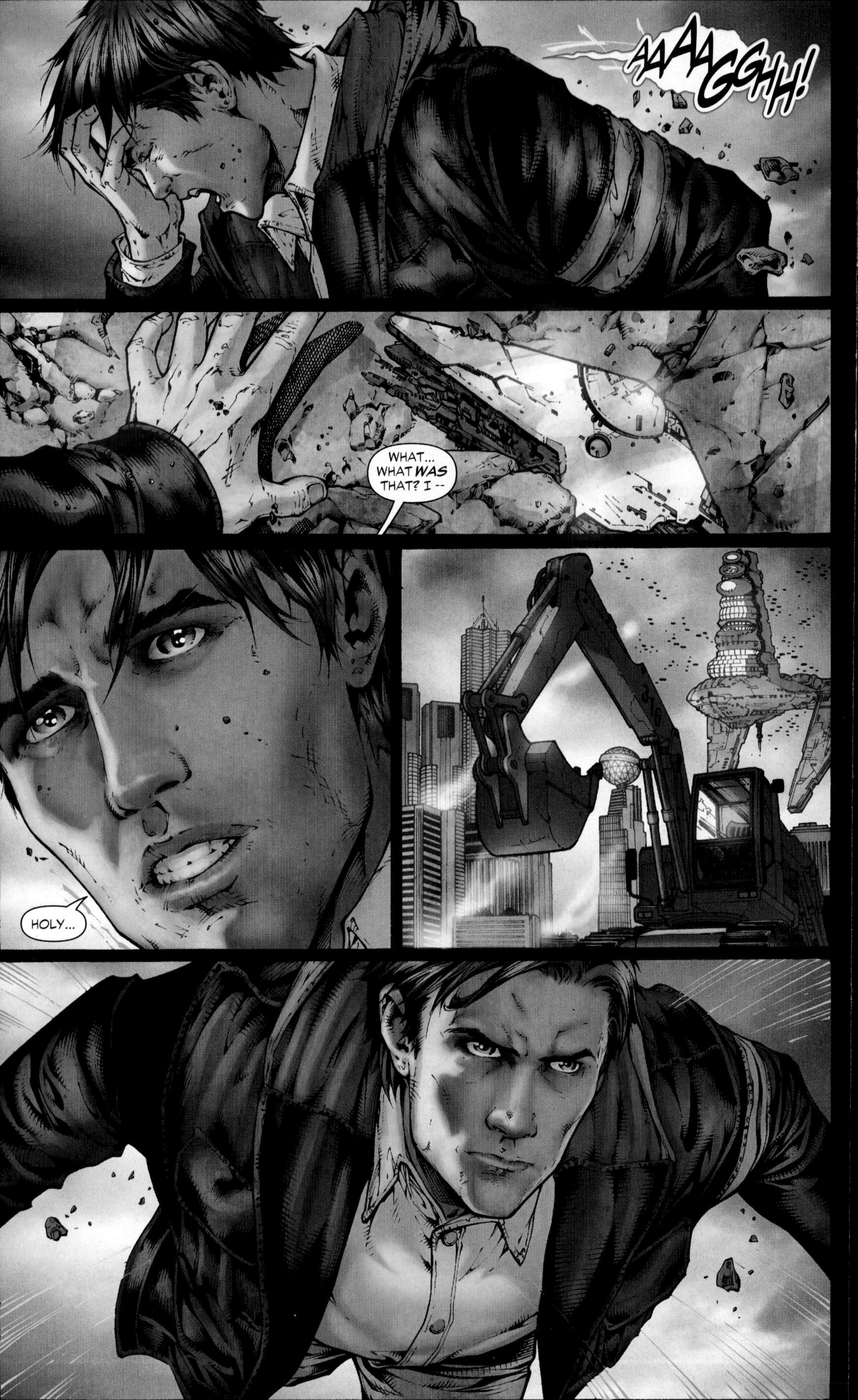
AAAAGGHH!
WHAT... WHAT WAS THAT? I --
HOLY...

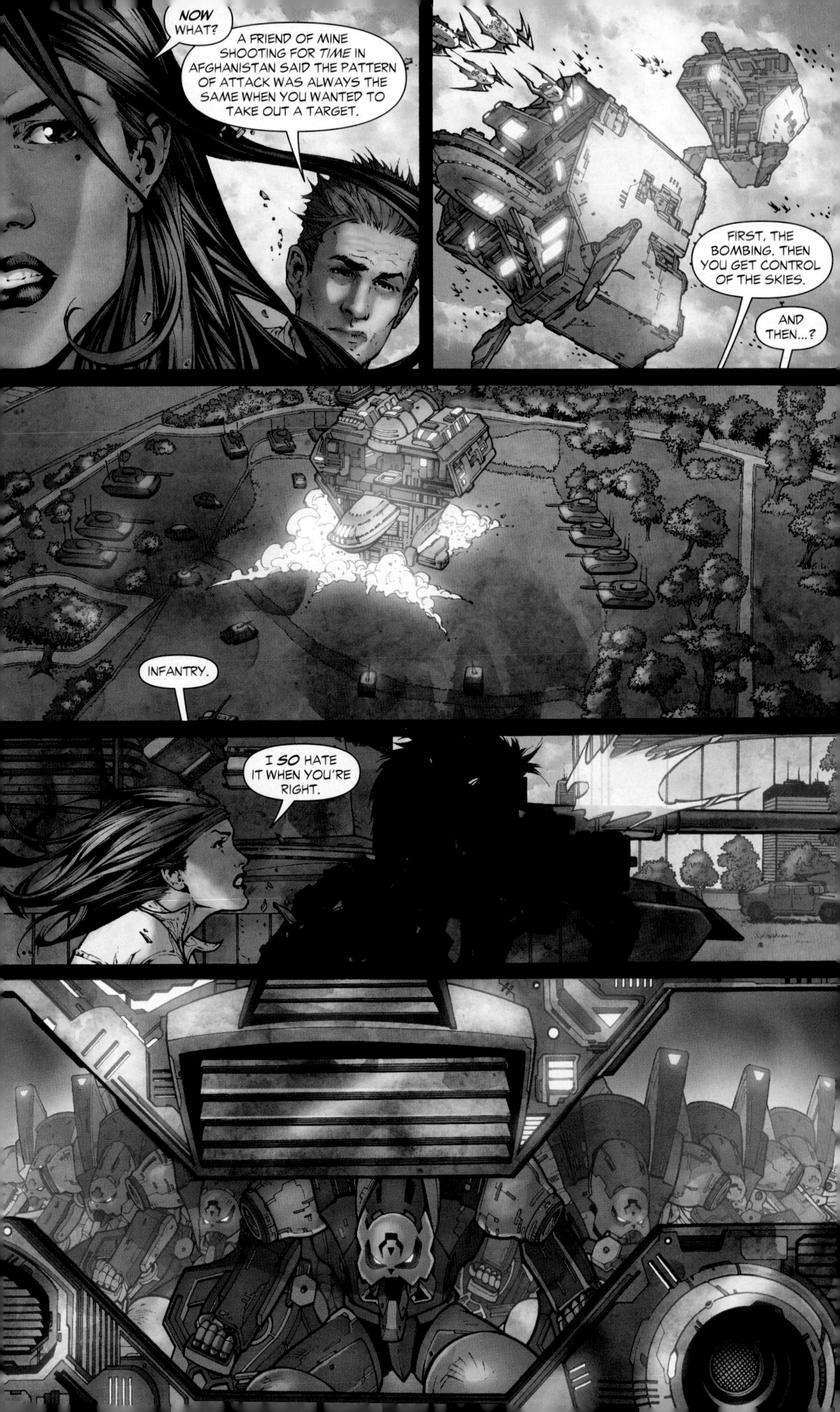
NOW WHAT?
A FRIEND OF MINE SHOOTING FOR TIME IN AFGHANISTAN SAID THE PATTERN OF ATTACK WAS ALWAYS THE SAME WHEN YOU WANTED TO TAKE OUT A TARGET.
FIRST, THE BOMBING. THEN YOU GET CONTROL OF THE SKIES.
AND THEN...?
INFANTRY.
I SO HATE IT WHEN YOU'RE RIGHT.

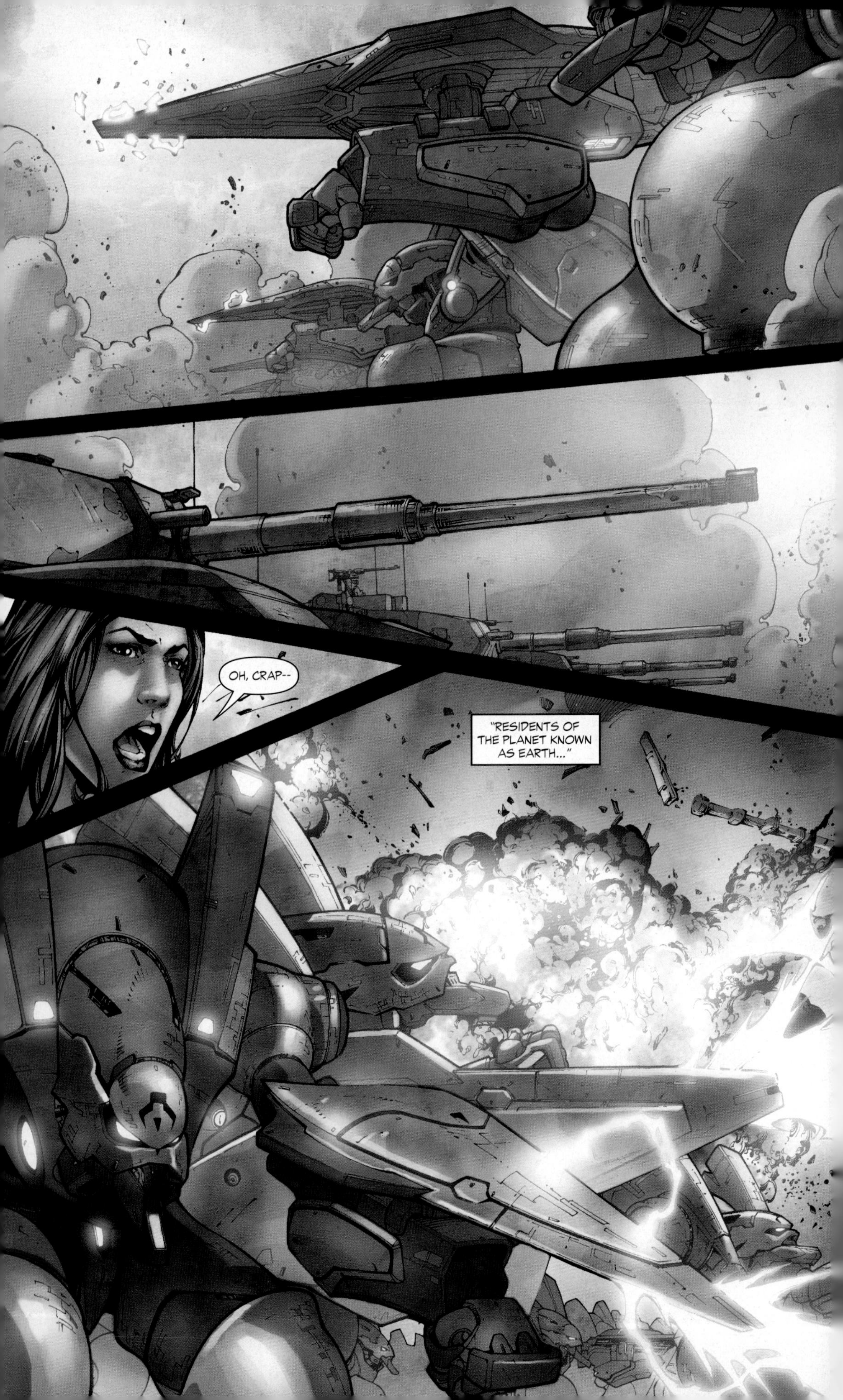
OH, CRAP--
"RESIDENTS OF THE PLANET KNOWN AS EARTH..."

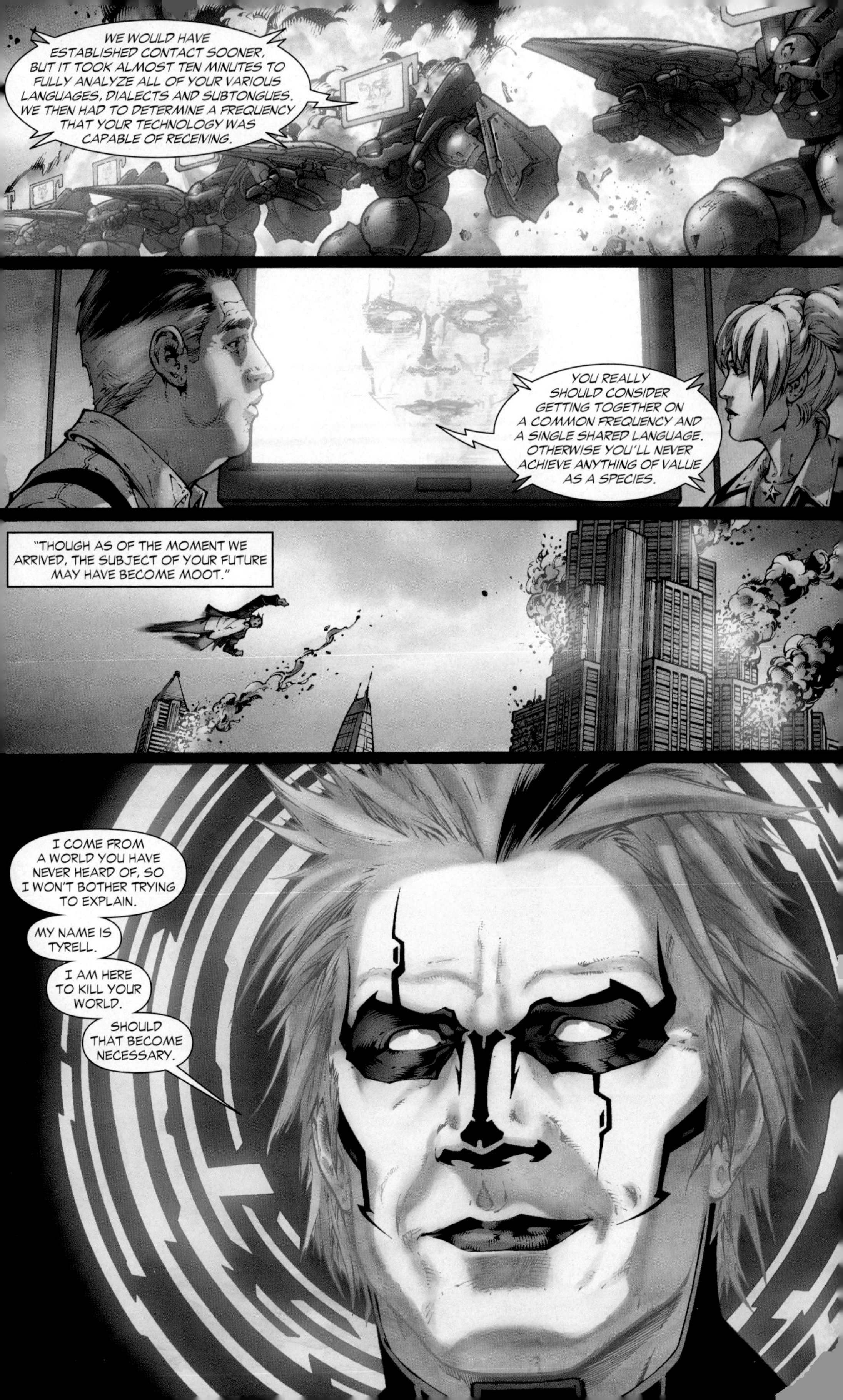
WE WOULD HAVE ESTABLISHED CONTACT SOONER, BUT IT TOOK ALMOST TEN MINUTES TO FULLY ANALYZE ALL OF YOUR VARIOUS LANGUAGES, DIALECTS AND SUBTONGUES. WE THEN HAD TO DETERMINE A FREQUENCY THAT YOUR TECHNOLOGY WAS CAPABLE OF RECEIVING.
YOU REALLY SHOULD CONSIDER GETTING TOGETHER ON A COMMON FREQUENCY AND A SINGLE SHARED LANGUAGE. OTHERWISE YOU'LL NEVER ACHIEVE ANYTHING OF VALUE AS A SPECIES.
"THOUGH AS OF THE MOMENT WE ARRIVED, THE SUBJECT OF YOUR FUTURE MAY HAVE BECOME MOOT."
I COME FROM A WORLD YOU HAVE NEVER HEARD OF, SO I WON'T BOTHER TRYING TO EXPLAIN.
MY NAME IS TYRELL.
I AM HERE TO KILL YOUR WORLD.
SHOULD THAT BECOME NECESSARY.

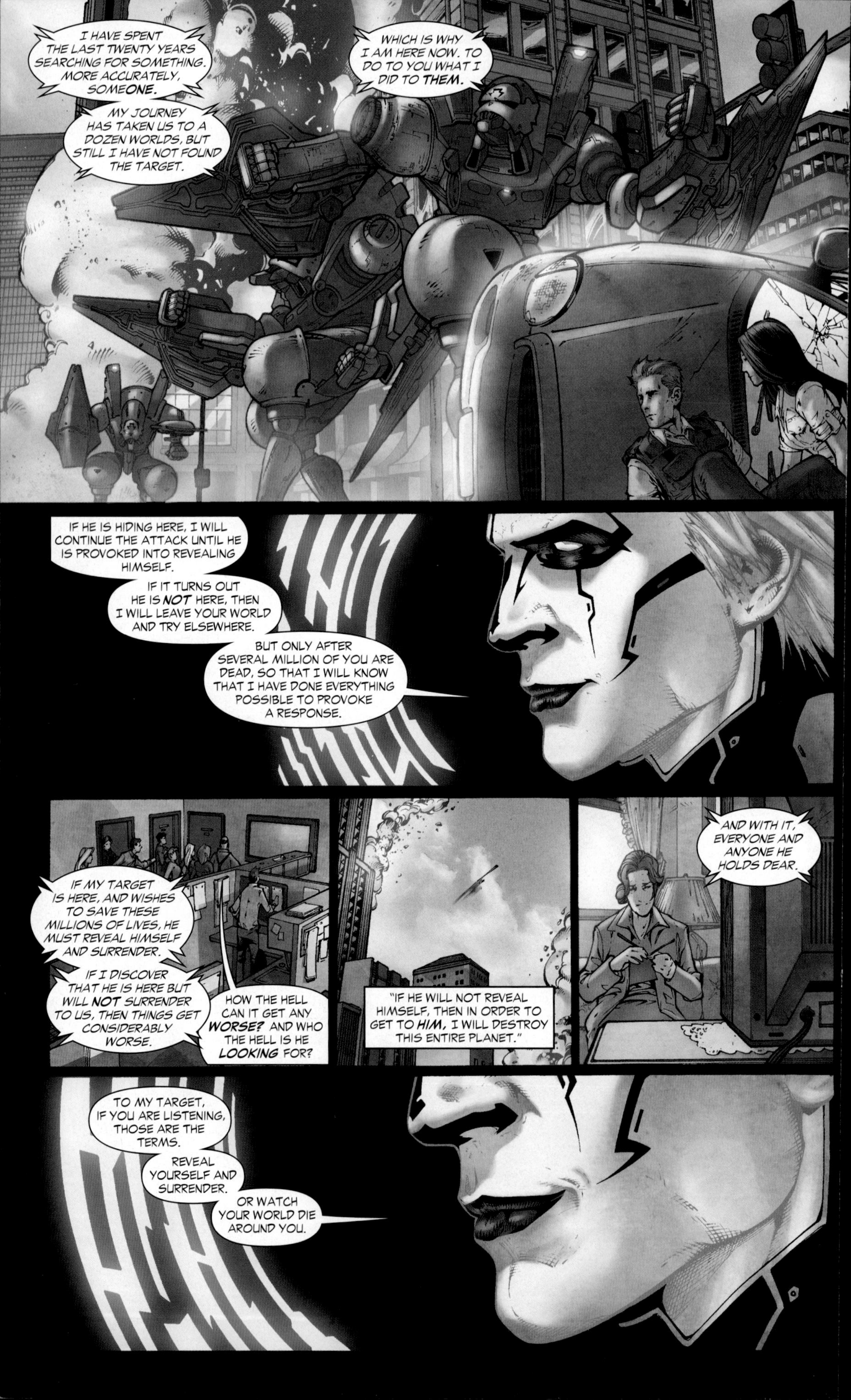
I HAVE SPENT THE LAST TWENTY YEARS SEARCHING FOR SOMETHING. MORE ACCURATELY, SOMEONE.
MY JOURNEY HAS TAKEN US TO A DOZEN WORLDS, BUT STILL I HAVE NOT FOUND THE TARGET.
WHICH IS WHY I AM HERE NOW. TO DO TO YOU WHAT I DID TO THEM.
IF HE IS HIDING HERE, I WILL CONTINUE THE ATTACK UNTIL HE IS PROVOKED INTO REVEALING HIMSELF.
IF IT TURNS OUT HE IS NOT HERE, THEN I WILL LEAVE YOUR WORLD AND TRY ELSEWHERE.
BUT ONLY AFTER SEVERAL MILLION OF YOU ARE DEAD, SO THAT I WILL KNOW THAT I HAVE DONE EVERYTHING POSSIBLE TO PROVOKE A RESPONSE.
IF MY TARGET IS HERE, AND WISHES TO SAVE THESE MILLIONS OF LIVES, HE MUST REVEAL HIMSELF AND SURRENDER.
IF I DISCOVER THAT HE IS HERE BUT WILL NOT SURRENDER TO US, THEN THINGS GET CONSIDERABLY WORSE.
HOW THE HELL CAN IT GET ANY WORSE? AND WHO THE HELL IS HE LOOKING FOR?
"IF HE WILL NOT REVEAL HIMSELF, THEN IN ORDER TO GET TO HIM, I WILL DESTROY THIS ENTIRE PLANET."
AND WITH IT, EVERYONE AND ANYONE HE HOLDS DEAR.
TO MY TARGET, IF YOU ARE LISTENING, THOSE ARE THE TERMS.
REVEAL YOURSELF AND SURRENDER.
OR WATCH YOUR WORLD DIE AROUND YOU.

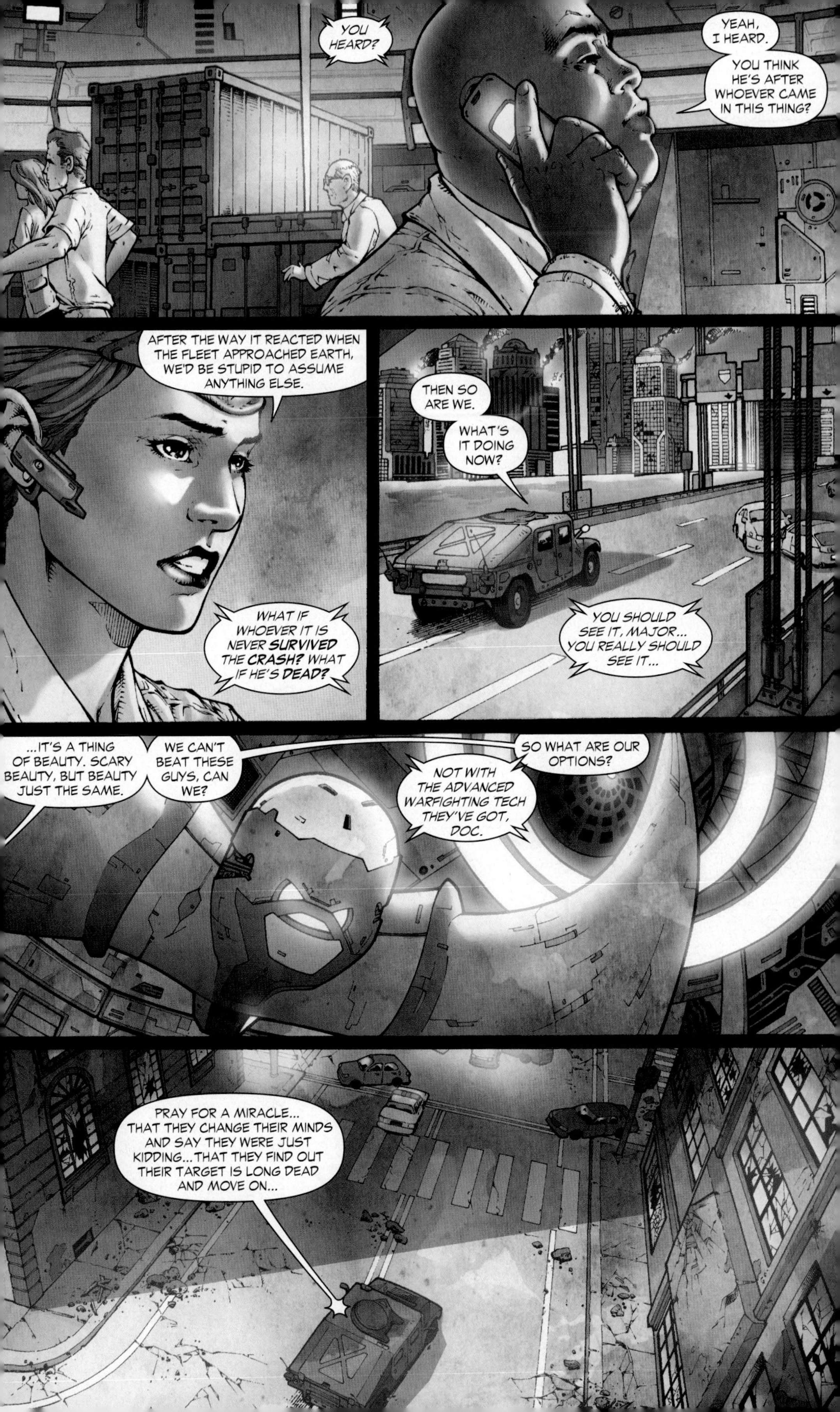
YOU HEARD?
YEAH, I HEARD.
YOU THINK HE'S AFTER WHOEVER CAME IN THIS THING?
AFTER THE WAY IT REACTED WHEN THE FLEET APPROACHED EARTH, WE'D BE STUPID TO ASSUME ANYTHING ELSE.
THEN SO ARE WE.
WHAT'S IT DOING NOW?
WHAT IF WHOEVER IT IS NEVER SURVIVED THE CRASH? WHAT IF HE'S DEAD?
YOU SHOULD SEE IT, MAJOR... YOU REALLY SHOULD SEE IT...
...IT'S A THING OF BEAUTY. SCARY BEAUTY, BUT BEAUTY JUST THE SAME.
WE CAN'T BEAT THESE GUYS, CAN WE?
NOT WITH THE ADVANCED WARFIGHTING TECH THEY'VE GOT, DOC.
SO WHAT ARE OUR OPTIONS?
PRAY FOR A MIRACLE... THAT THEY CHANGE THEIR MINDS AND SAY THEY WERE JUST KIDDING... THAT THEY FIND OUT THEIR TARGET IS LONG DEAD AND MOVE ON...

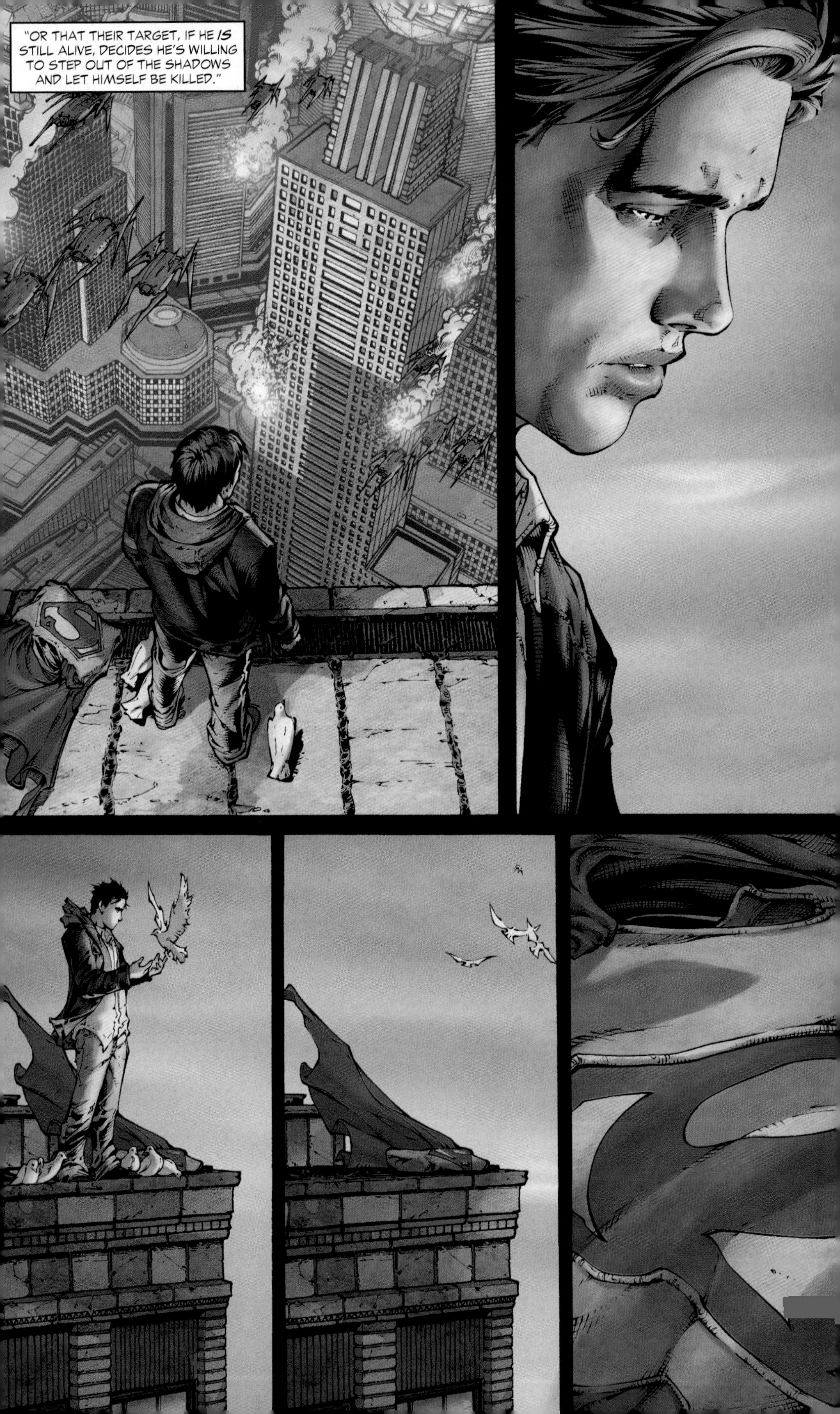
"OR THAT THEIR TARGET, IF HE *IS* STILL ALIVE, DECIDES HE'S WILLING TO STEP OUT OF THE SHADOWS AND LET HIMSELF BE KILLED."

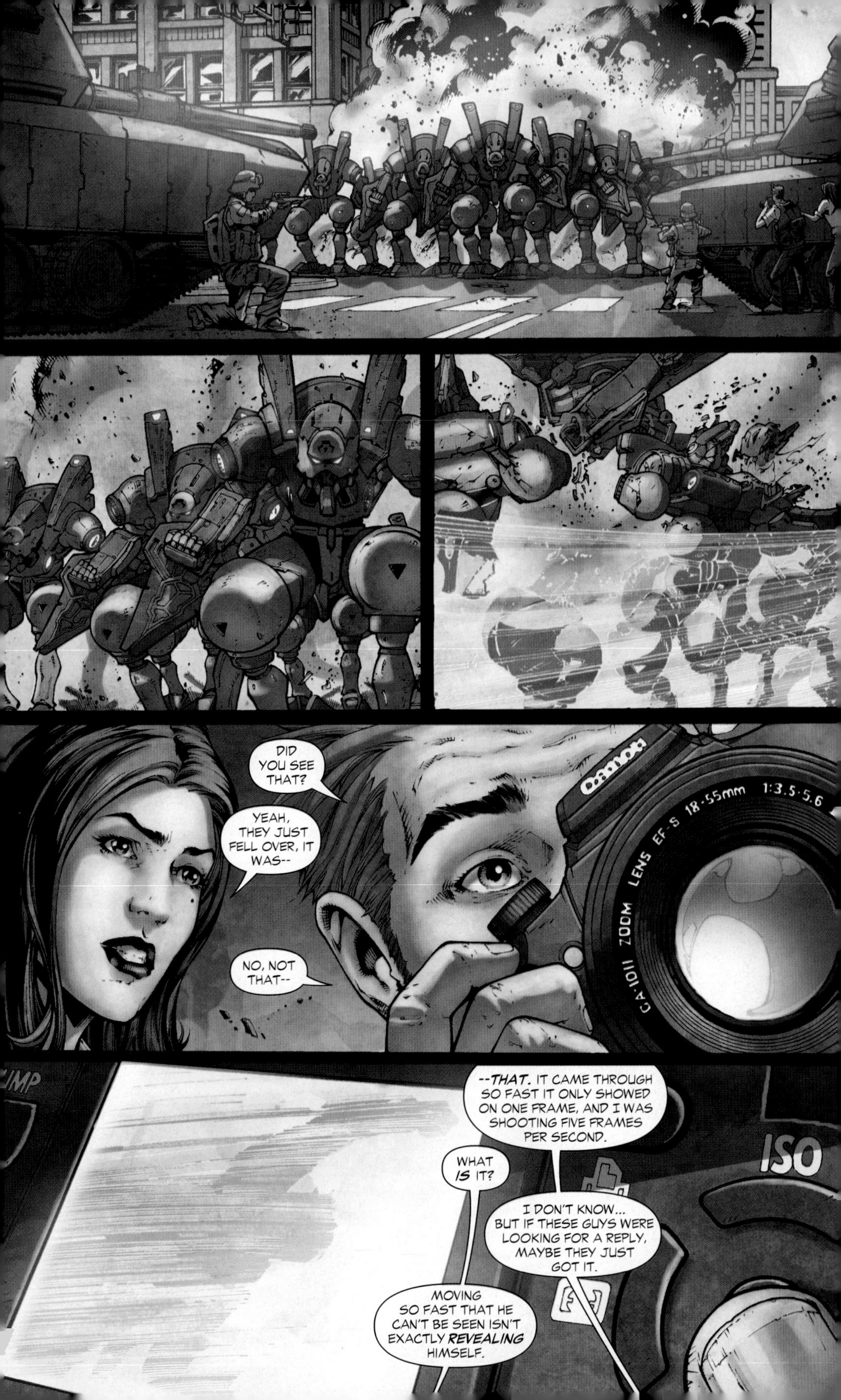
DID YOU SEE THAT?
YEAH, THEY JUST FELL OVER, IT WAS--
NO, NOT THAT--
--THAT. IT CAME THROUGH SO FAST IT ONLY SHOWED ON ONE FRAME, AND I WAS SHOOTING FIVE FRAMES PER SECOND.
WHAT IS IT?
I DON'T KNOW... BUT IF THESE GUYS WERE LOOKING FOR A REPLY, MAYBE THEY JUST GOT IT.
MOVING SO FAST THAT HE CAN'T BE SEEN ISN'T EXACTLY REVEALING HIMSELF.

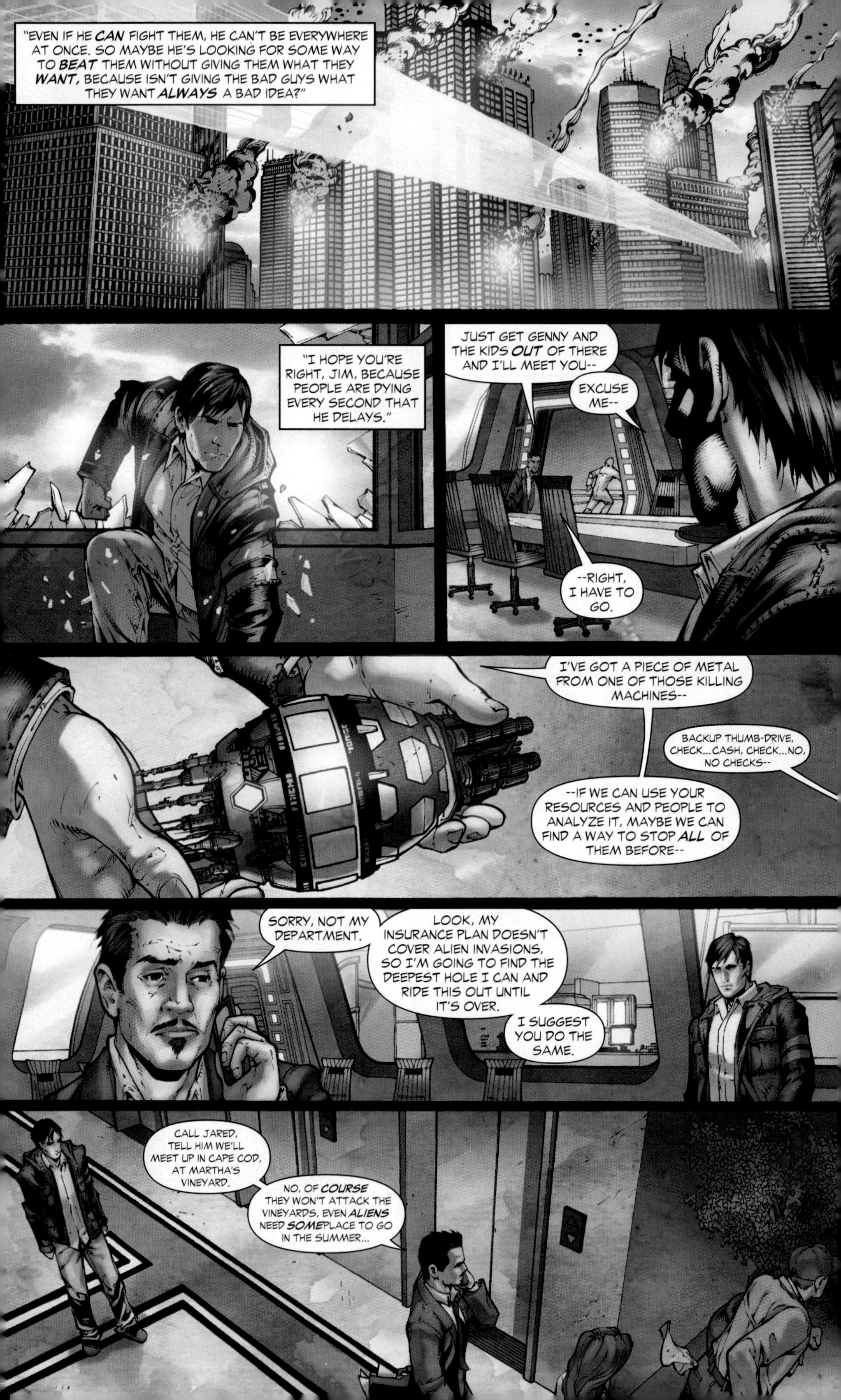
"EVEN IF HE CAN FIGHT THEM, HE CAN'T BE EVERYWHERE AT ONCE. SO MAYBE HE'S LOOKING FOR SOME WAY TO BEAT THEM WITHOUT GIVING THEM WHAT THEY WANT, BECAUSE ISN'T GIVING THE BAD GUYS WHAT THEY WANT ALWAYS A BAD IDEA?"
"I HOPE YOU'RE RIGHT, JIM, BECAUSE PEOPLE ARE DYING EVERY SECOND THAT HE DELAYS."
JUST GET GENNY AND THE KIDS OUT OF THERE AND I'LL MEET YOU--
EXCUSE ME--
--RIGHT, I HAVE TO GO.
I'VE GOT A PIECE OF METAL FROM ONE OF THOSE KILLING MACHINES--
BACKUP THUMB-DRIVE, CHECK...CASH, CHECK...NO, NO CHECKS--
--IF WE CAN USE YOUR RESOURCES AND PEOPLE TO ANALYZE IT, MAYBE WE CAN FIND A WAY TO STOP ALL OF THEM BEFORE--
SORRY, NOT MY DEPARTMENT.
LOOK, MY INSURANCE PLAN DOESN'T COVER ALIEN INVASIONS, SO I'M GOING TO FIND THE DEEPEST HOLE I CAN AND RIDE THIS OUT UNTIL IT'S OVER.
I SUGGEST YOU DO THE SAME.
CALL JARED, TELL HIM WE'LL MEET UP IN CAPE COD, AT MARTHA'S VINEYARD.
NO, OF COURSE THEY WON'T ATTACK THE VINEYARDS, EVEN ALIENS NEED SOMEPLACE TO GO IN THE SUMMER...

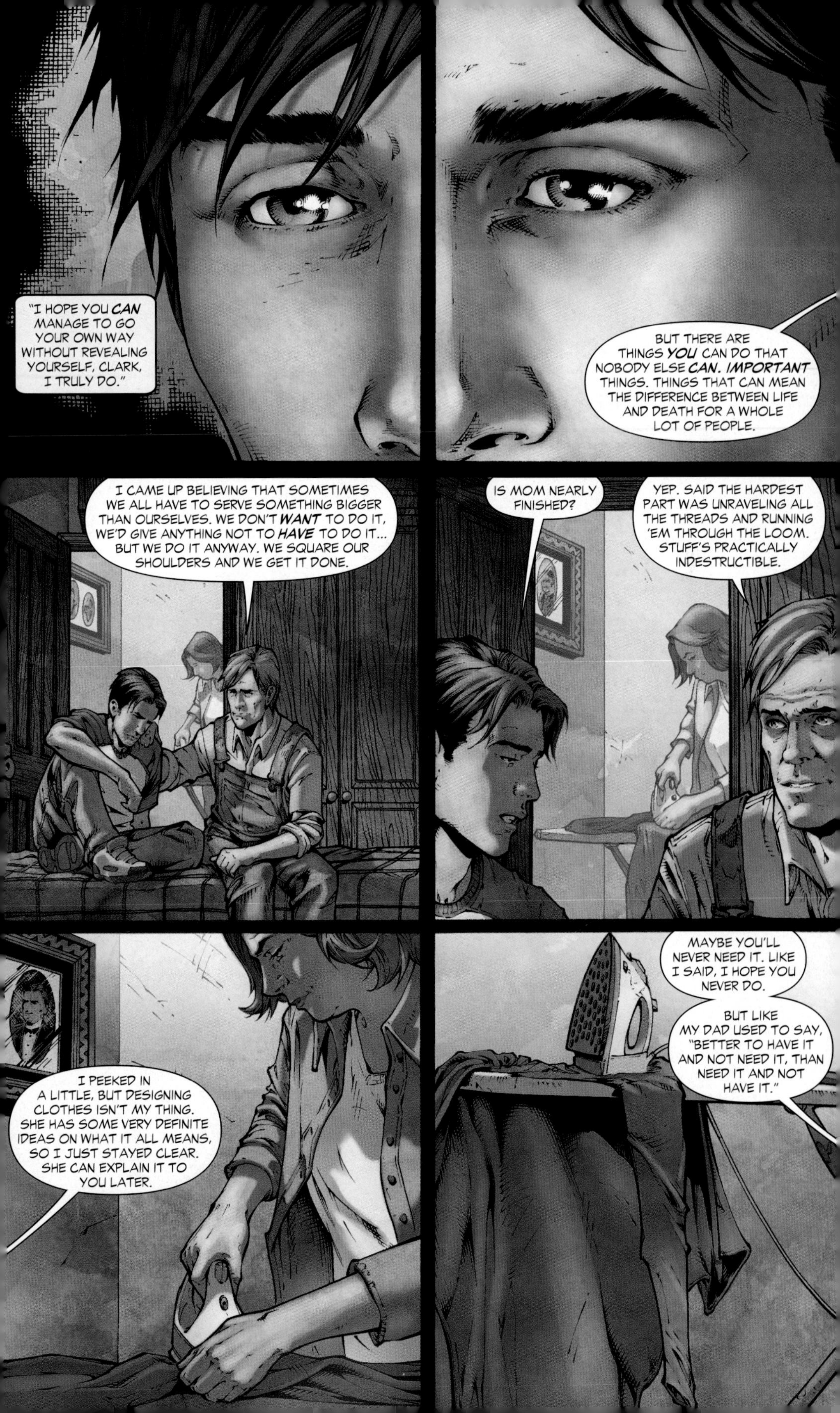
"I HOPE YOU CAN MANAGE TO GO YOUR OWN WAY WITHOUT REVEALING YOURSELF, CLARK, I TRULY DO."
BUT THERE ARE THINGS YOU CAN DO THAT NOBODY ELSE CAN. IMPORTANT THINGS. THINGS THAT CAN MEAN THE DIFFERENCE BETWEEN LIFE AND DEATH FOR A WHOLE LOT OF PEOPLE.
I CAME UP BELIEVING THAT SOMETIMES WE ALL HAVE TO SERVE SOMETHING BIGGER THAN OURSELVES. WE DON'T WANT TO DO IT, WE'D GIVE ANYTHING NOT TO HAVE TO DO IT... BUT WE DO IT ANYWAY. WE SQUARE OUR SHOULDERS AND WE GET IT DONE.
IS MOM NEARLY FINISHED?
YEP. SAID THE HARDEST PART WAS UNRAVELING ALL THE THREADS AND RUNNING 'EM THROUGH THE LOOM. STUFF'S PRACTICALLY INDESTRUCTIBLE.
I PEEKED IN A LITTLE, BUT DESIGNING CLOTHES ISN'T MY THING. SHE HAS SOME VERY DEFINITE IDEAS ON WHAT IT ALL MEANS, SO I JUST STAYED CLEAR. SHE CAN EXPLAIN IT TO YOU LATER.
MAYBE YOU'LL NEVER NEED IT. LIKE I SAID, I HOPE YOU NEVER DO.
BUT LIKE MY DAD USED TO SAY, "BETTER TO HAVE IT AND NOT NEED IT, THAN NEED IT AND NOT HAVE IT."

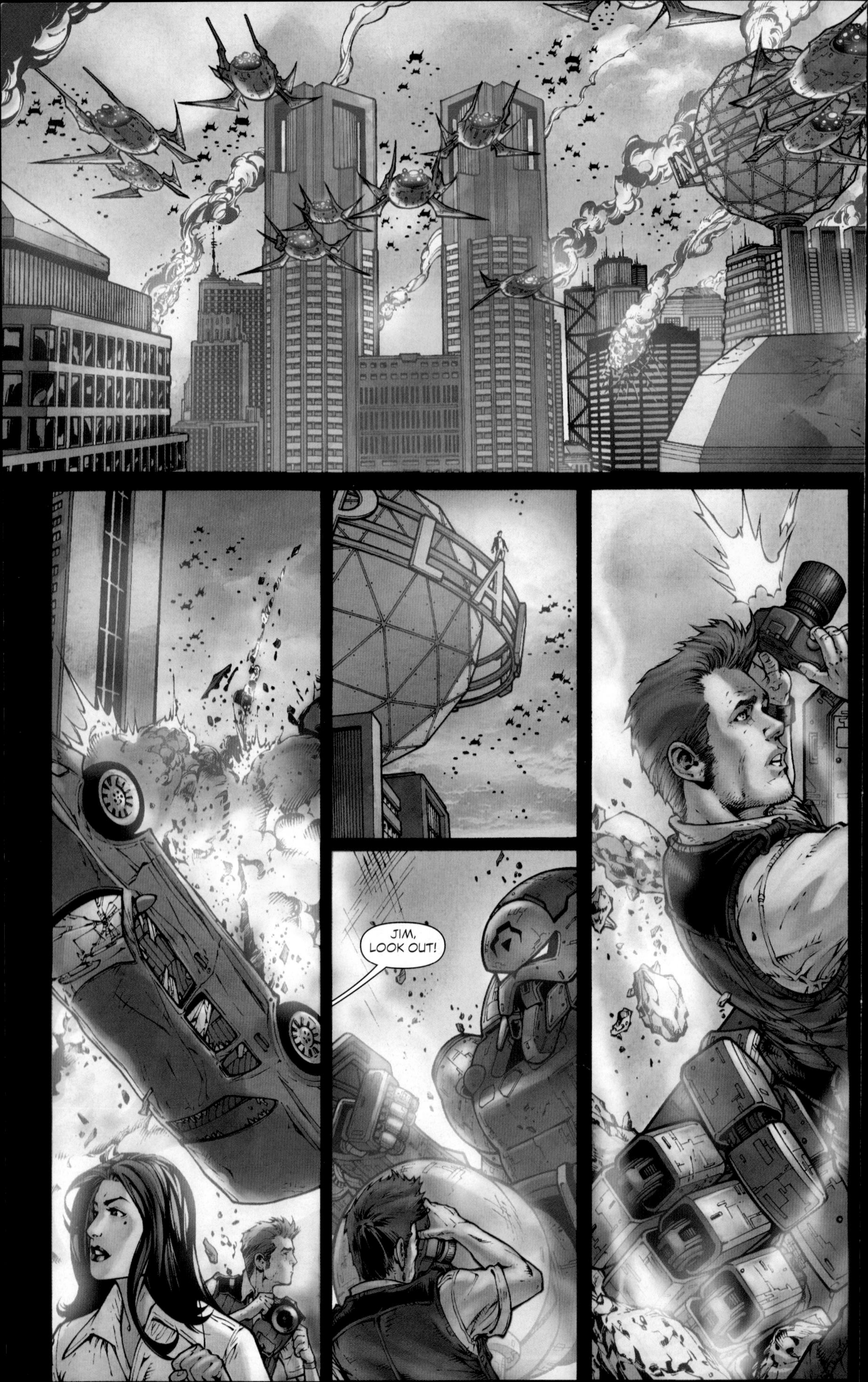

NE
LA
JIM, LOOK OUT!

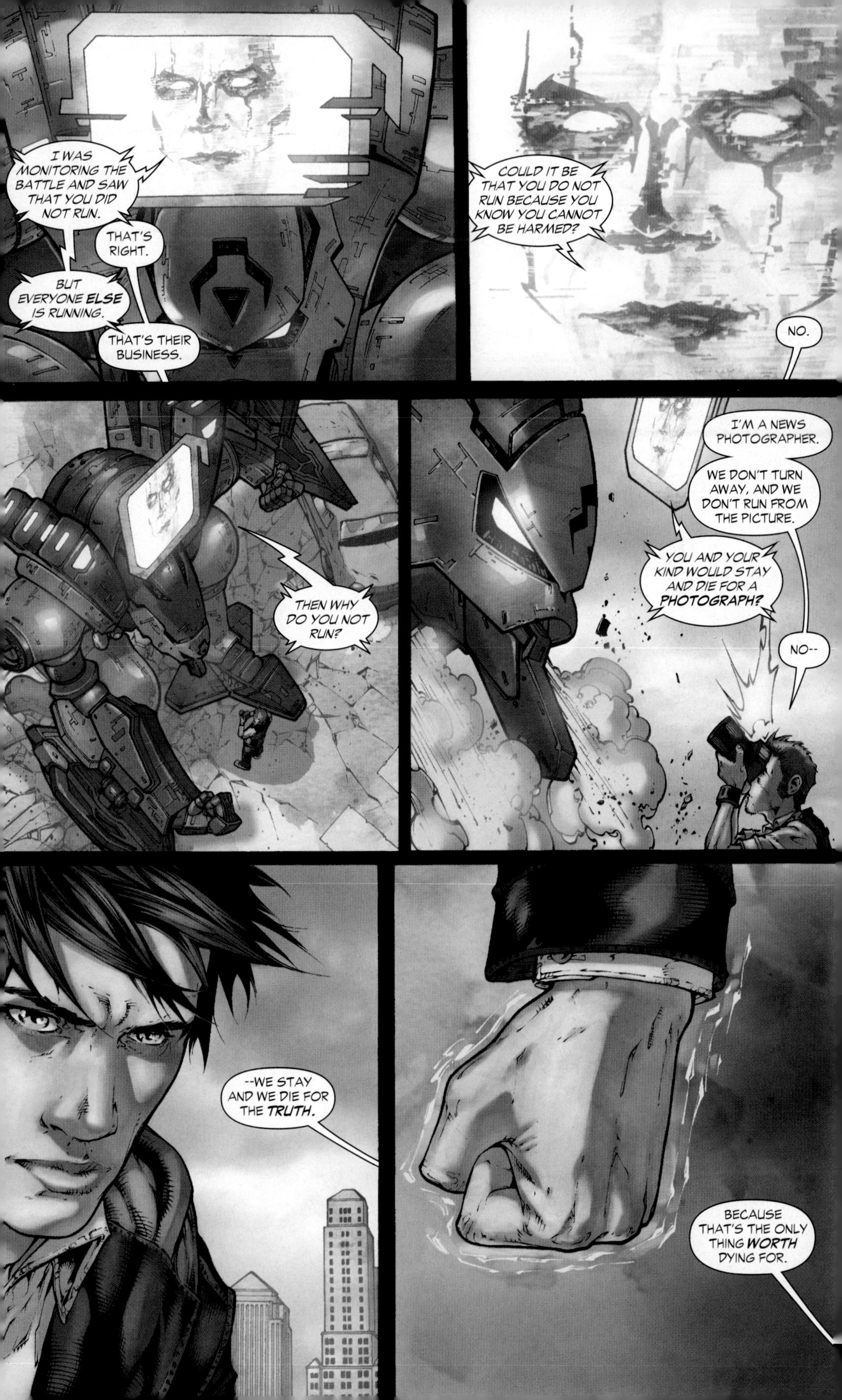
I WAS MONITORING THE BATTLE AND SAW THAT YOU DID NOT RUN.
THAT'S RIGHT.
BUT EVERYONE ELSE IS RUNNING.
THAT'S THEIR BUSINESS.
COULD IT BE THAT YOU DO NOT RUN BECAUSE YOU KNOW YOU CANNOT BE HARMED?
NO.
THEN WHY DO YOU NOT RUN?
I'M A NEWS PHOTOGRAPHER.
WE DON'T TURN AWAY, AND WE DON'T RUN FROM THE PICTURE.
YOU AND YOUR KIND WOULD STAY AND DIE FOR A PHOTOGRAPH?
NO--
--WE STAY AND WE DIE FOR THE TRUTH.
BECAUSE THAT'S THE ONLY THING WORTH DYING FOR.

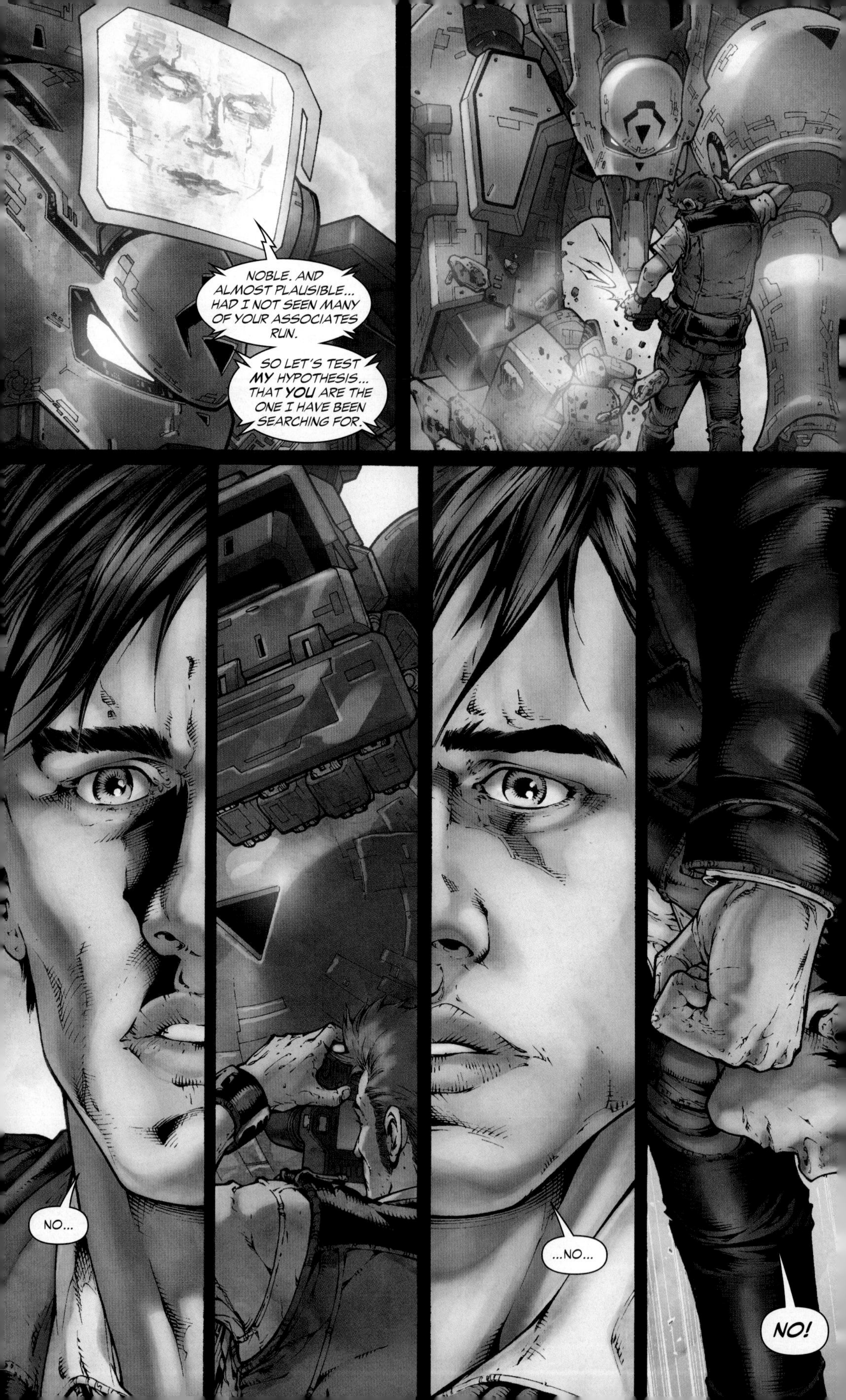
NOBLE. AND ALMOST PLAUSIBLE... HAD I NOT SEEN MANY OF YOUR ASSOCIATES RUN.
SO LET'S TEST **MY** HYPOTHESIS... THAT **YOU** ARE THE ONE I HAVE BEEN SEARCHING FOR.
NO...
...NO...
NO!

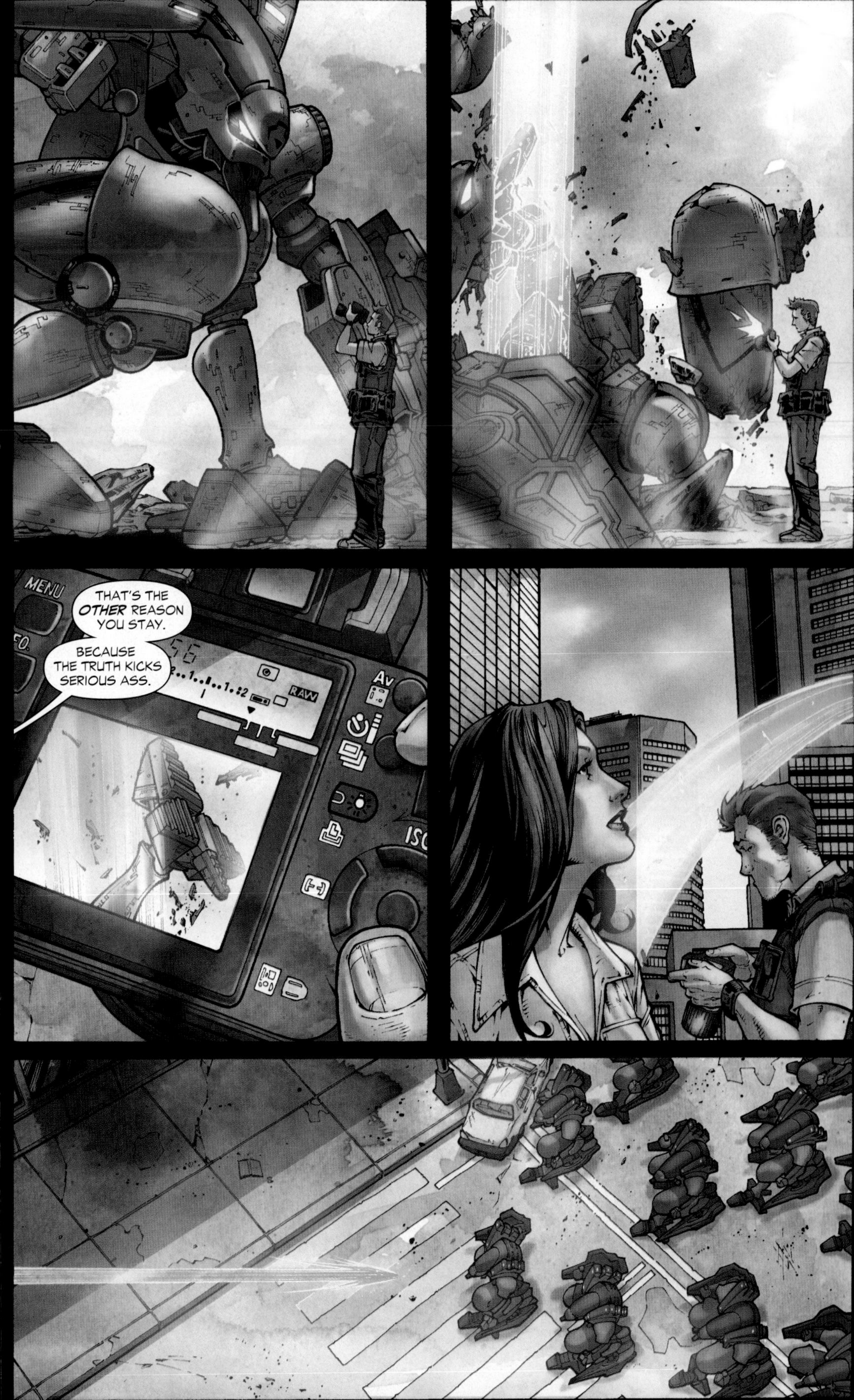
MENU
THAT'S THE *OTHER* REASON YOU STAY.
BECAUSE THE TRUTH KICKS SERIOUS ASS.
RAW
Av

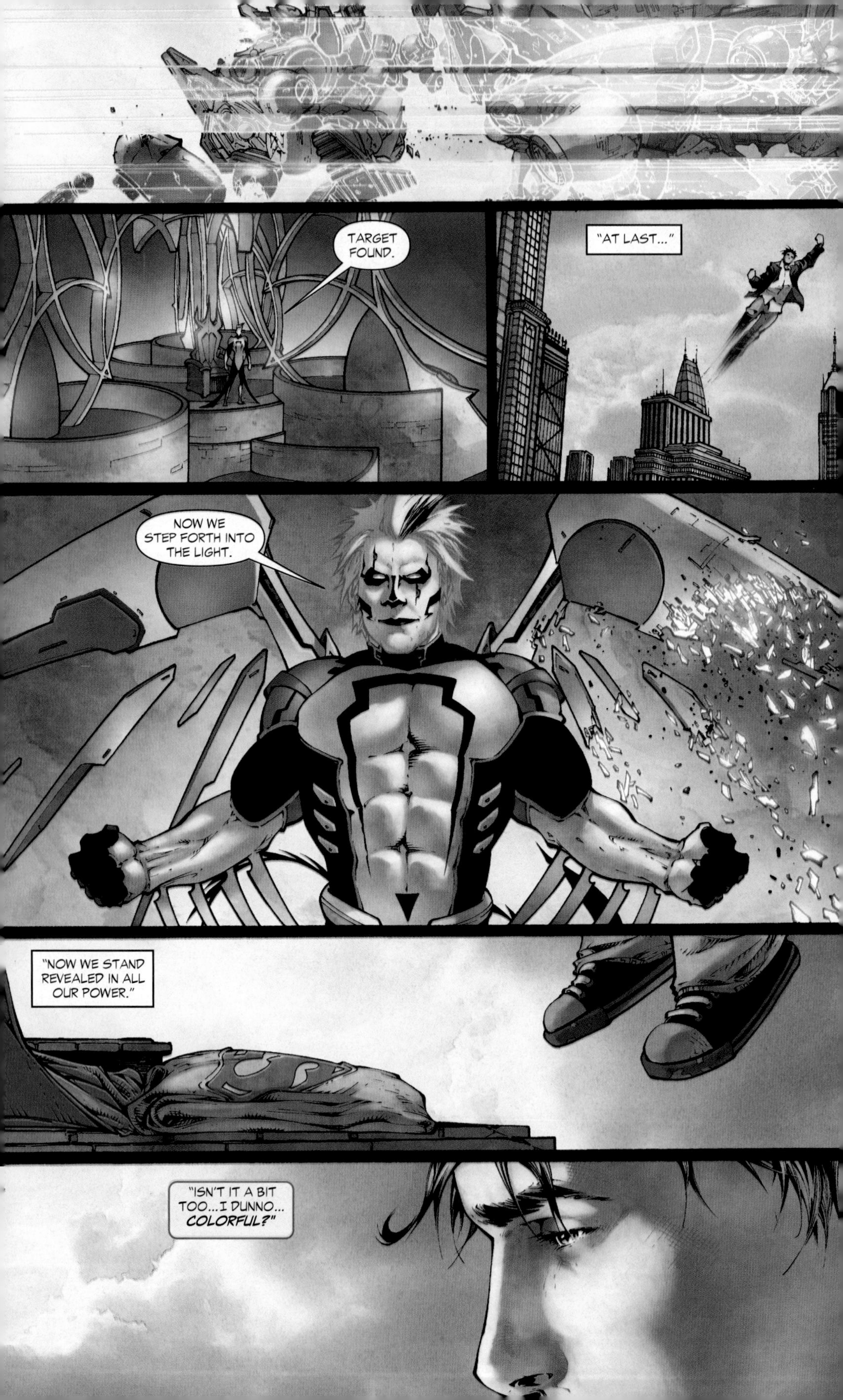

TARGET FOUND.
"AT LAST..."
NOW WE STEP FORTH INTO THE LIGHT.
"NOW WE STAND REVEALED IN ALL OUR POWER."
"ISN'T IT A BIT TOO...I DUNNO... COLORFUL?"

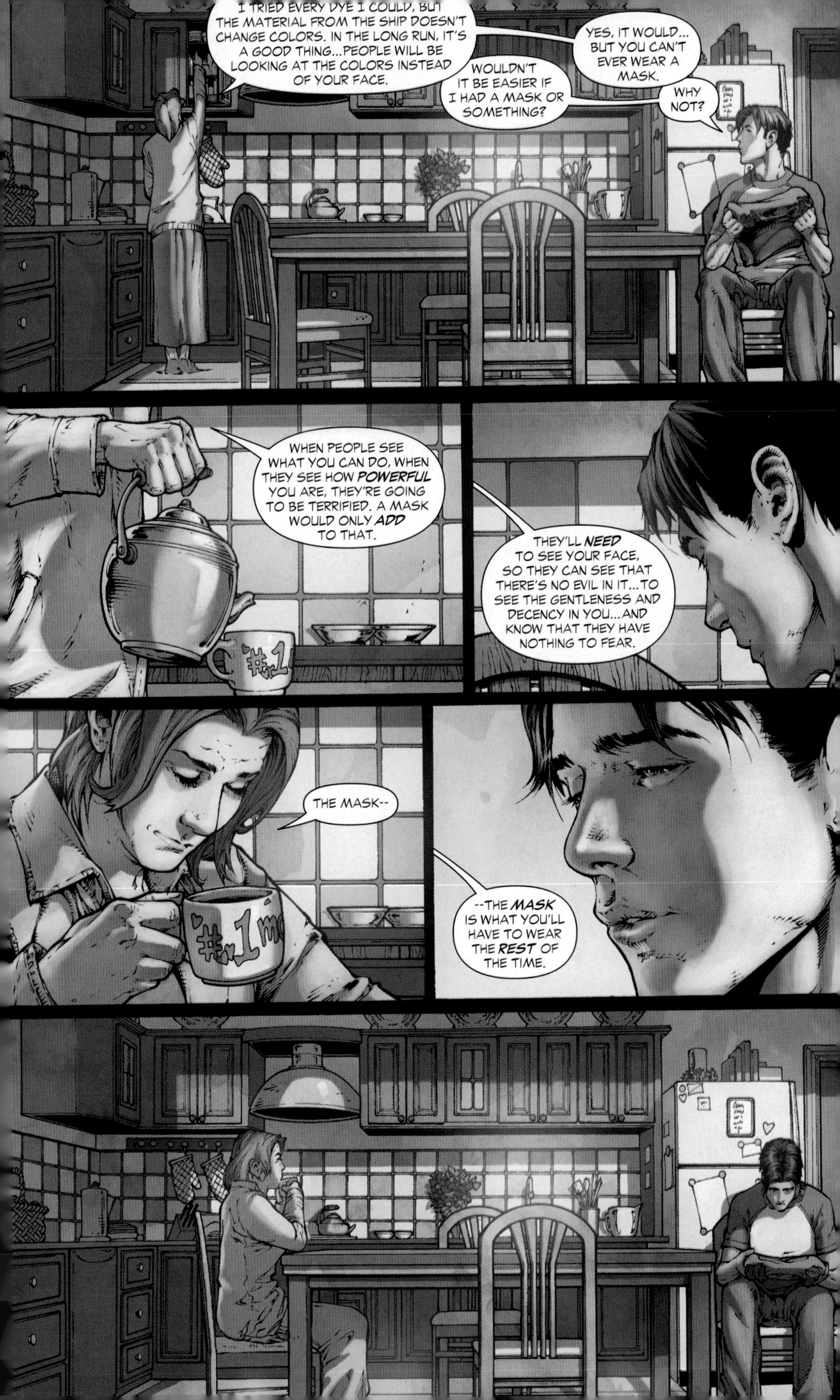
I TRIED EVERY DYE I COULD, BUT THE MATERIAL FROM THE SHIP DOESN'T CHANGE COLORS. IN THE LONG RUN, IT'S A GOOD THING...PEOPLE WILL BE LOOKING AT THE COLORS INSTEAD OF YOUR FACE.
WOULDN'T IT BE EASIER IF I HAD A MASK OR SOMETHING?
YES, IT WOULD... BUT YOU CAN'T EVER WEAR A MASK.
WHY NOT?
WHEN PEOPLE SEE WHAT YOU CAN DO, WHEN THEY SEE HOW POWERFUL YOU ARE, THEY'RE GOING TO BE TERRIFIED. A MASK WOULD ONLY ADD TO THAT.
THEY'LL NEED TO SEE YOUR FACE, SO THEY CAN SEE THAT THERE'S NO EVIL IN IT...TO SEE THE GENTLENESS AND DECENCY IN YOU...AND KNOW THAT THEY HAVE NOTHING TO FEAR.
THE MASK--
--THE MASK IS WHAT YOU'LL HAVE TO WEAR THE REST OF THE TIME.

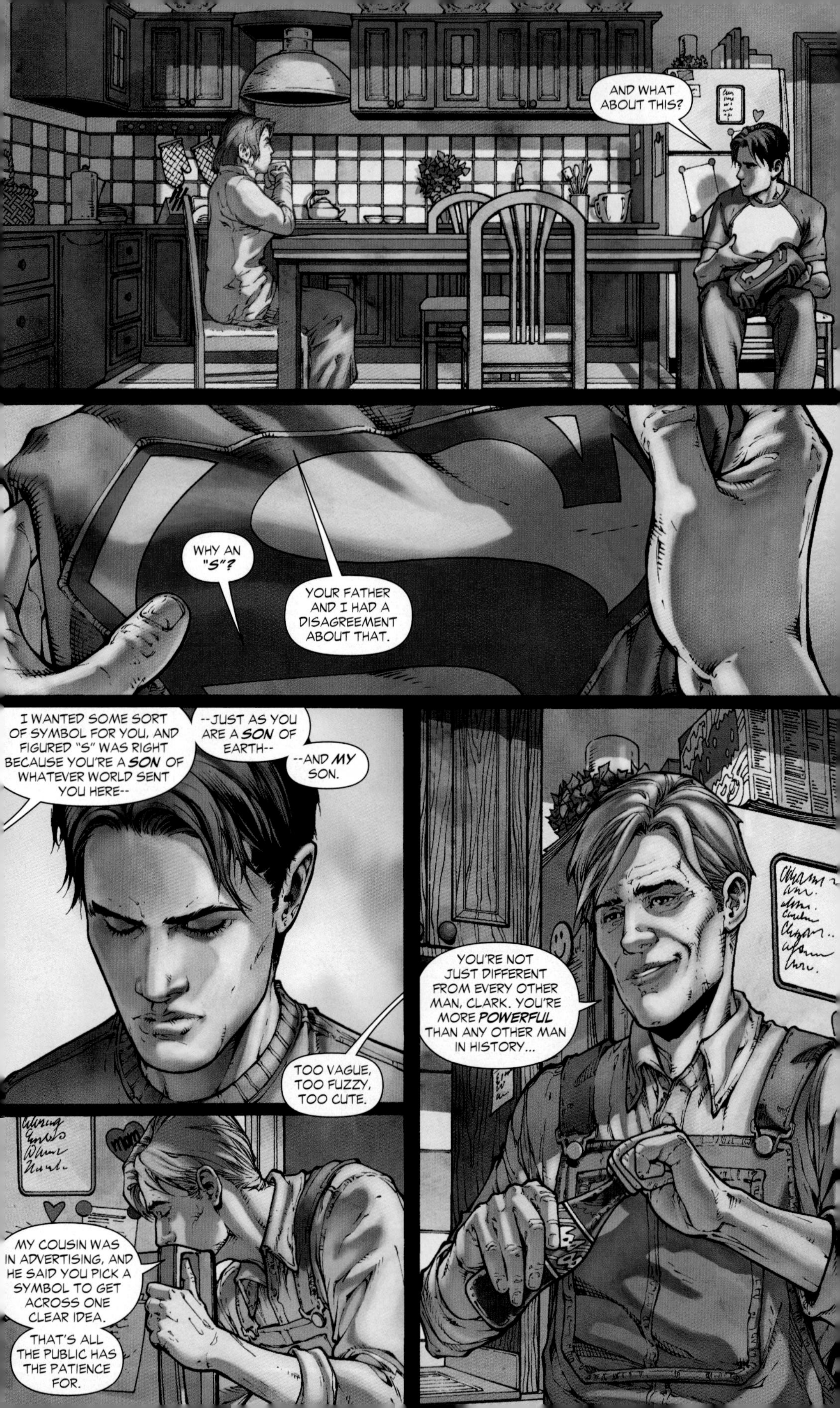
AND WHAT ABOUT THIS?
WHY AN "S"?
YOUR FATHER AND I HAD A DISAGREEMENT ABOUT THAT.
I WANTED SOME SORT OF SYMBOL FOR YOU, AND FIGURED "S" WAS RIGHT BECAUSE YOU'RE A SON OF WHATEVER WORLD SENT YOU HERE--
--JUST AS YOU ARE A SON OF EARTH--
--AND MY SON.
TOO VAGUE, TOO FUZZY, TOO CUTE.
YOU'RE NOT JUST DIFFERENT FROM EVERY OTHER MAN, CLARK. YOU'RE MORE POWERFUL THAN ANY OTHER MAN IN HISTORY...
MY COUSIN WAS IN ADVERTISING, AND HE SAID YOU PICK A SYMBOL TO GET ACROSS ONE CLEAR IDEA.
THAT'S ALL THE PUBLIC HAS THE PATIENCE FOR.

"...YOU'RE UNIQUE IN ALL THE WORLD.

"EXTRAORDINARY.

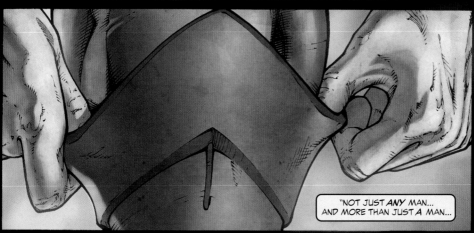

"NOT JUST *ANY* MAN... AND MORE THAN JUST *A* MAN...

"...A *SUPER-MAN*..."

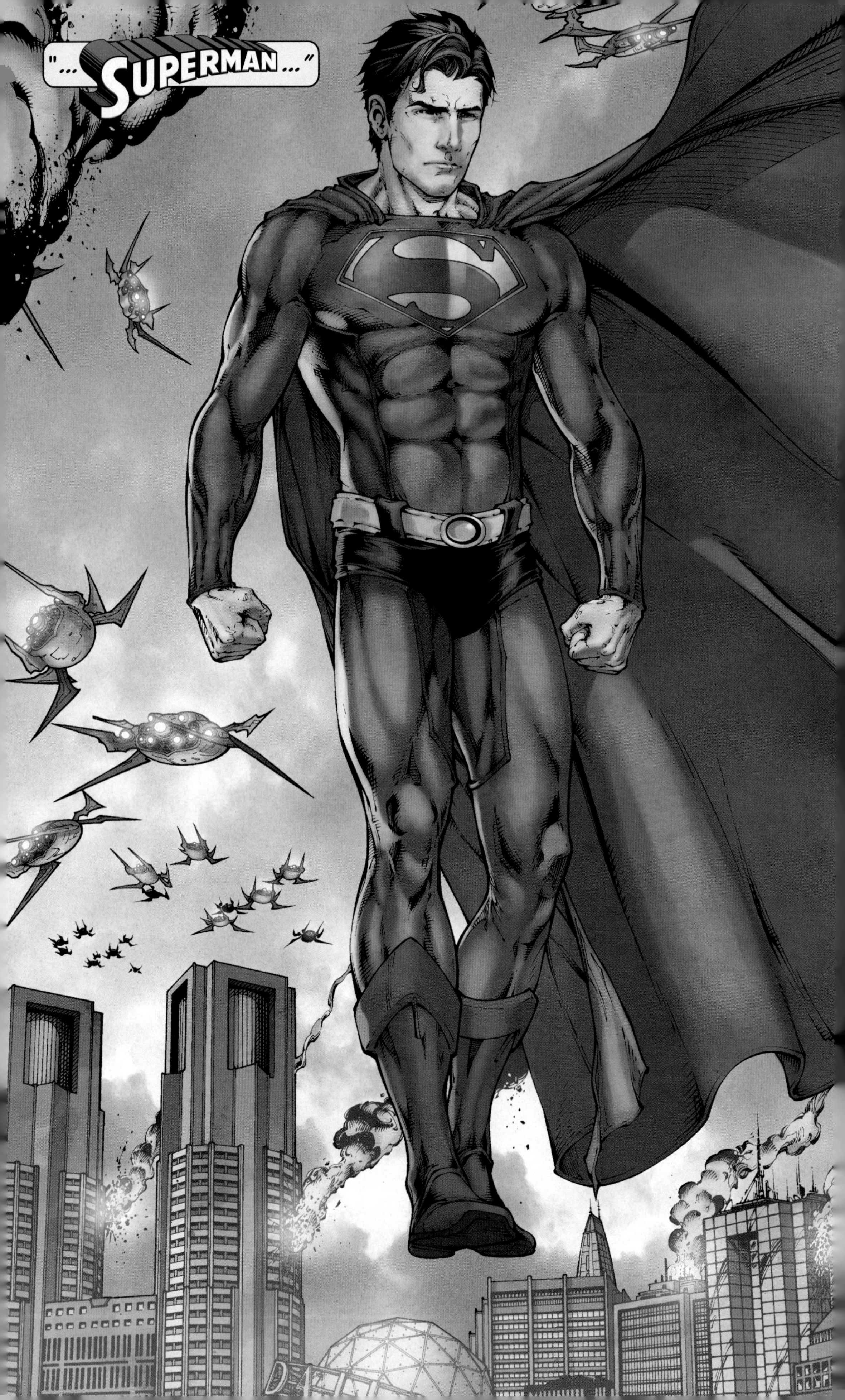
"...SUPERMAN..."

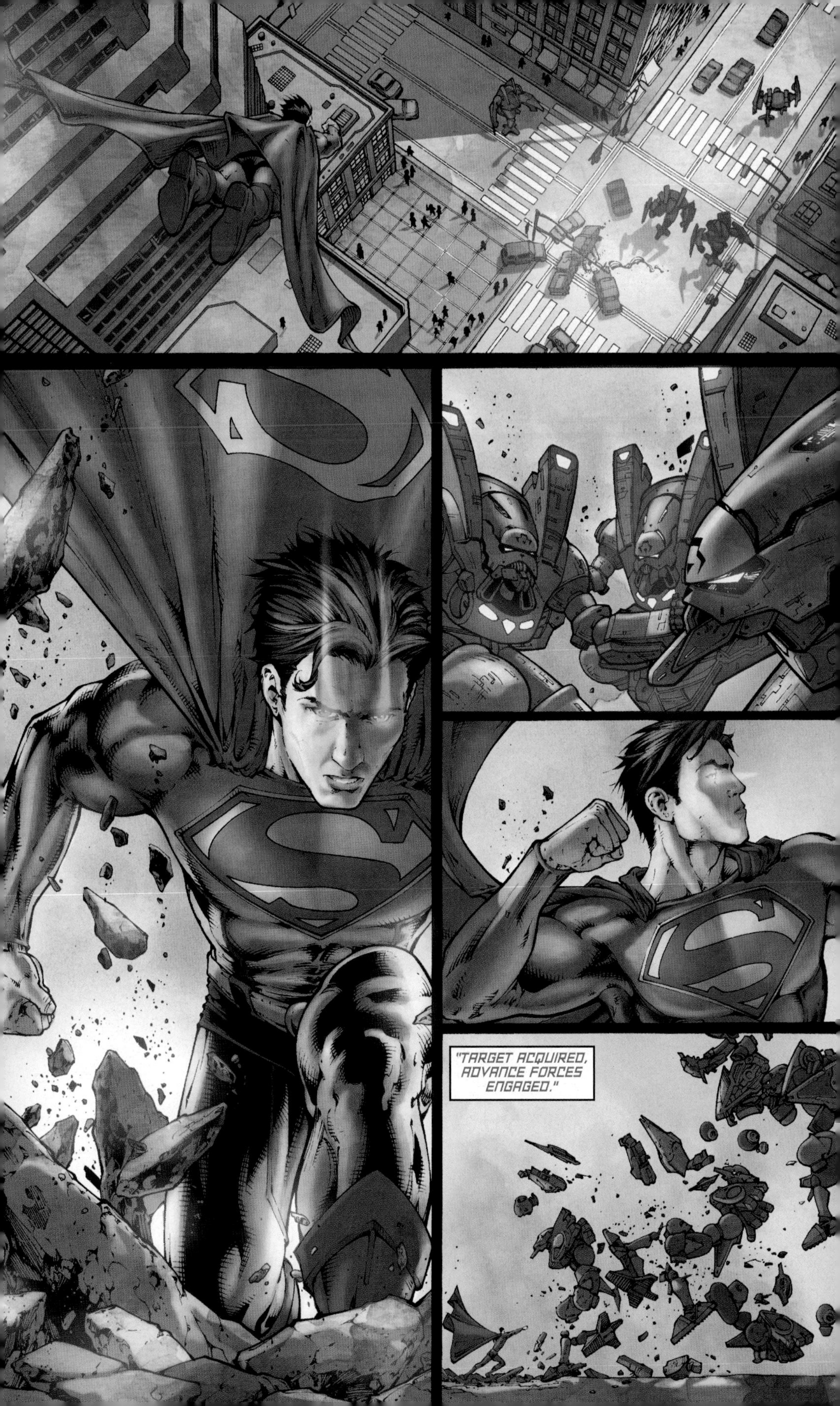
"TARGET ACQUIRED, ADVANCE FORCES ENGAGED."

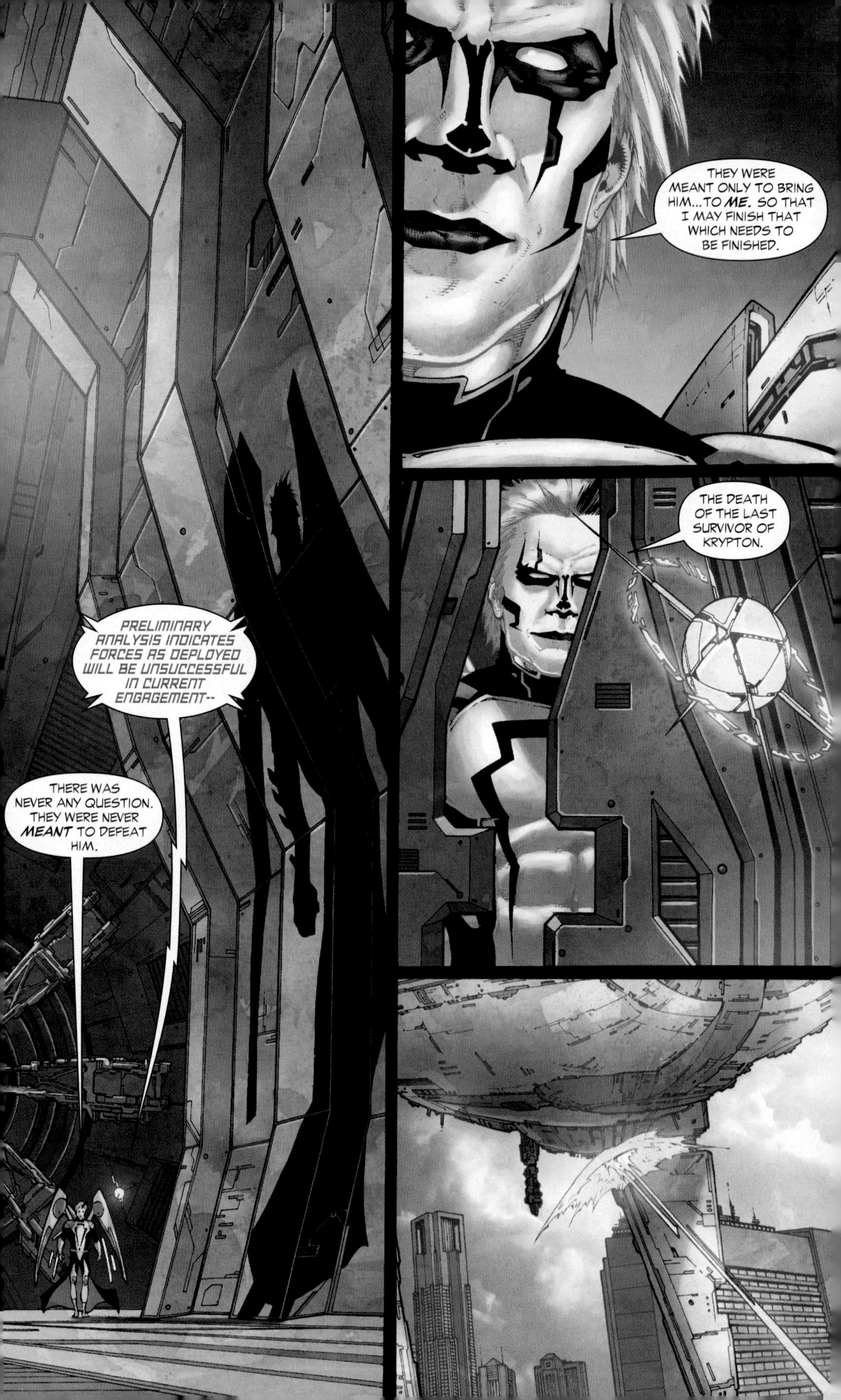
PRELIMINARY ANALYSIS INDICATES FORCES AS DEPLOYED WILL BE UNSUCCESSFUL IN CURRENT ENGAGEMENT--
THERE WAS NEVER ANY QUESTION. THEY WERE NEVER MEANT TO DEFEAT HIM.
THEY WERE MEANT ONLY TO BRING HIM...TO ME. SO THAT I MAY FINISH THAT WHICH NEEDS TO BE FINISHED.
THE DEATH OF THE LAST SURVIVOR OF KRYPTON.

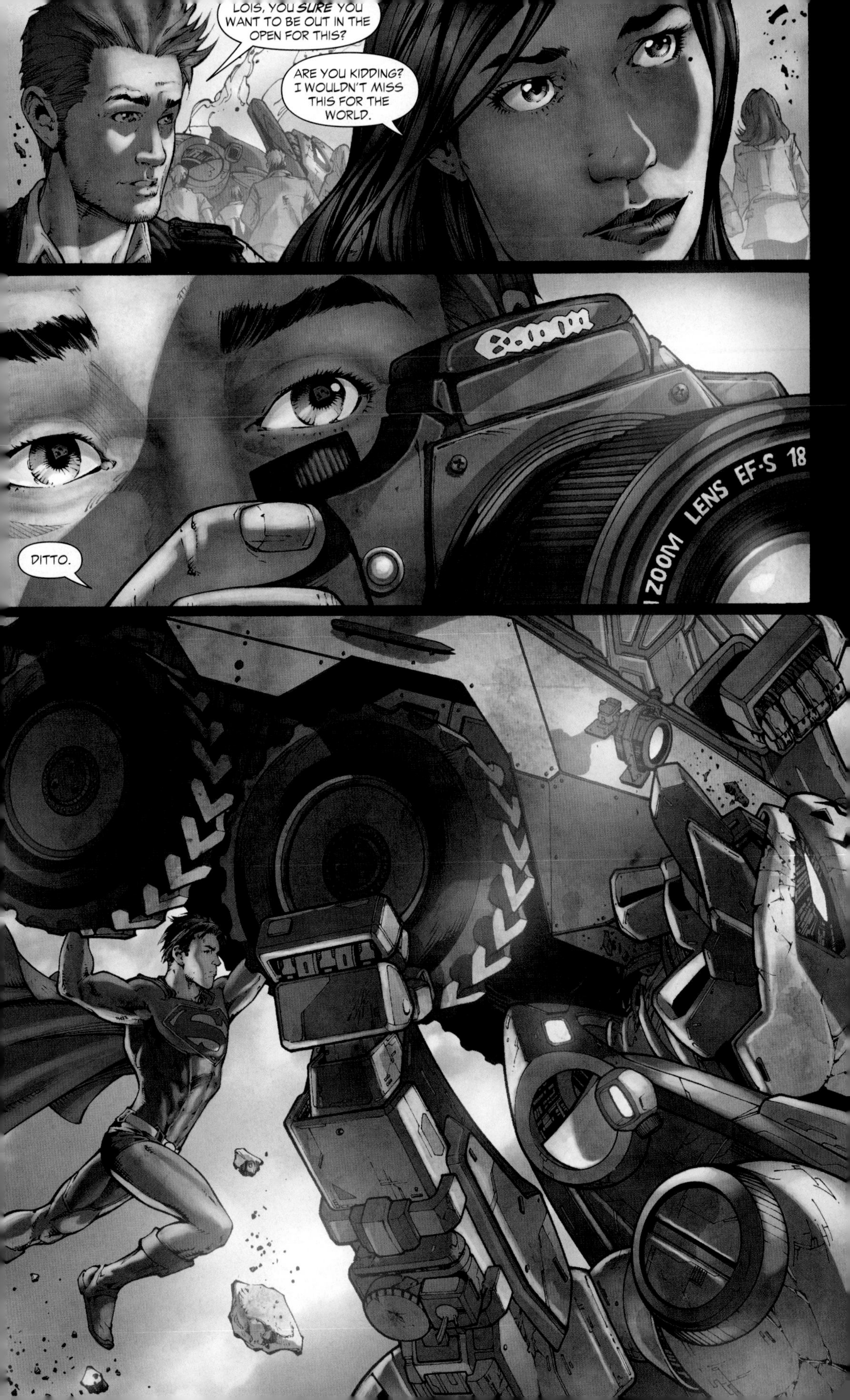
LOIS, YOU SURE YOU WANT TO BE OUT IN THE OPEN FOR THIS?
ARE YOU KIDDING? I WOULDN'T MISS THIS FOR THE WORLD.
ZOOM LENS EF-S 18
DITTO.

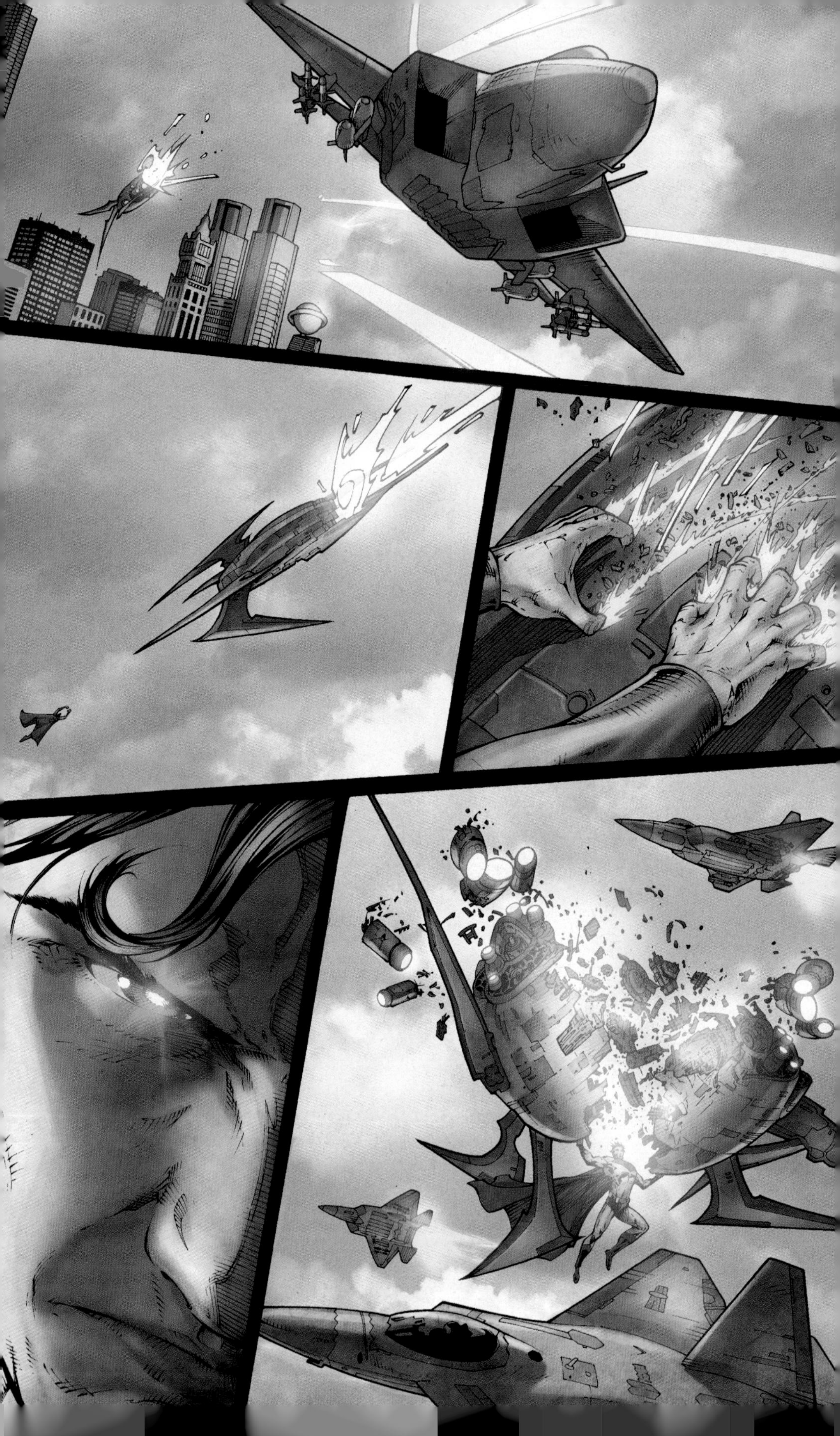

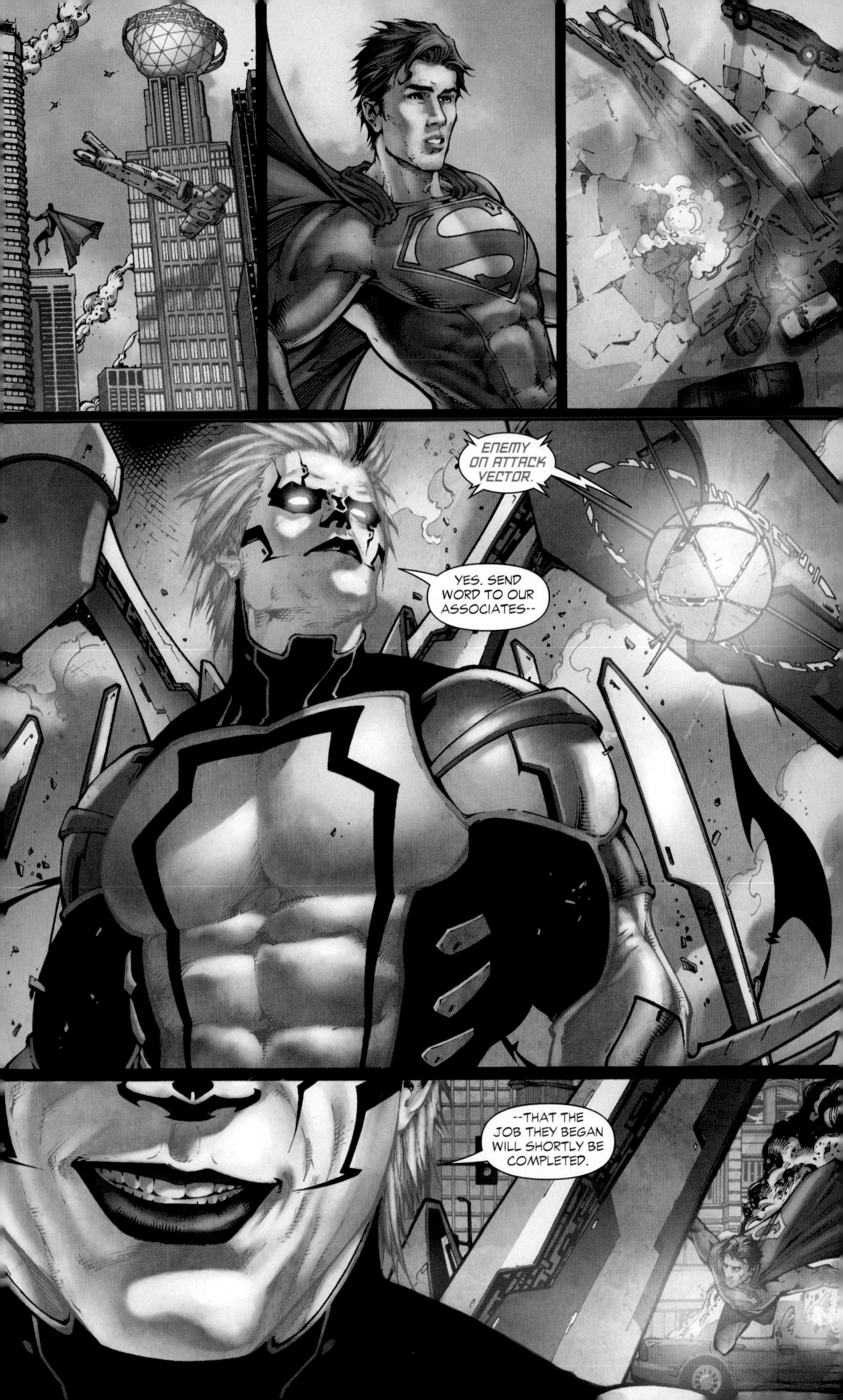
ENEMY ON ATTACK VECTOR.
YES. SEND WORD TO OUR ASSOCIATES--
--THAT THE JOB THEY BEGAN WILL SHORTLY BE COMPLETED.

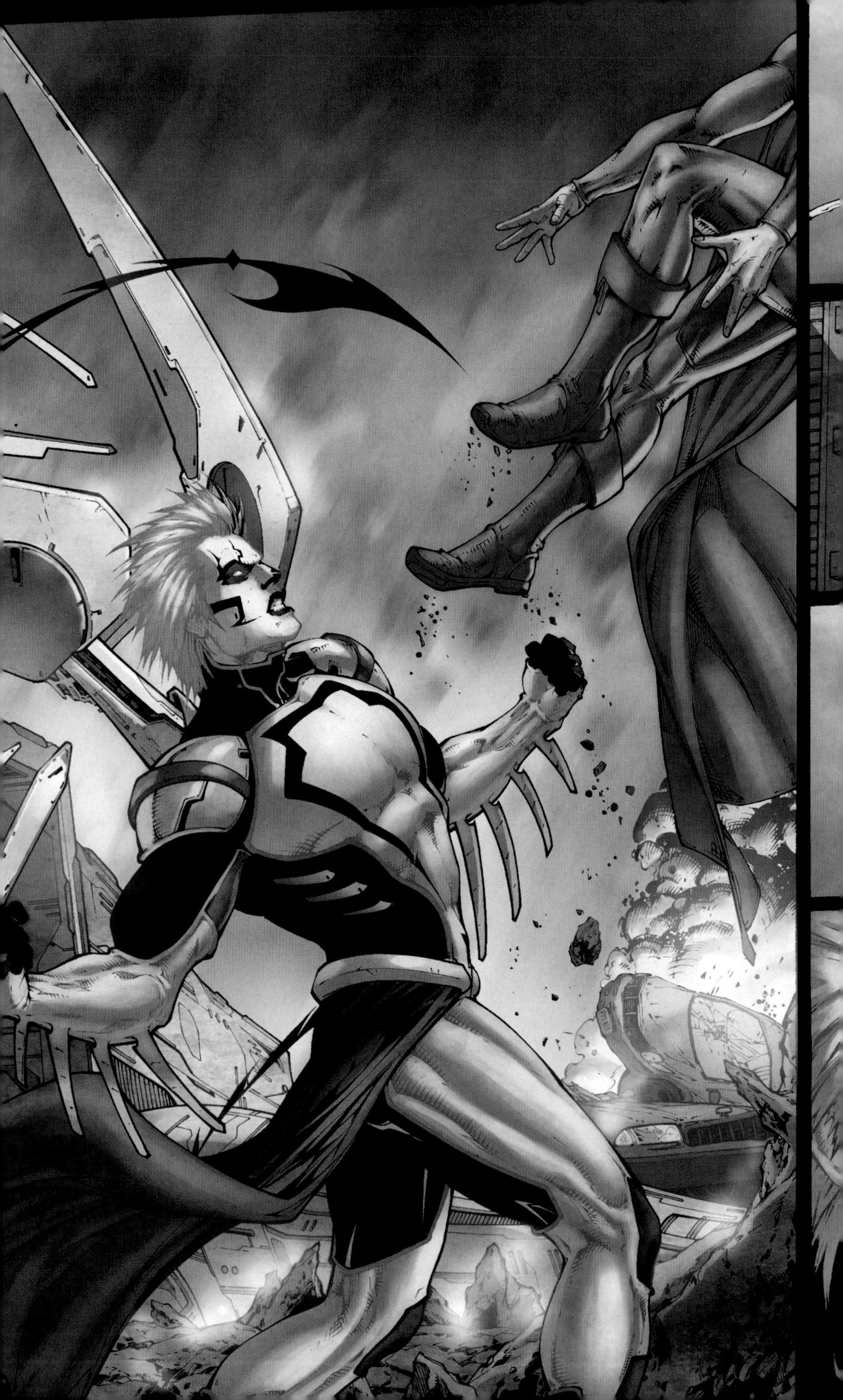

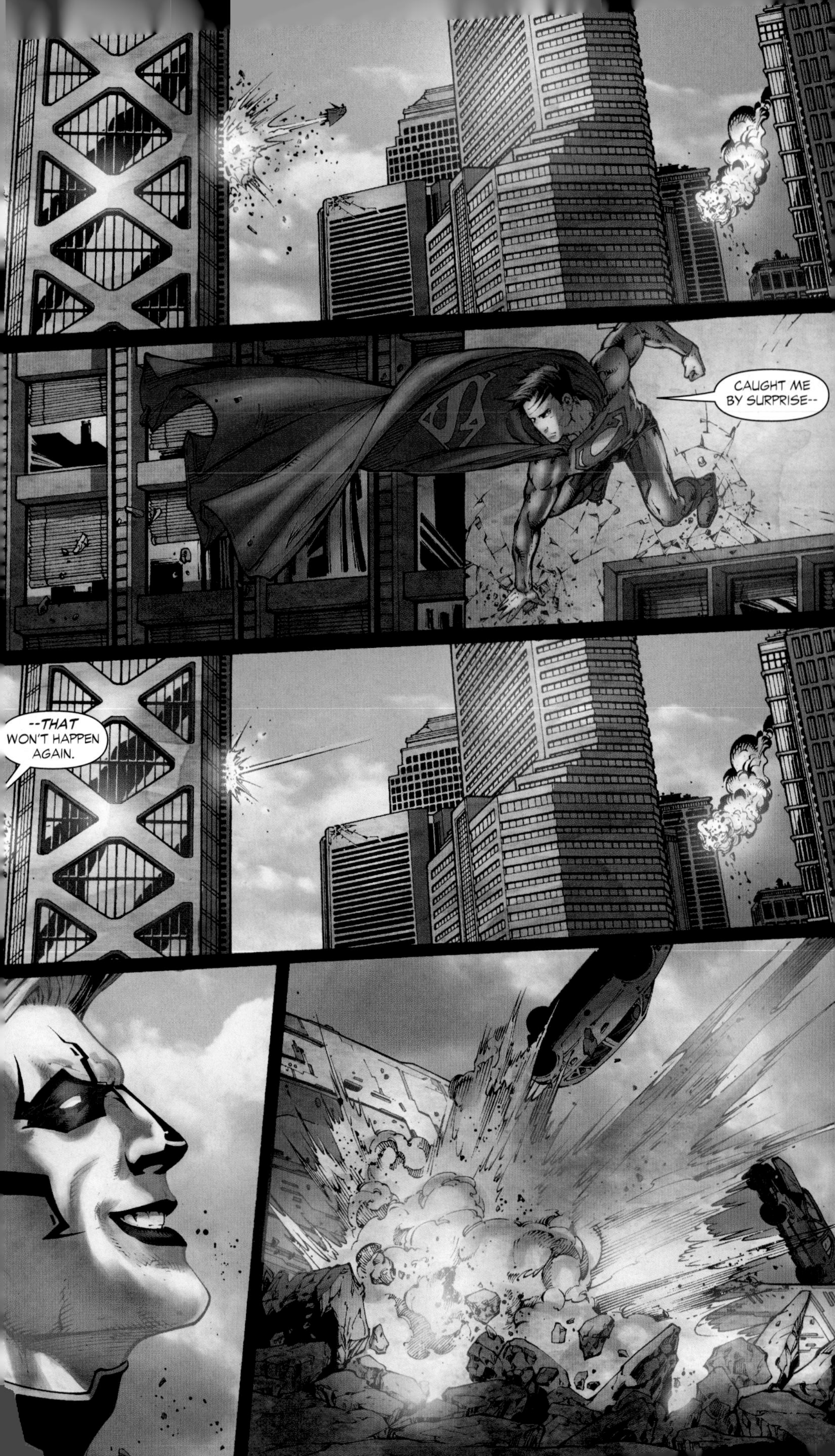
CAUGHT ME BY SURPRISE--
--THAT WON'T HAPPEN AGAIN.

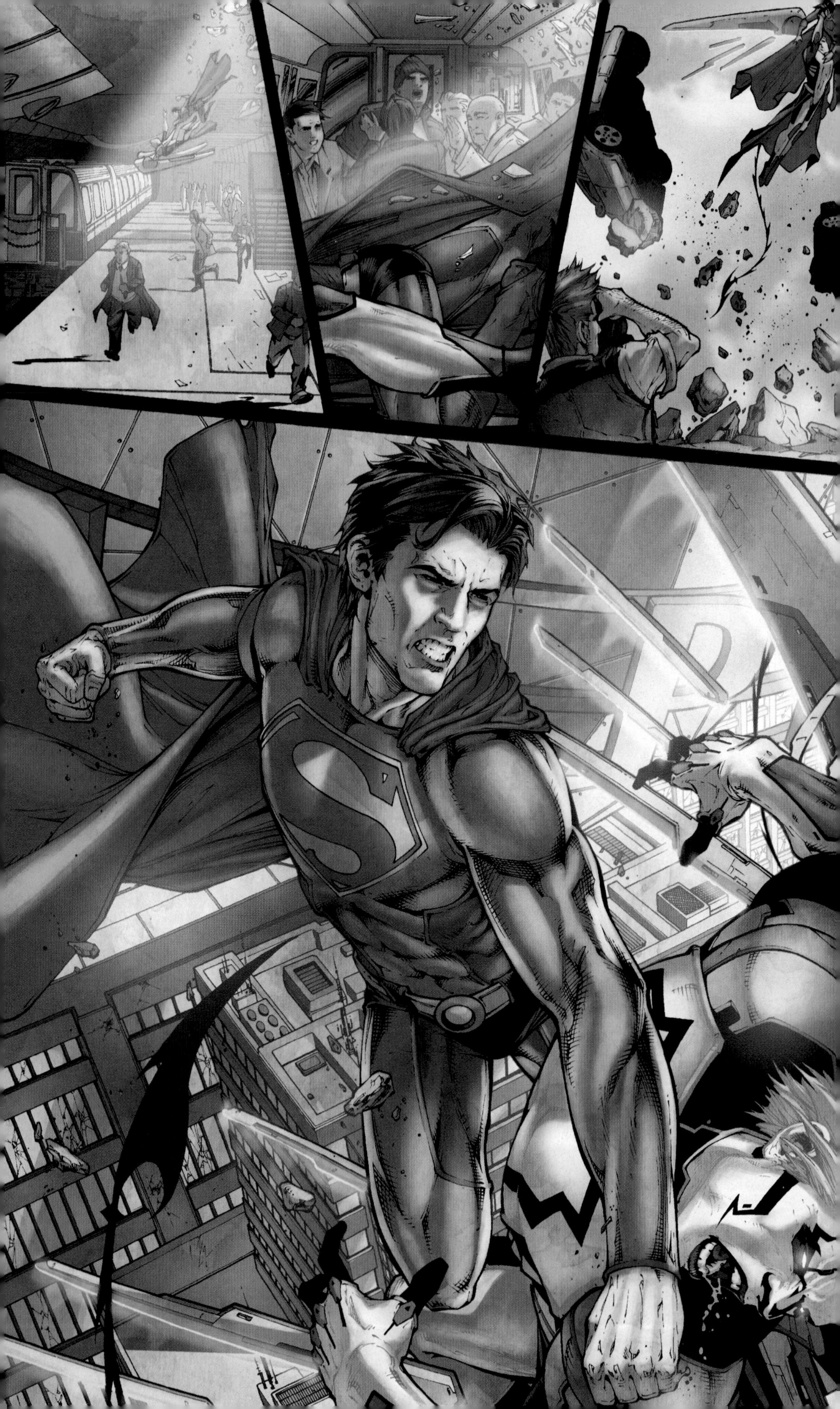

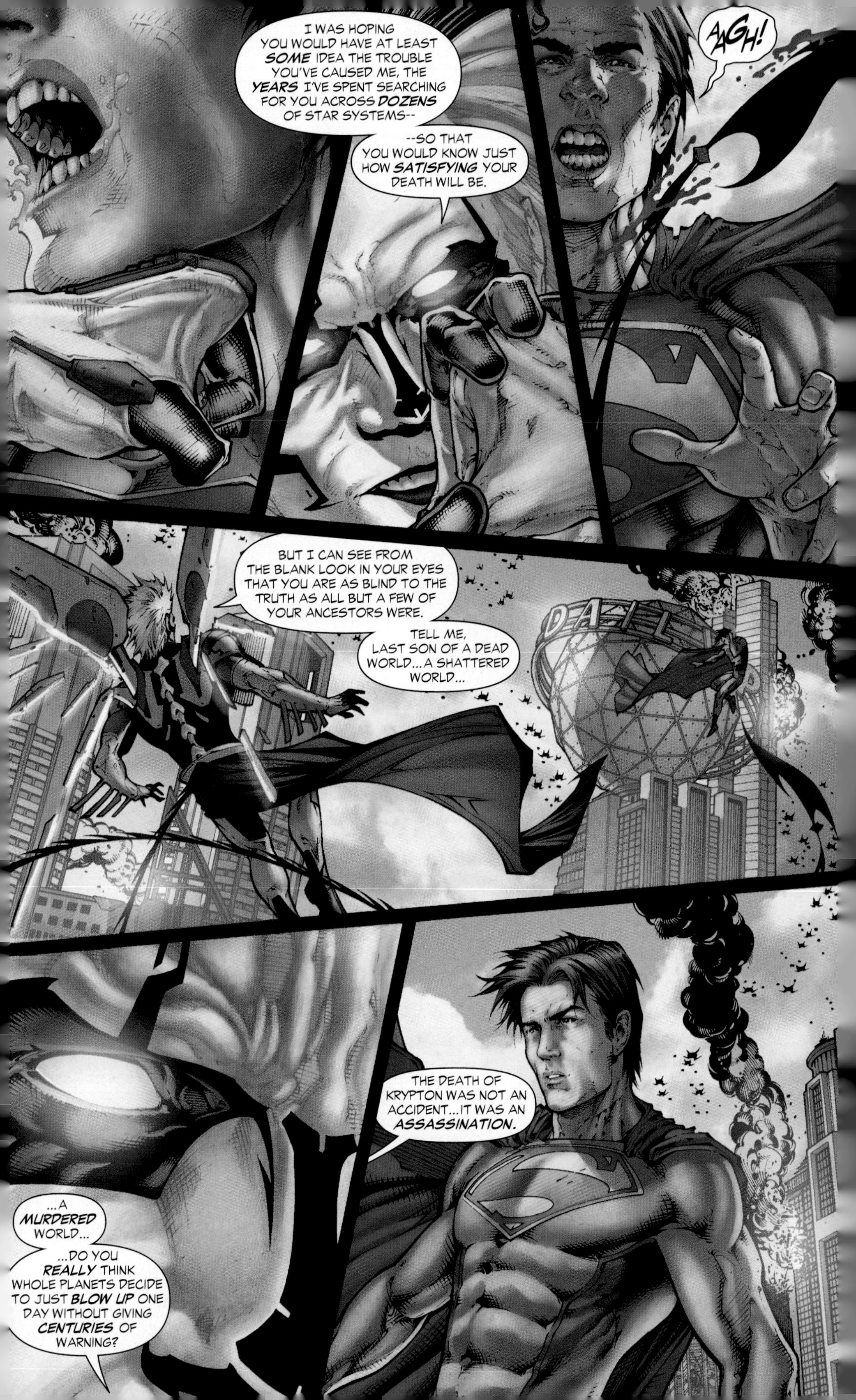

I WAS HOPING YOU WOULD HAVE AT LEAST SOME IDEA THE TROUBLE YOU'VE CAUSED ME, THE YEARS I'VE SPENT SEARCHING FOR YOU ACROSS DOZENS OF STAR SYSTEMS--
--SO THAT YOU WOULD KNOW JUST HOW SATISFYING YOUR DEATH WILL BE.
AAGH!
BUT I CAN SEE FROM THE BLANK LOOK IN YOUR EYES THAT YOU ARE AS BLIND TO THE TRUTH AS ALL BUT A FEW OF YOUR ANCESTORS WERE.
TELL ME, LAST SON OF A DEAD WORLD...A SHATTERED WORLD...
...A MURDERED WORLD...
...DO YOU REALLY THINK WHOLE PLANETS DECIDE TO JUST BLOW UP ONE DAY WITHOUT GIVING CENTURIES OF WARNING?
THE DEATH OF KRYPTON WAS NOT AN ACCIDENT...IT WAS AN ASSASSINATION.

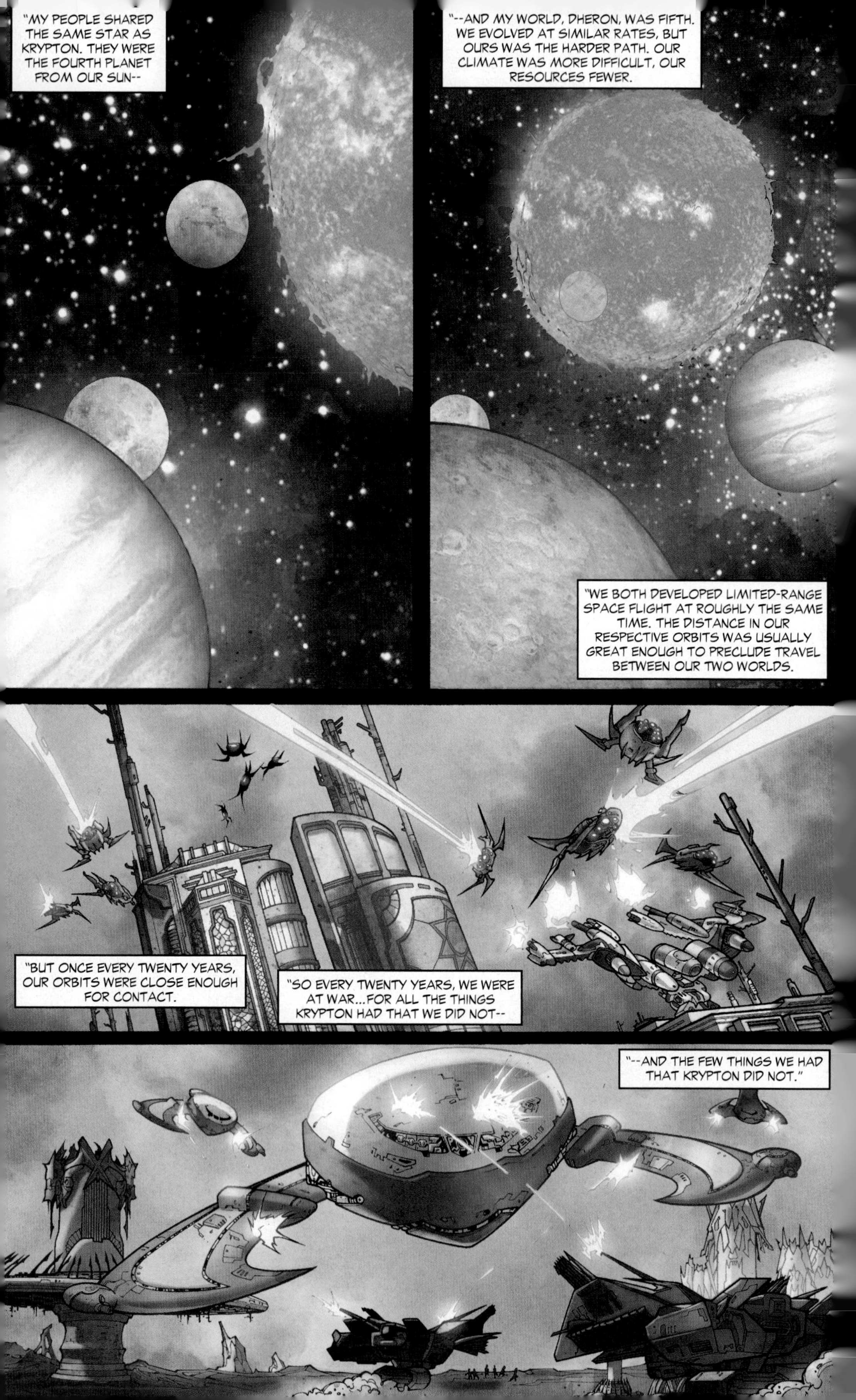
"MY PEOPLE SHARED THE SAME STAR AS KRYPTON. THEY WERE THE FOURTH PLANET FROM OUR SUN--
"--AND MY WORLD, DHERON, WAS FIFTH. WE EVOLVED AT SIMILAR RATES, BUT OURS WAS THE HARDER PATH. OUR CLIMATE WAS MORE DIFFICULT, OUR RESOURCES FEWER.
"WE BOTH DEVELOPED LIMITED-RANGE SPACE FLIGHT AT ROUGHLY THE SAME TIME. THE DISTANCE IN OUR RESPECTIVE ORBITS WAS USUALLY GREAT ENOUGH TO PRECLUDE TRAVEL BETWEEN OUR TWO WORLDS.
"BUT ONCE EVERY TWENTY YEARS, OUR ORBITS WERE CLOSE ENOUGH FOR CONTACT.
"SO EVERY TWENTY YEARS, WE WERE AT WAR...FOR ALL THE THINGS KRYPTON HAD THAT WE DID NOT--
"--AND THE FEW THINGS WE HAD THAT KRYPTON DID NOT."

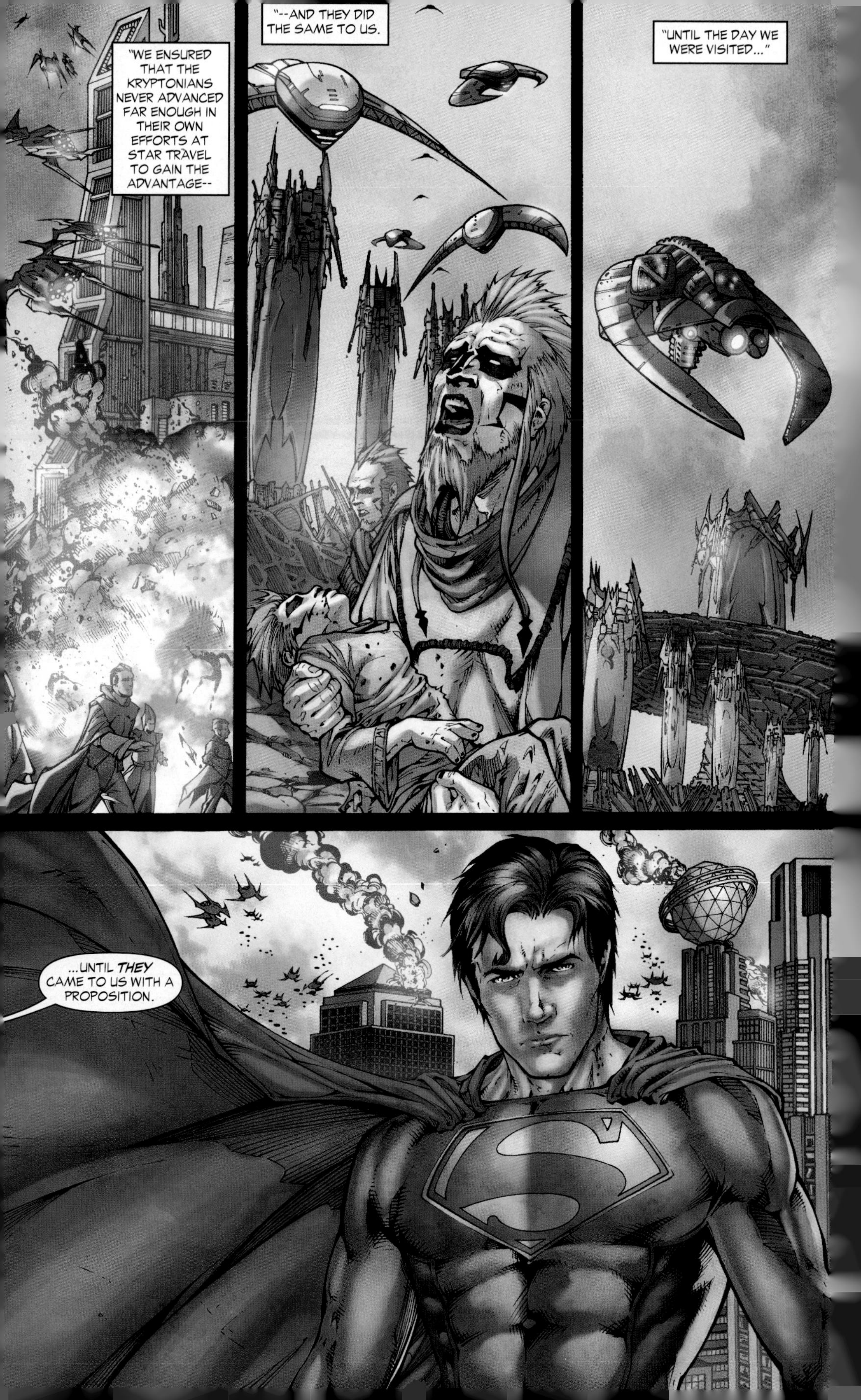
"WE ENSURED THAT THE KRYPTONIANS NEVER ADVANCED FAR ENOUGH IN THEIR OWN EFFORTS AT STAR TRAVEL TO GAIN THE ADVANTAGE--
"--AND THEY DID THE SAME TO US.
"UNTIL THE DAY WE WERE VISITED..."
...UNTIL *THEY* CAME TO US WITH A PROPOSITION.

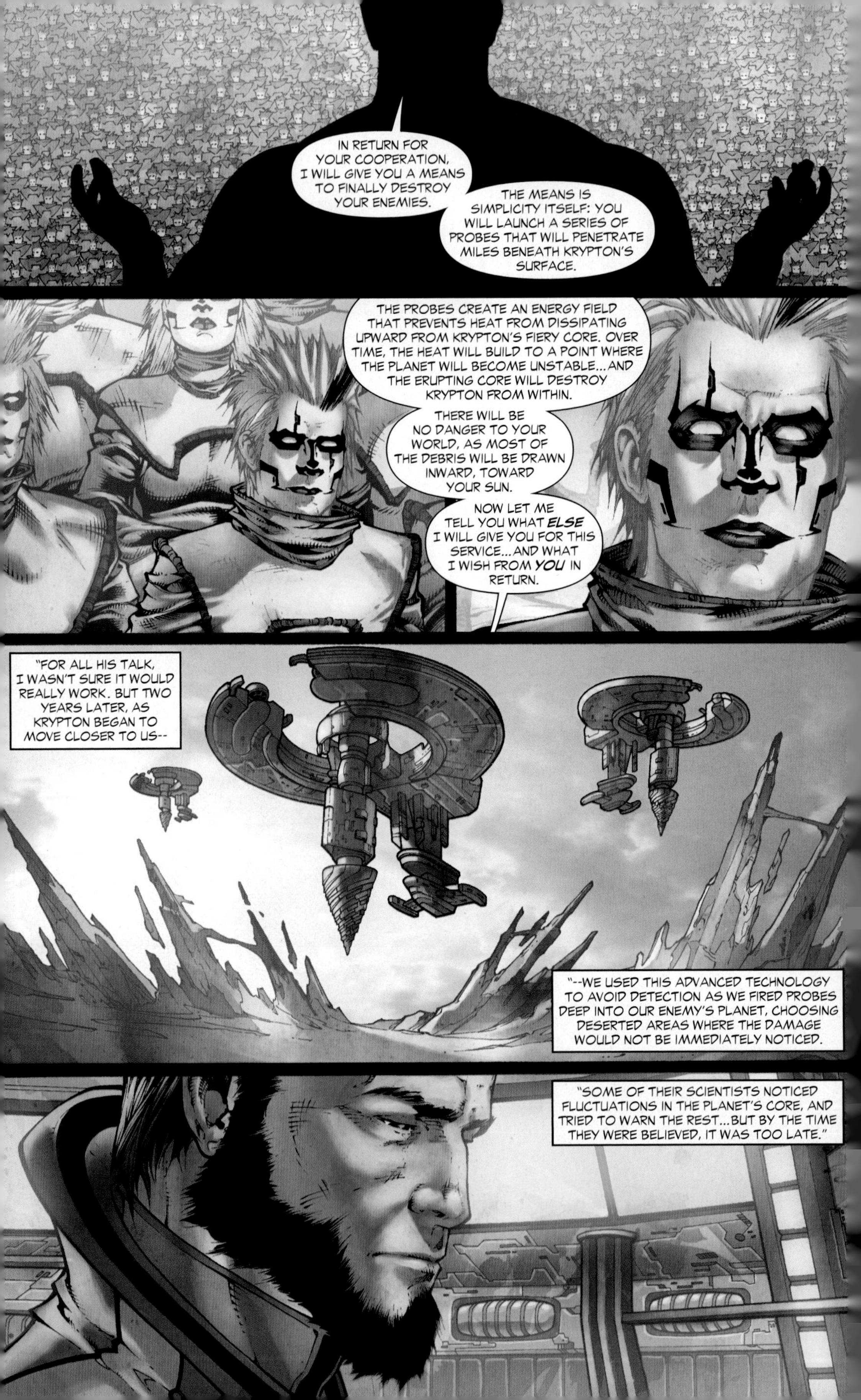
IN RETURN FOR YOUR COOPERATION, I WILL GIVE YOU A MEANS TO FINALLY DESTROY YOUR ENEMIES.
THE MEANS IS SIMPLICITY ITSELF: YOU WILL LAUNCH A SERIES OF PROBES THAT WILL PENETRATE MILES BENEATH KRYPTON'S SURFACE.
THE PROBES CREATE AN ENERGY FIELD THAT PREVENTS HEAT FROM DISSIPATING UPWARD FROM KRYPTON'S FIERY CORE. OVER TIME, THE HEAT WILL BUILD TO A POINT WHERE THE PLANET WILL BECOME UNSTABLE...AND THE ERUPTING CORE WILL DESTROY KRYPTON FROM WITHIN.
THERE WILL BE NO DANGER TO YOUR WORLD, AS MOST OF THE DEBRIS WILL BE DRAWN INWARD, TOWARD YOUR SUN.
NOW LET ME TELL YOU WHAT *ELSE* I WILL GIVE YOU FOR THIS SERVICE...AND WHAT I WISH FROM *YOU* IN RETURN.
"FOR ALL HIS TALK, I WASN'T SURE IT WOULD REALLY WORK. BUT TWO YEARS LATER, AS KRYPTON BEGAN TO MOVE CLOSER TO US--
"--WE USED THIS ADVANCED TECHNOLOGY TO AVOID DETECTION AS WE FIRED PROBES DEEP INTO OUR ENEMY'S PLANET, CHOOSING DESERTED AREAS WHERE THE DAMAGE WOULD NOT BE IMMEDIATELY NOTICED.
"SOME OF THEIR SCIENTISTS NOTICED FLUCTUATIONS IN THE PLANET'S CORE, AND TRIED TO WARN THE REST...BUT BY THE TIME THEY WERE BELIEVED, IT WAS TOO LATE."

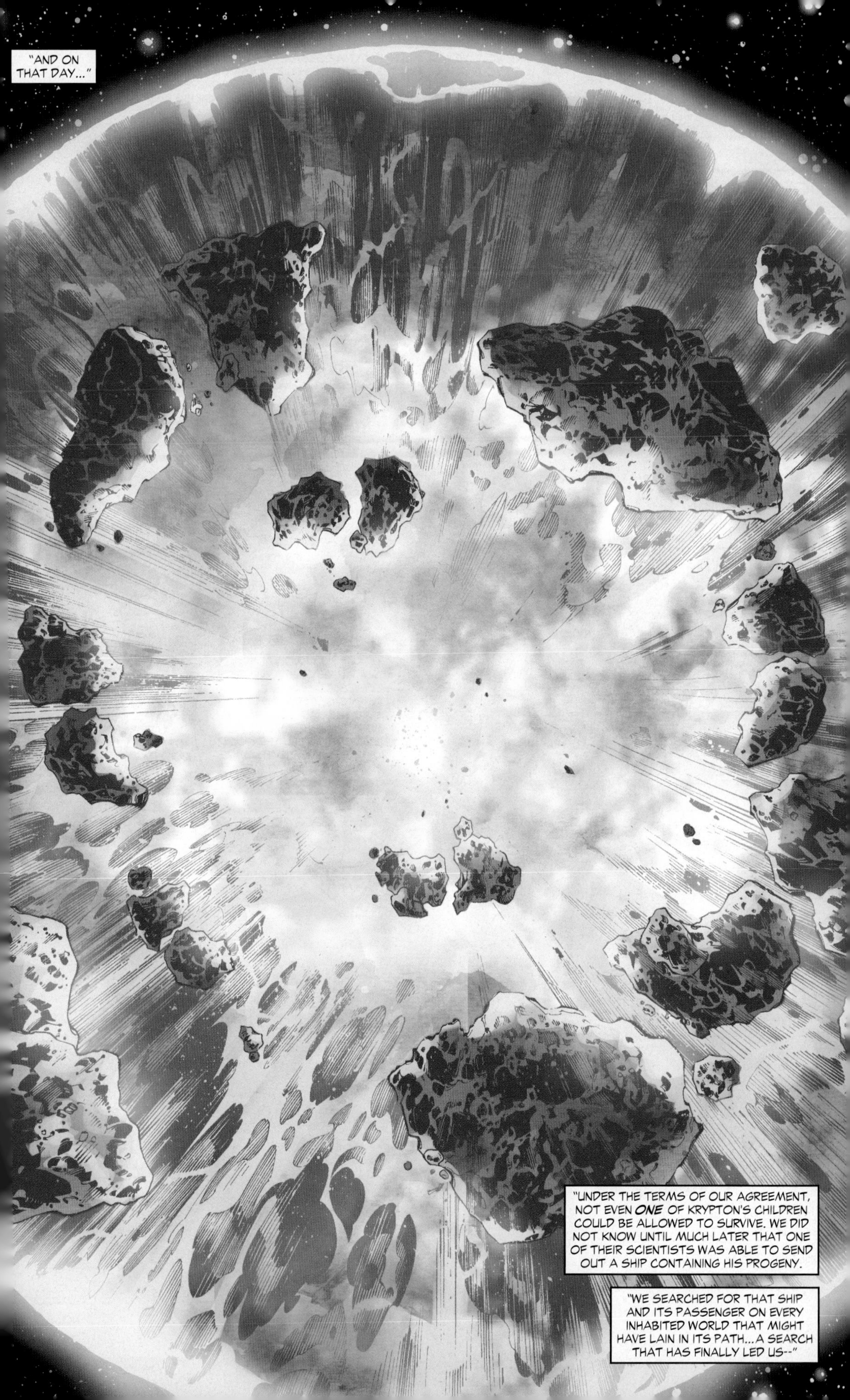
"AND ON THAT DAY..."
"UNDER THE TERMS OF OUR AGREEMENT, NOT EVEN ONE OF KRYPTON'S CHILDREN COULD BE ALLOWED TO SURVIVE. WE DID NOT KNOW UNTIL MUCH LATER THAT ONE OF THEIR SCIENTISTS WAS ABLE TO SEND OUT A SHIP CONTAINING HIS PROGENY.
"WE SEARCHED FOR THAT SHIP AND ITS PASSENGER ON EVERY INHABITED WORLD THAT MIGHT HAVE LAIN IN ITS PATH...A SEARCH THAT HAS FINALLY LED US--"

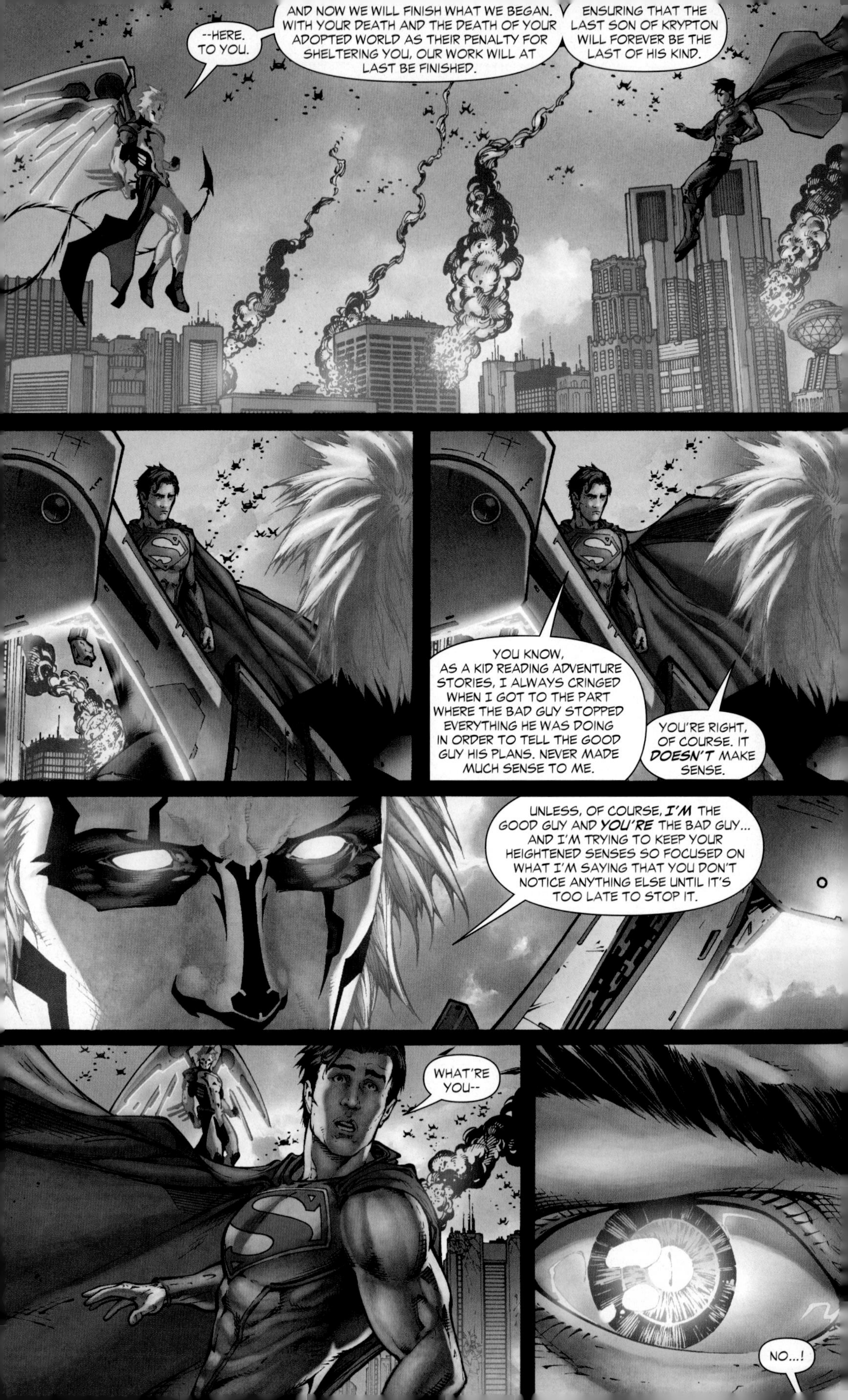
--HERE. TO YOU.
AND NOW WE WILL FINISH WHAT WE BEGAN. WITH YOUR DEATH AND THE DEATH OF YOUR ADOPTED WORLD AS THEIR PENALTY FOR SHELTERING YOU, OUR WORK WILL AT LAST BE FINISHED.
ENSURING THAT THE LAST SON OF KRYPTON WILL FOREVER BE THE LAST OF HIS KIND.
YOU KNOW, AS A KID READING ADVENTURE STORIES, I ALWAYS CRINGED WHEN I GOT TO THE PART WHERE THE BAD GUY STOPPED EVERYTHING HE WAS DOING IN ORDER TO TELL THE GOOD GUY HIS PLANS. NEVER MADE MUCH SENSE TO ME.
YOU'RE RIGHT, OF COURSE. IT ***DOESN'T*** MAKE SENSE.
UNLESS, OF COURSE, ***I'M*** THE GOOD GUY AND ***YOU'RE*** THE BAD GUY... AND I'M TRYING TO KEEP YOUR HEIGHTENED SENSES SO FOCUSED ON WHAT I'M SAYING THAT YOU DON'T NOTICE ANYTHING ELSE UNTIL IT'S TOO LATE TO STOP IT.
WHAT'RE YOU--
NO...!

RUSSIA.

EGYPT.

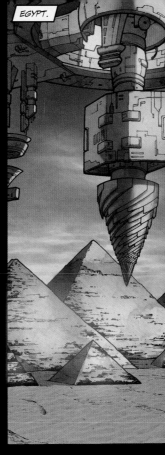

FRANCE.

TIBET.

AFRICA.

UNITED STATES.

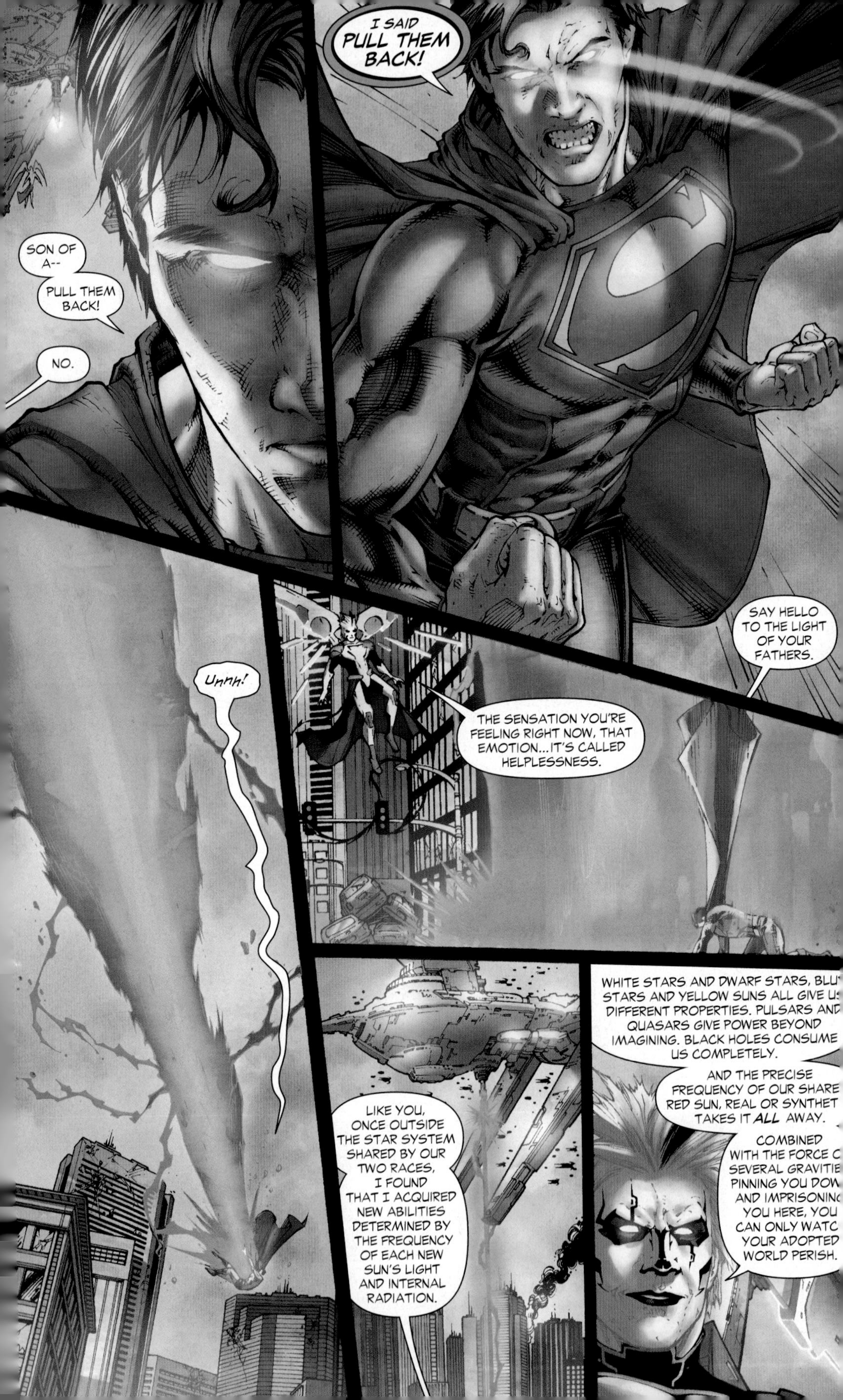

I SAID PULL THEM BACK!
SON OF A--
PULL THEM BACK!
NO.
SAY HELLO TO THE LIGHT OF YOUR FATHERS.
Unnh!
THE SENSATION YOU'RE FEELING RIGHT NOW, THAT EMOTION...IT'S CALLED HELPLESSNESS.
LIKE YOU, ONCE OUTSIDE THE STAR SYSTEM SHARED BY OUR TWO RACES, I FOUND THAT I ACQUIRED NEW ABILITIES DETERMINED BY THE FREQUENCY OF EACH NEW SUN'S LIGHT AND INTERNAL RADIATION.
WHITE STARS AND DWARF STARS, BLU STARS AND YELLOW SUNS ALL GIVE US DIFFERENT PROPERTIES. PULSARS AND QUASARS GIVE POWER BEYOND IMAGINING. BLACK HOLES CONSUME US COMPLETELY.
AND THE PRECISE FREQUENCY OF OUR SHARE RED SUN, REAL OR SYNTHET TAKES IT ALL AWAY.
COMBINED WITH THE FORCE O SEVERAL GRAVITIE PINNING YOU DOW AND IMPRISONING YOU HERE, YOU CAN ONLY WATC YOUR ADOPTED WORLD PERISH.

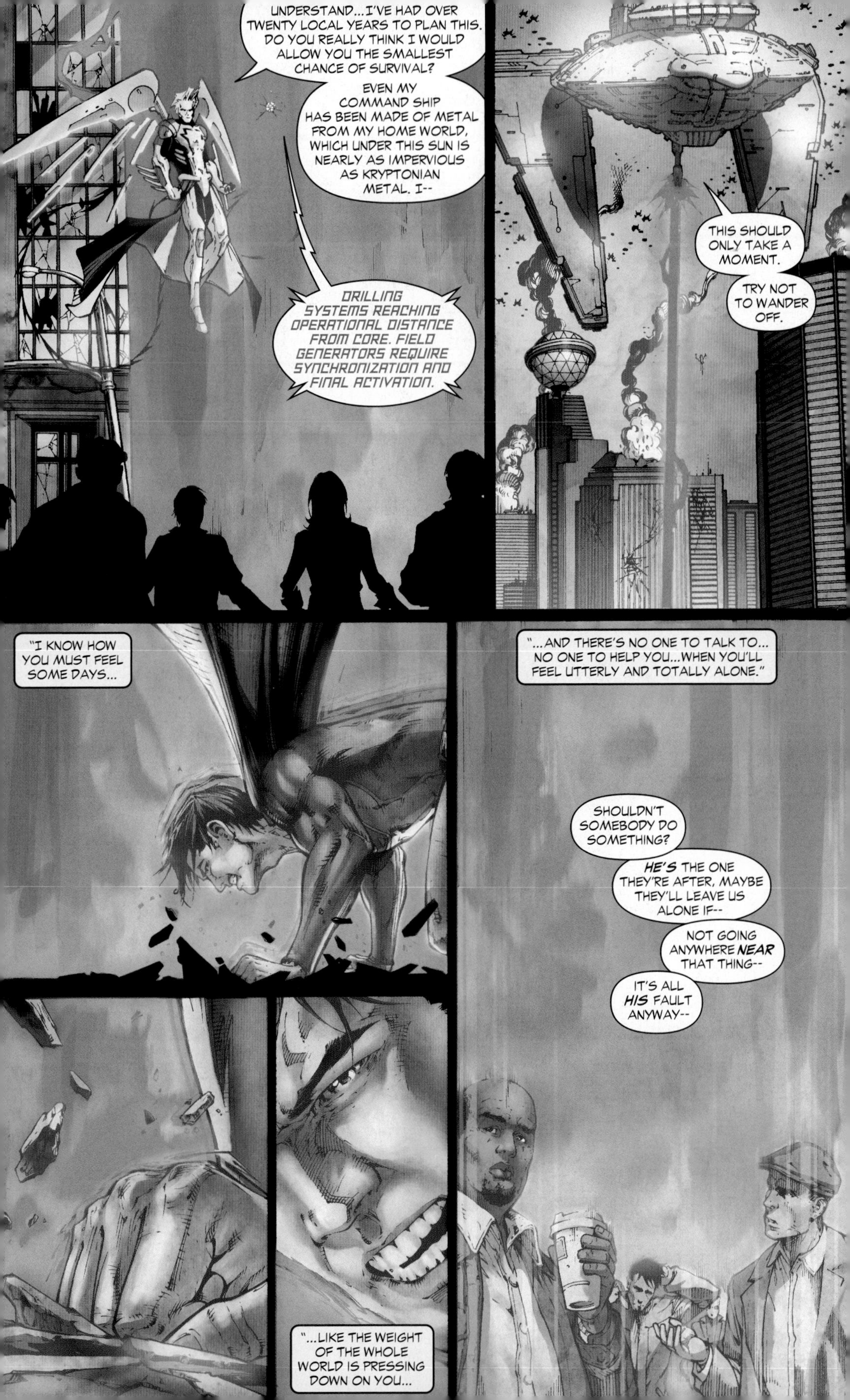
UNDERSTAND...I'VE HAD OVER TWENTY LOCAL YEARS TO PLAN THIS. DO YOU REALLY THINK I WOULD ALLOW YOU THE SMALLEST CHANCE OF SURVIVAL?
EVEN MY COMMAND SHIP HAS BEEN MADE OF METAL FROM MY HOME WORLD, WHICH UNDER THIS SUN IS NEARLY AS IMPERVIOUS AS KRYPTONIAN METAL. I--
DRILLING SYSTEMS REACHING OPERATIONAL DISTANCE FROM CORE. FIELD GENERATORS REQUIRE SYNCHRONIZATION AND FINAL ACTIVATION.
THIS SHOULD ONLY TAKE A MOMENT.
TRY NOT TO WANDER OFF.
"I KNOW HOW YOU MUST FEEL SOME DAYS...
"...LIKE THE WEIGHT OF THE WHOLE WORLD IS PRESSING DOWN ON YOU...
"...AND THERE'S NO ONE TO TALK TO... NO ONE TO HELP YOU...WHEN YOU'LL FEEL UTTERLY AND TOTALLY ALONE."
SHOULDN'T SOMEBODY DO SOMETHING?
HE'S THE ONE THEY'RE AFTER, MAYBE THEY'LL LEAVE US ALONE IF--
NOT GOING ANYWHERE NEAR THAT THING--
IT'S ALL HIS FAULT ANYWAY--

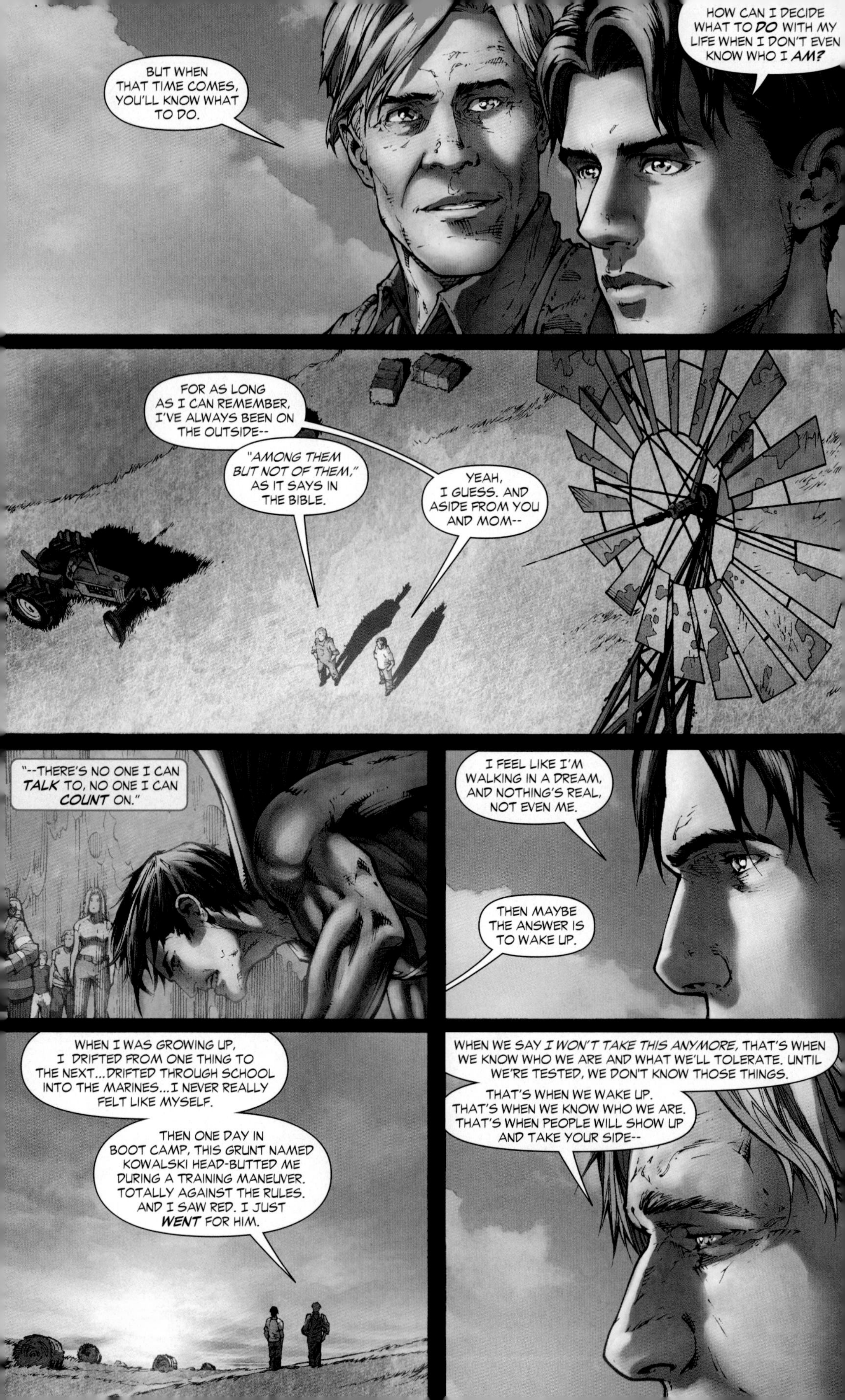
BUT WHEN THAT TIME COMES, YOU'LL KNOW WHAT TO DO.
HOW CAN I DECIDE WHAT TO DO WITH MY LIFE WHEN I DON'T EVEN KNOW WHO I AM?
FOR AS LONG AS I CAN REMEMBER, I'VE ALWAYS BEEN ON THE OUTSIDE--
"AMONG THEM BUT NOT OF THEM," AS IT SAYS IN THE BIBLE.
YEAH, I GUESS. AND ASIDE FROM YOU AND MOM--
"--THERE'S NO ONE I CAN TALK TO, NO ONE I CAN COUNT ON."
I FEEL LIKE I'M WALKING IN A DREAM, AND NOTHING'S REAL, NOT EVEN ME.
THEN MAYBE THE ANSWER IS TO WAKE UP.
WHEN I WAS GROWING UP, I DRIFTED FROM ONE THING TO THE NEXT...DRIFTED THROUGH SCHOOL INTO THE MARINES...I NEVER REALLY FELT LIKE MYSELF.
THEN ONE DAY IN BOOT CAMP, THIS GRUNT NAMED KOWALSKI HEAD-BUTTED ME DURING A TRAINING MANEUVER. TOTALLY AGAINST THE RULES. AND I SAW RED. I JUST WENT FOR HIM.
WHEN WE SAY I WON'T TAKE THIS ANYMORE, THAT'S WHEN WE KNOW WHO WE ARE AND WHAT WE'LL TOLERATE. UNTIL WE'RE TESTED, WE DON'T KNOW THOSE THINGS.
THAT'S WHEN WE WAKE UP. THAT'S WHEN WE KNOW WHO WE ARE. THAT'S WHEN PEOPLE WILL SHOW UP AND TAKE YOUR SIDE--

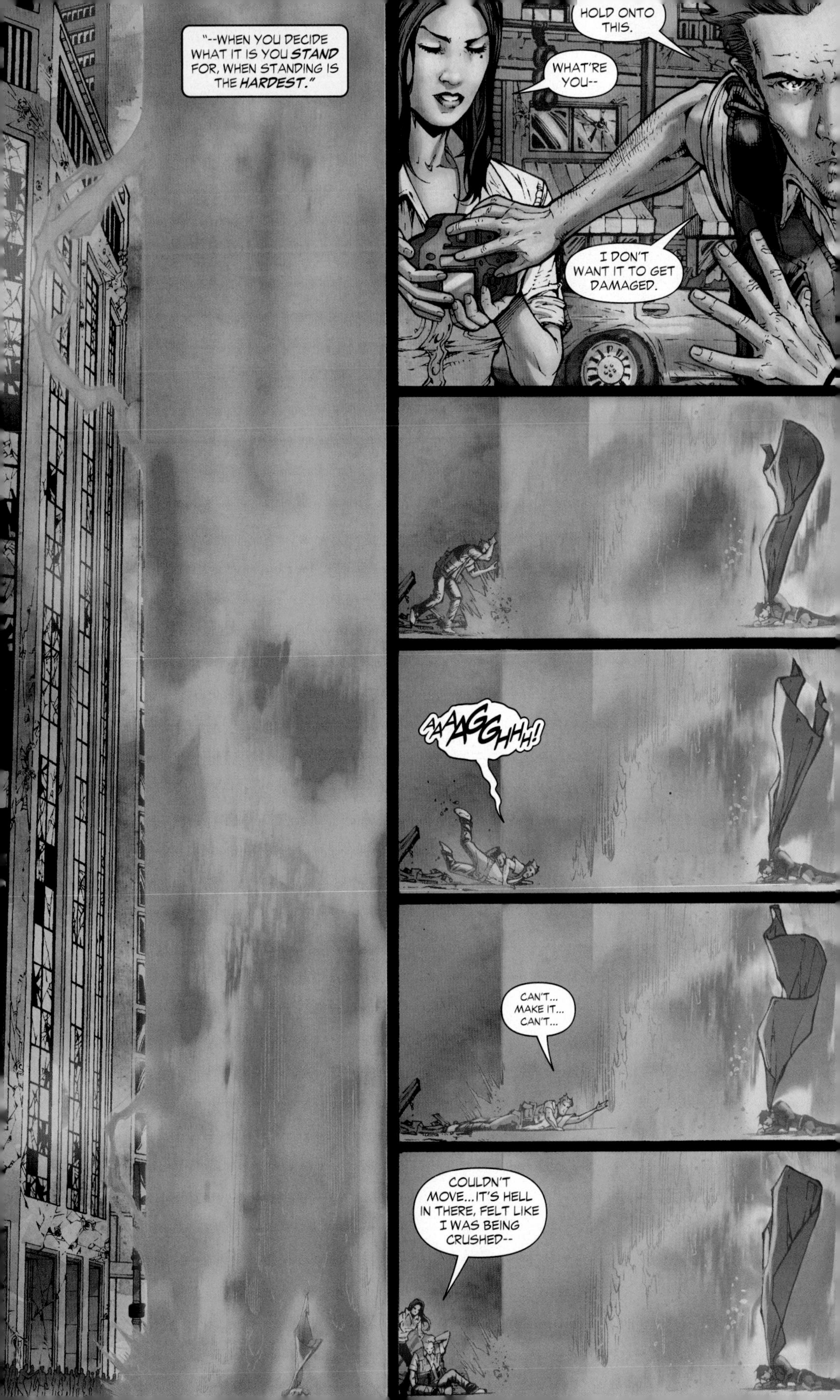
"--WHEN YOU DECIDE WHAT IT IS YOU STAND FOR, WHEN STANDING IS THE HARDEST."
HOLD ONTO THIS.
WHAT'RE YOU--
I DON'T WANT IT TO GET DAMAGED.
AAAAGGHHH!
CAN'T... MAKE IT... CAN'T...
COULDN'T MOVE... IT'S HELL IN THERE, FELT LIKE I WAS BEING CRUSHED--

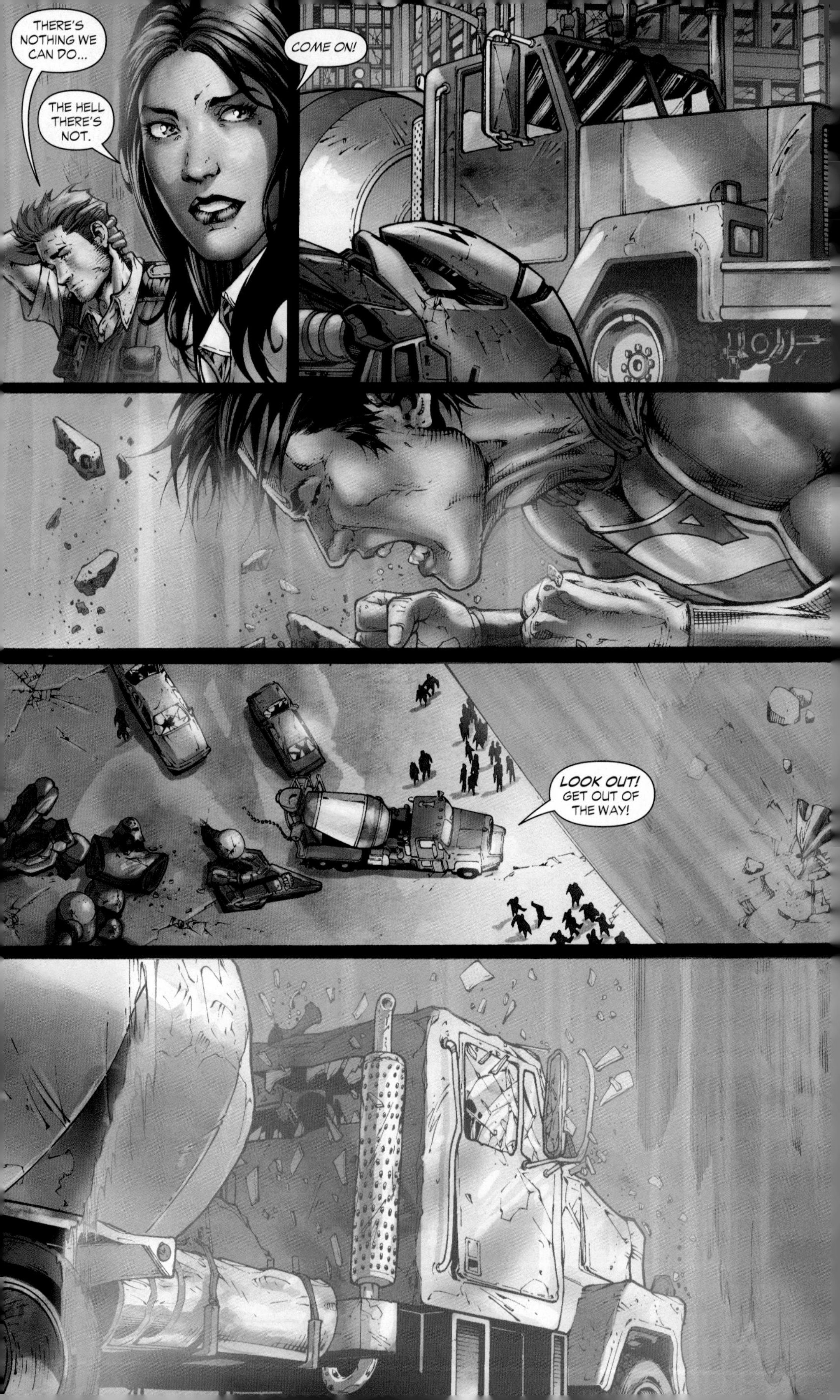
THERE'S NOTHING WE CAN DO...
THE HELL THERE'S NOT.
COME ON!
LOOK OUT! GET OUT OF THE WAY!

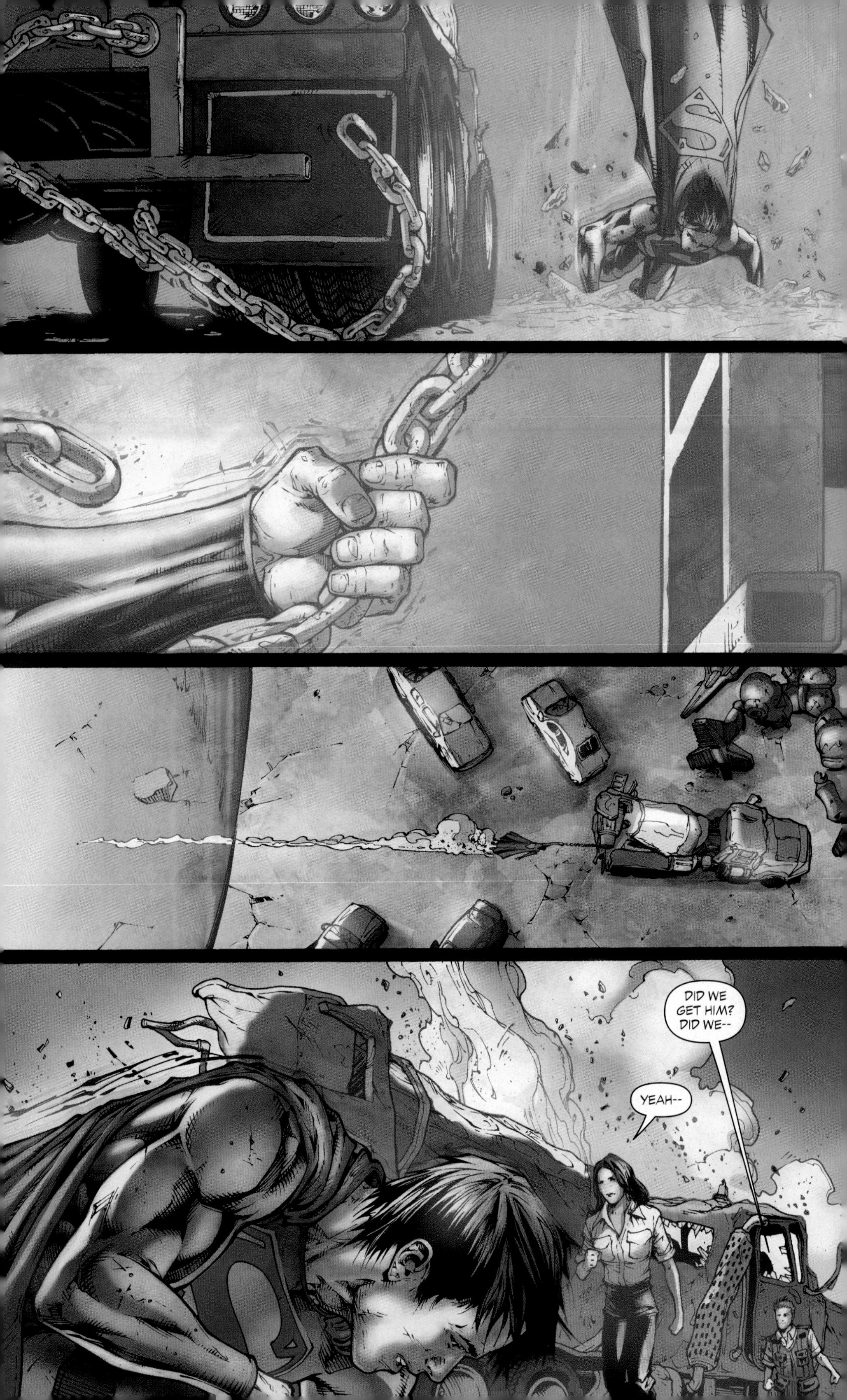
DID WE GET HIM? DID WE--
YEAH--

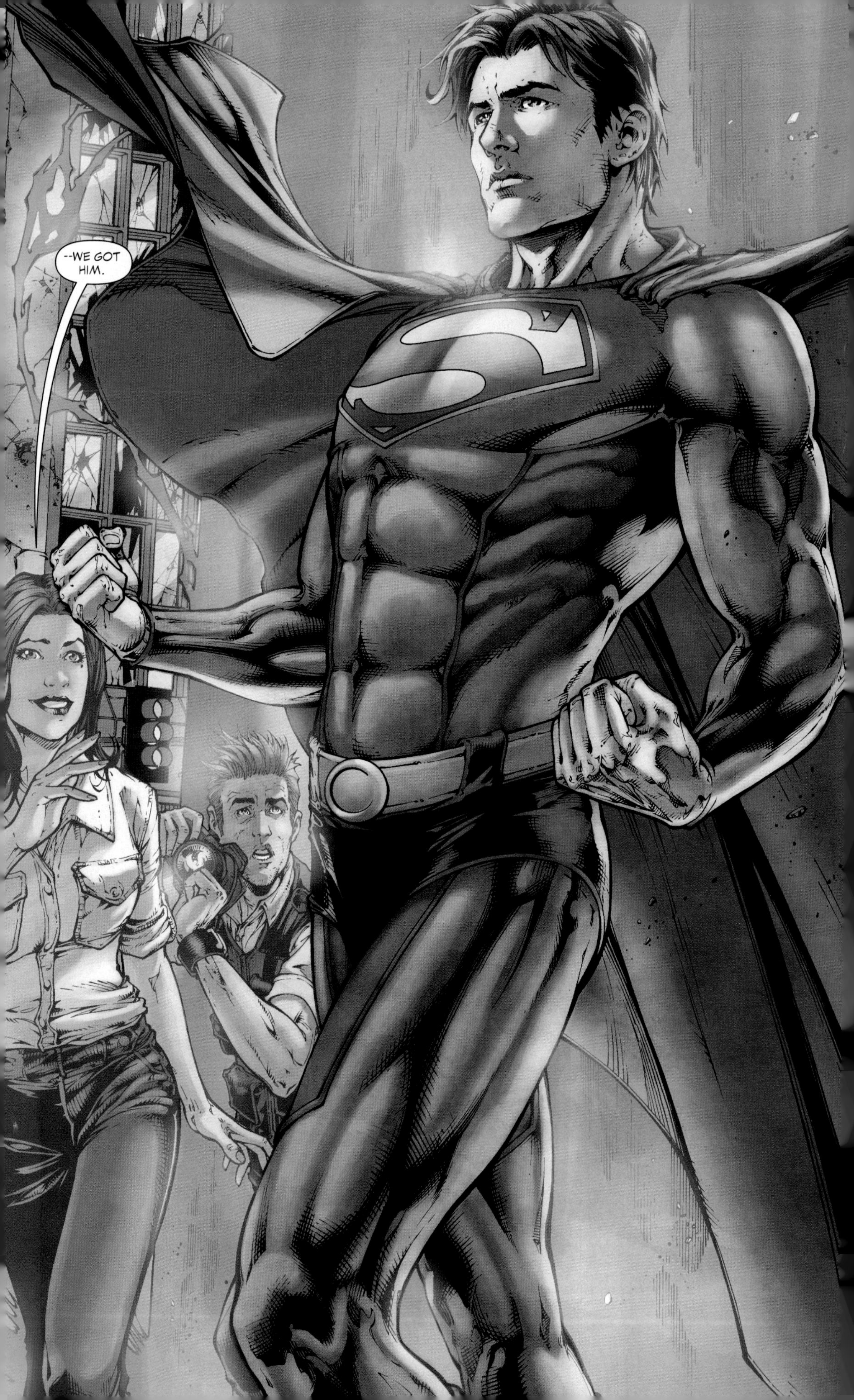
--WE GOT HIM.

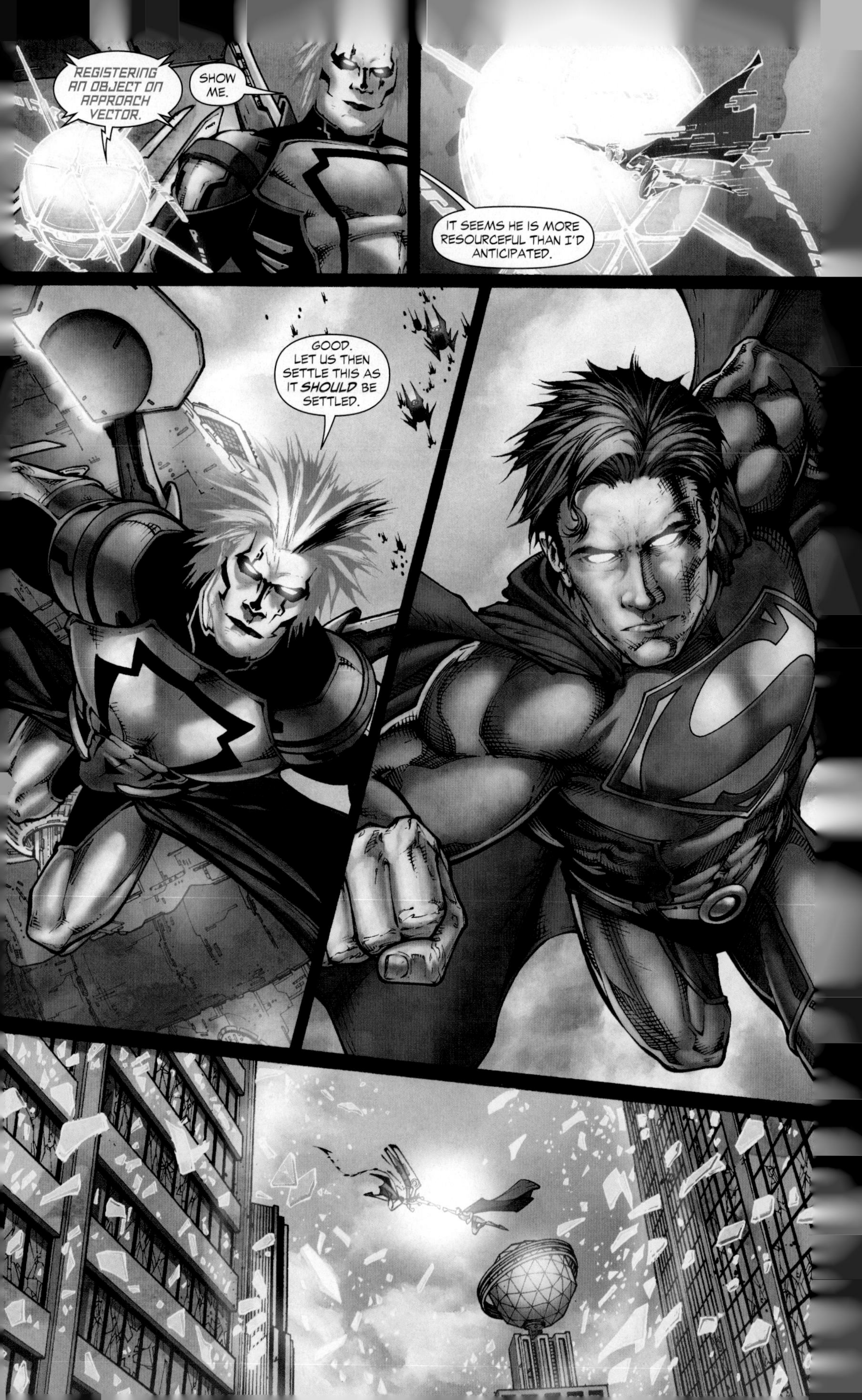
REGISTERING AN OBJECT ON APPROACH VECTOR.
SHOW ME.
IT SEEMS HE IS MORE RESOURCEFUL THAN I'D ANTICIPATED.
GOOD. LET US THEN SETTLE THIS AS IT SHOULD BE SETTLED.

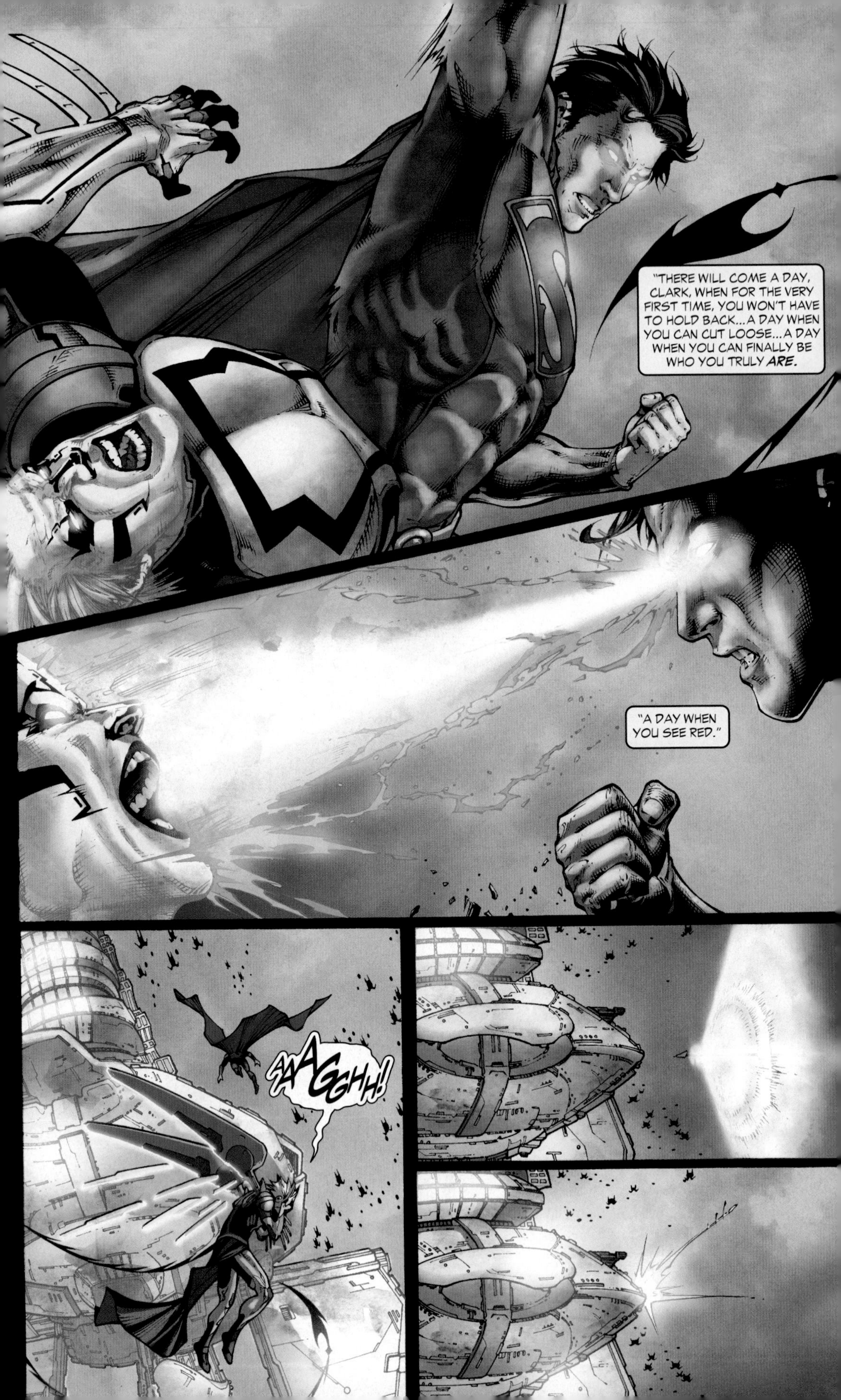
"THERE WILL COME A DAY, CLARK, WHEN FOR THE VERY FIRST TIME, YOU WON'T HAVE TO HOLD BACK...A DAY WHEN YOU CAN CUT LOOSE...A DAY WHEN YOU CAN FINALLY BE WHO YOU TRULY *ARE*.
"A DAY WHEN YOU SEE RED."
AAAGGHH!

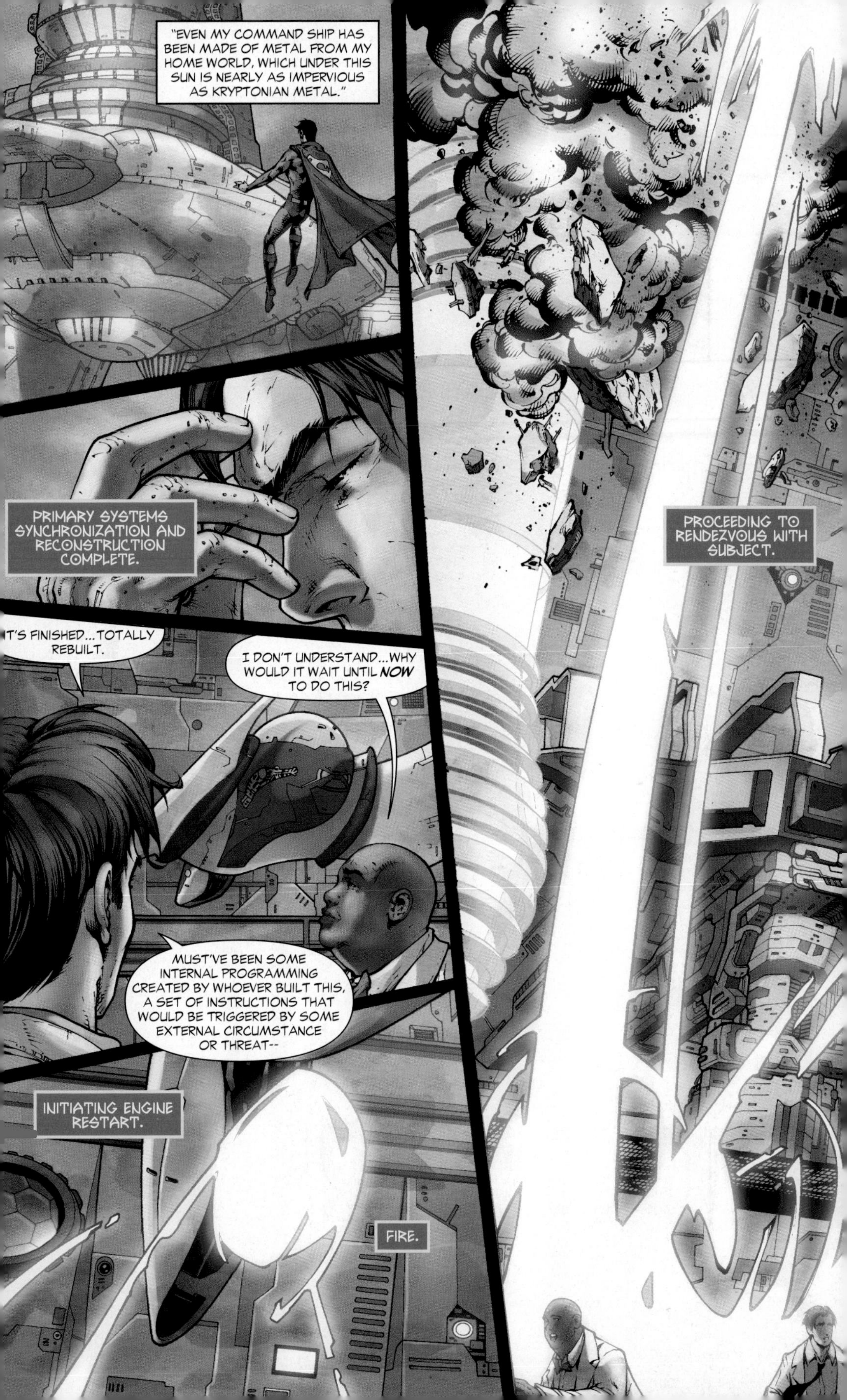
"EVEN MY COMMAND SHIP HAS BEEN MADE OF METAL FROM MY HOME WORLD, WHICH UNDER THIS SUN IS NEARLY AS IMPERVIOUS AS KRYPTONIAN METAL."
PRIMARY SYSTEMS SYNCHRONIZATION AND RECONSTRUCTION COMPLETE.
T'S FINISHED...TOTALLY REBUILT.
I DON'T UNDERSTAND...WHY WOULD IT WAIT UNTIL NOW TO DO THIS?
MUST'VE BEEN SOME INTERNAL PROGRAMMING CREATED BY WHOEVER BUILT THIS, A SET OF INSTRUCTIONS THAT WOULD BE TRIGGERED BY SOME EXTERNAL CIRCUMSTANCE OR THREAT--
INITIATING ENGINE RESTART.
FIRE.
PROCEEDING TO RENDEZVOUS WITH SUBJECT.

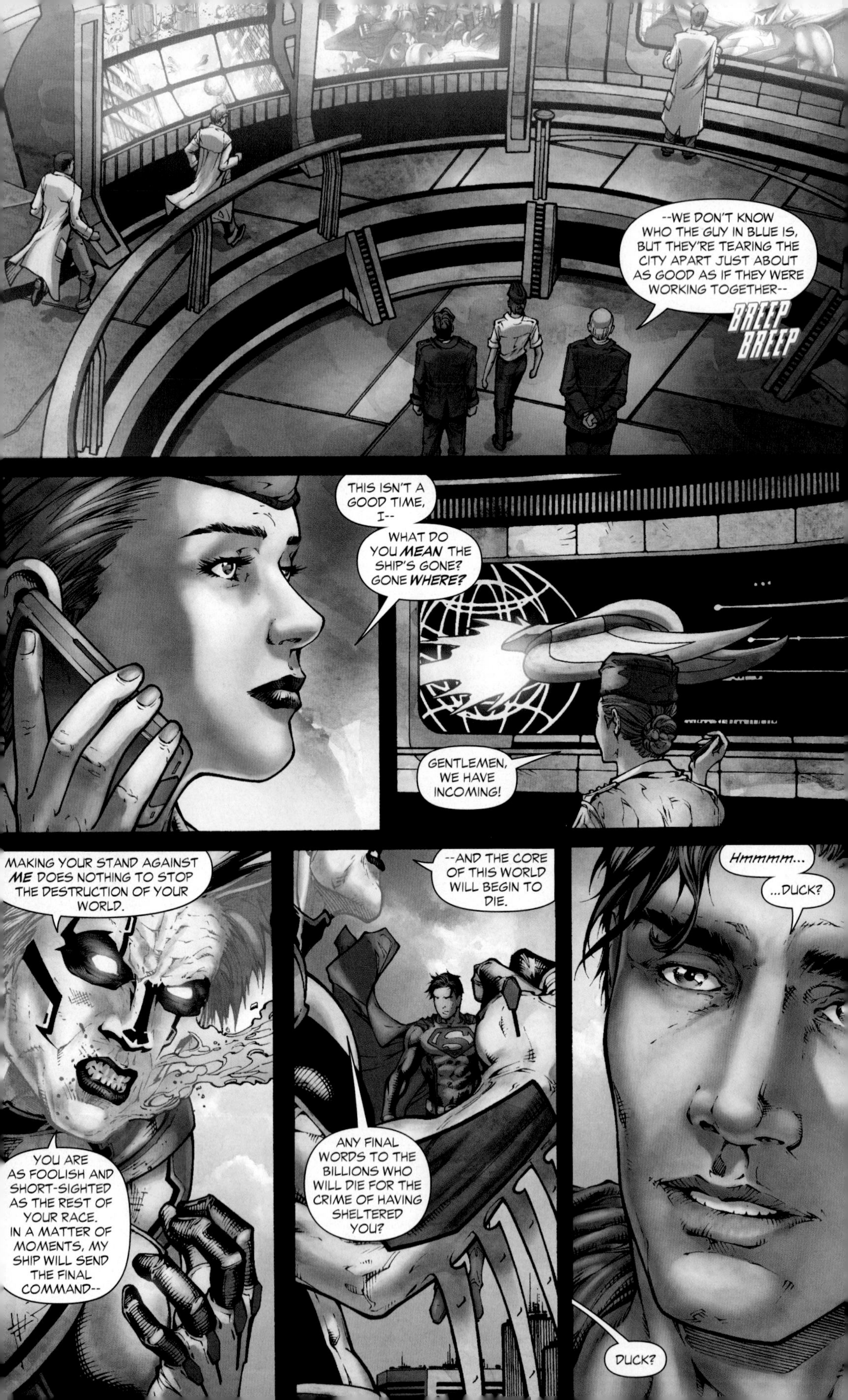
--WE DON'T KNOW WHO THE GUY IN BLUE IS, BUT THEY'RE TEARING THE CITY APART JUST ABOUT AS GOOD AS IF THEY WERE WORKING TOGETHER--
BREEP BREEP
THIS ISN'T A GOOD TIME, I--
WHAT DO YOU MEAN THE SHIP'S GONE? GONE WHERE?
GENTLEMEN, WE HAVE INCOMING!
MAKING YOUR STAND AGAINST ME DOES NOTHING TO STOP THE DESTRUCTION OF YOUR WORLD.
YOU ARE AS FOOLISH AND SHORT-SIGHTED AS THE REST OF YOUR RACE. IN A MATTER OF MOMENTS, MY SHIP WILL SEND THE FINAL COMMAND--
--AND THE CORE OF THIS WORLD WILL BEGIN TO DIE.
ANY FINAL WORDS TO THE BILLIONS WHO WILL DIE FOR THE CRIME OF HAVING SHELTERED YOU?
Hmmmm...
...DUCK?
DUCK?

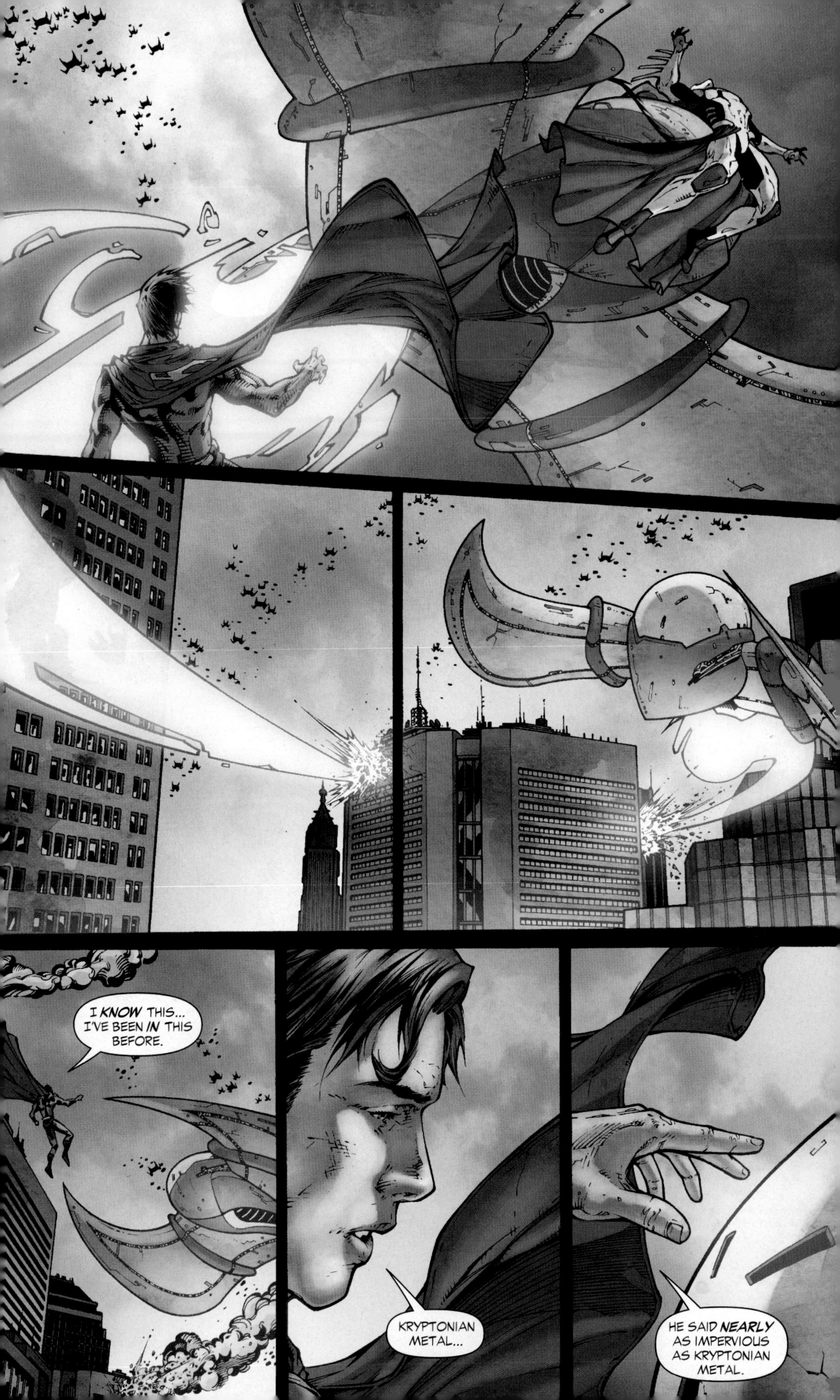
I KNOW THIS... I'VE BEEN IN THIS BEFORE.
KRYPTONIAN METAL...
HE SAID NEARLY AS IMPERVIOUS AS KRYPTONIAN METAL.

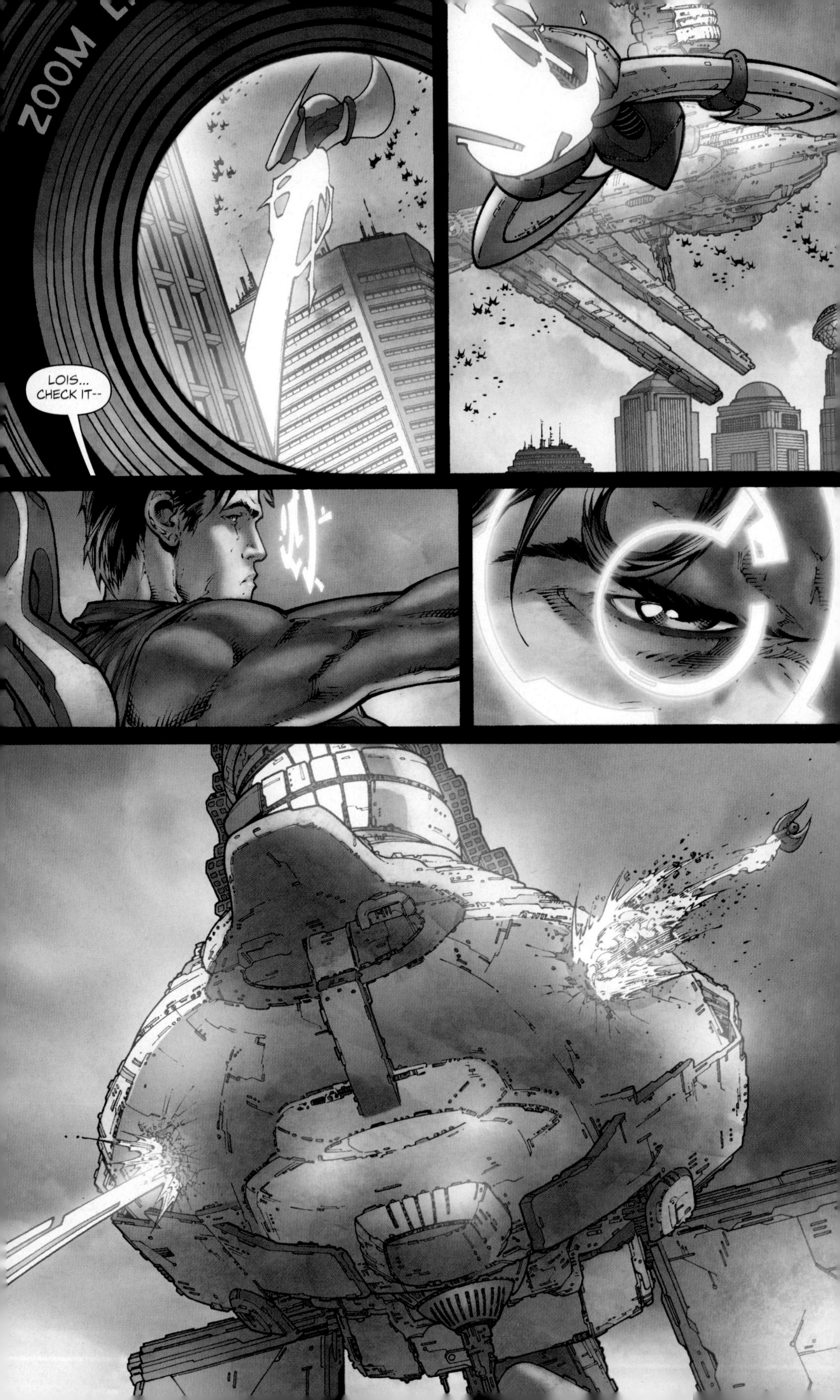
ZOOM
LOIS... CHECK IT--

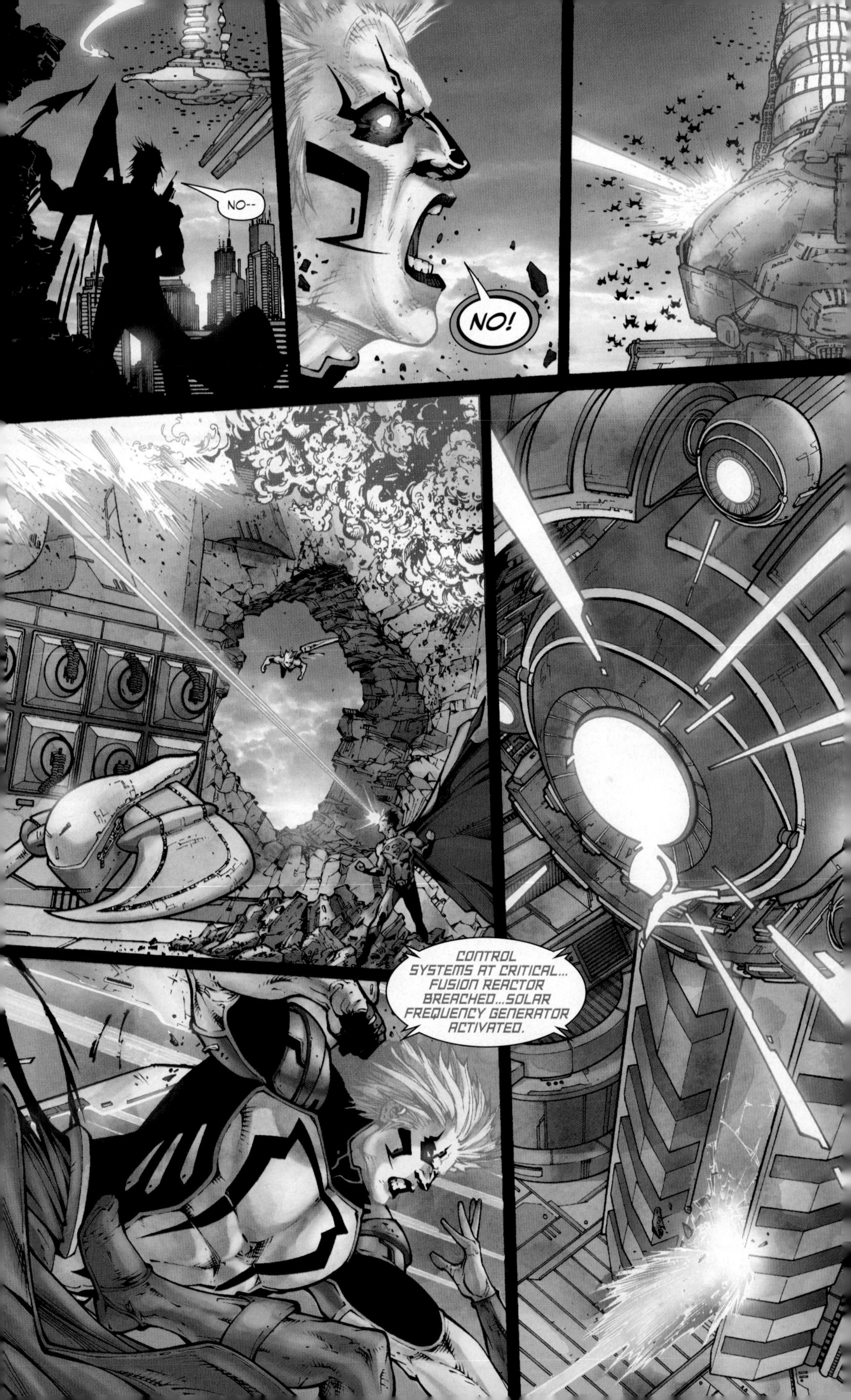
NO--
NO!
CONTROL SYSTEMS AT CRITICAL... ...FUSION REACTOR BREACHED...SOLAR FREQUENCY GENERATOR ACTIVATED.

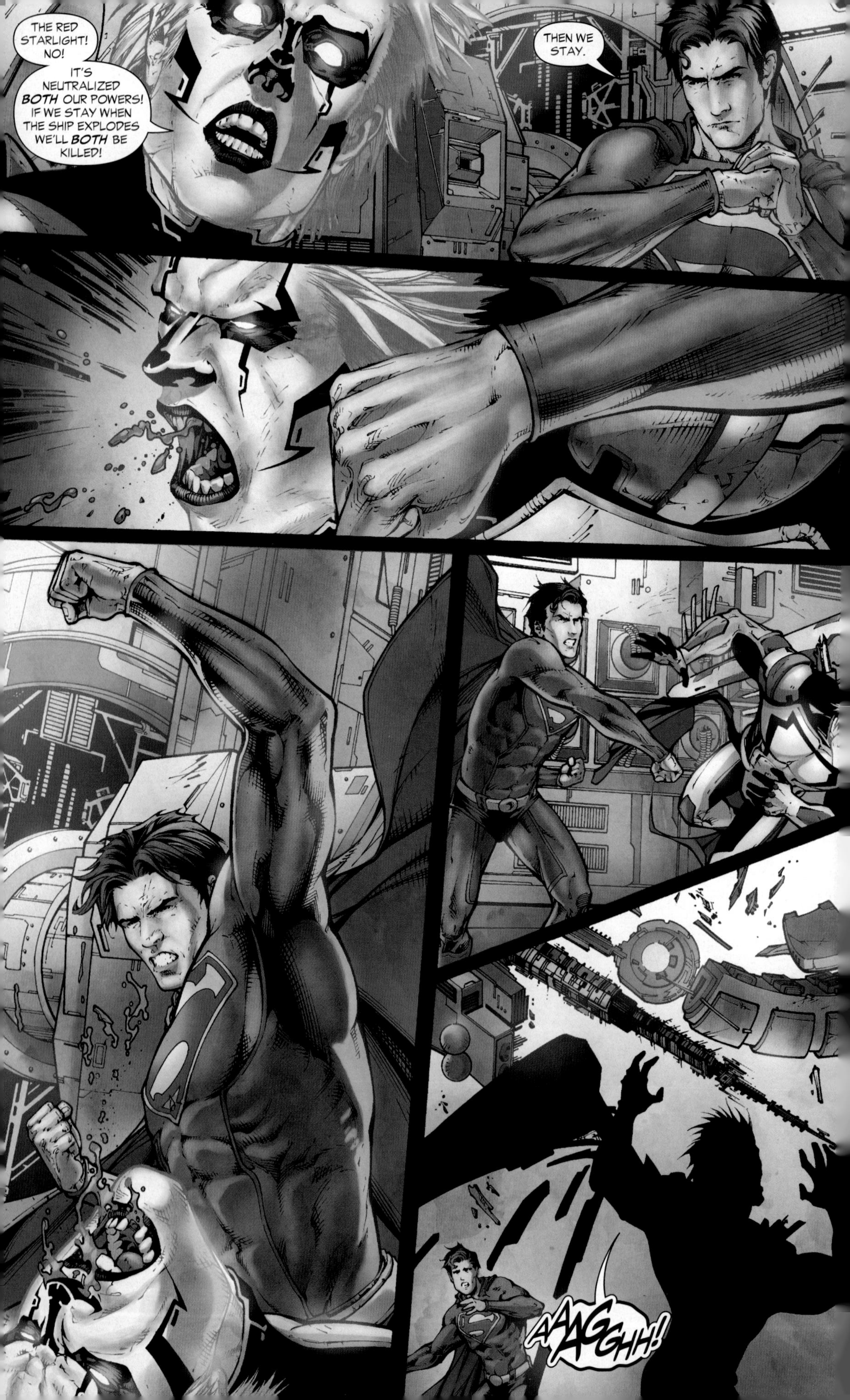
THE RED STARLIGHT! NO!
IT'S NEUTRALIZED BOTH OUR POWERS! IF WE STAY WHEN THE SHIP EXPLODES WE'LL BOTH BE KILLED!
THEN WE STAY.
AAAGGHH!

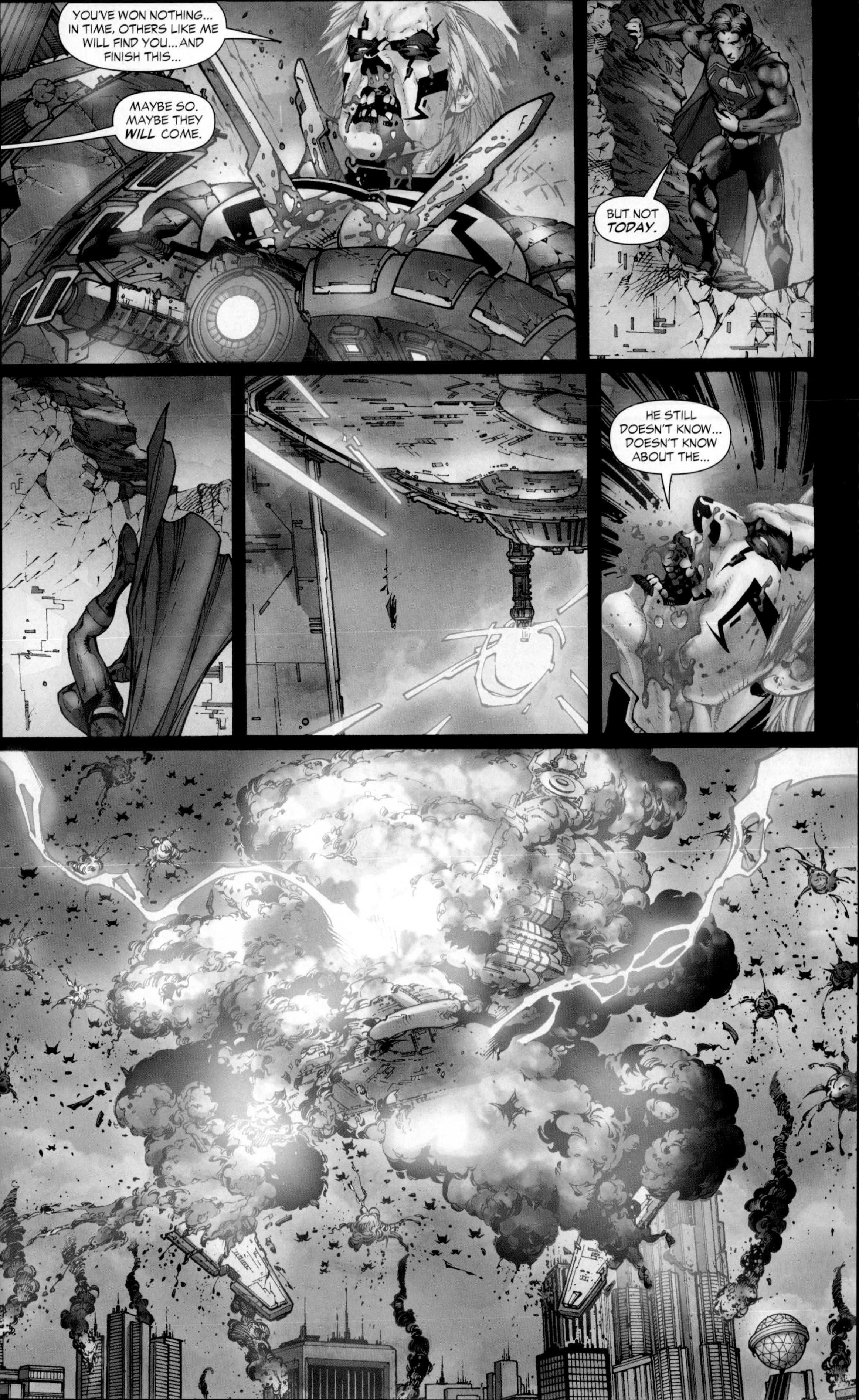
YOU'VE WON NOTHING... IN TIME, OTHERS LIKE ME WILL FIND YOU...AND FINISH THIS...
MAYBE SO. MAYBE THEY *WILL* COME.
BUT NOT *TODAY*.
HE STILL DOESN'T KNOW... DOESN'T KNOW ABOUT THE...

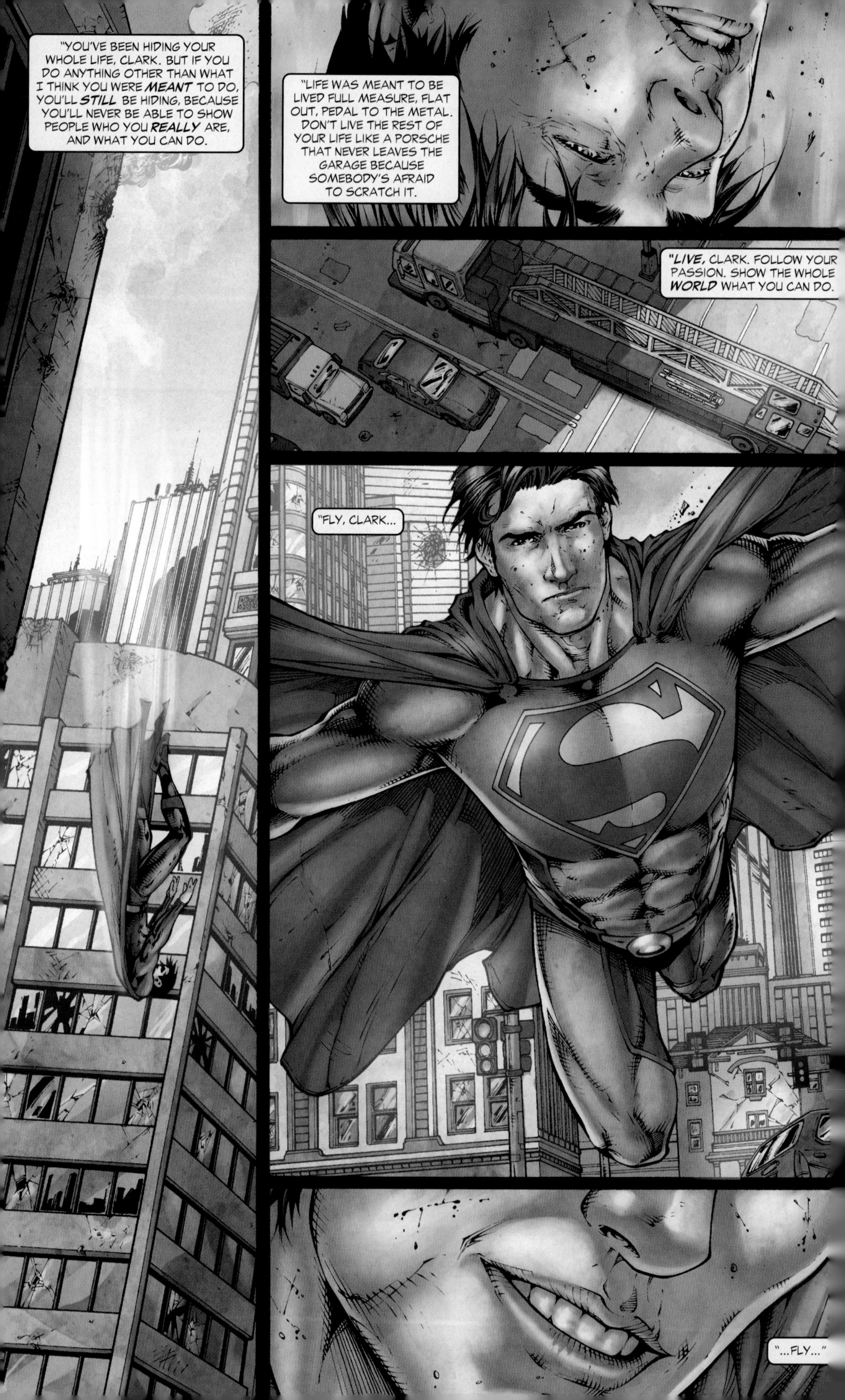
"YOU'VE BEEN HIDING YOUR WHOLE LIFE, CLARK. BUT IF YOU DO ANYTHING OTHER THAN WHAT I THINK YOU WERE MEANT TO DO, YOU'LL STILL BE HIDING, BECAUSE YOU'LL NEVER BE ABLE TO SHOW PEOPLE WHO YOU REALLY ARE, AND WHAT YOU CAN DO.
"LIFE WAS MEANT TO BE LIVED FULL MEASURE, FLAT OUT, PEDAL TO THE METAL. DON'T LIVE THE REST OF YOUR LIFE LIKE A PORSCHE THAT NEVER LEAVES THE GARAGE BECAUSE SOMEBODY'S AFRAID TO SCRATCH IT.
"LIVE, CLARK. FOLLOW YOUR PASSION. SHOW THE WHOLE WORLD WHAT YOU CAN DO.
"FLY, CLARK...
"...FLY..."

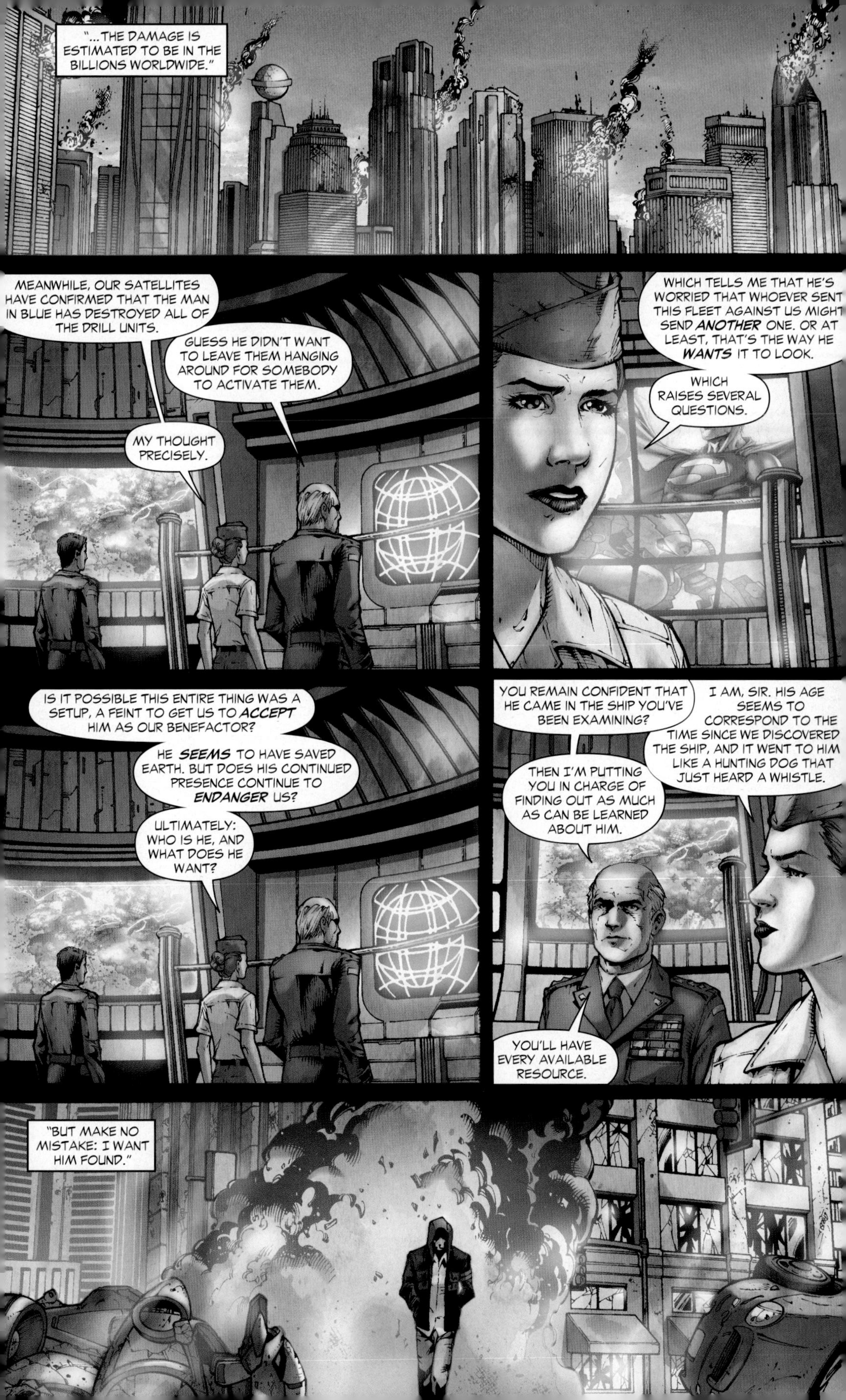
"...THE DAMAGE IS ESTIMATED TO BE IN THE BILLIONS WORLDWIDE."
MEANWHILE, OUR SATELLITES HAVE CONFIRMED THAT THE MAN IN BLUE HAS DESTROYED ALL OF THE DRILL UNITS.
GUESS HE DIDN'T WANT TO LEAVE THEM HANGING AROUND FOR SOMEBODY TO ACTIVATE THEM.
MY THOUGHT PRECISELY.
WHICH TELLS ME THAT HE'S WORRIED THAT WHOEVER SENT THIS FLEET AGAINST US MIGHT SEND ANOTHER ONE. OR AT LEAST, THAT'S THE WAY HE WANTS IT TO LOOK.
WHICH RAISES SEVERAL QUESTIONS.
IS IT POSSIBLE THIS ENTIRE THING WAS A SETUP, A FEINT TO GET US TO ACCEPT HIM AS OUR BENEFACTOR?
HE SEEMS TO HAVE SAVED EARTH. BUT DOES HIS CONTINUED PRESENCE CONTINUE TO ENDANGER US?
ULTIMATELY: WHO IS HE, AND WHAT DOES HE WANT?
YOU REMAIN CONFIDENT THAT HE CAME IN THE SHIP YOU'VE BEEN EXAMINING?
I AM, SIR. HIS AGE SEEMS TO CORRESPOND TO THE TIME SINCE WE DISCOVERED THE SHIP, AND IT WENT TO HIM LIKE A HUNTING DOG THAT JUST HEARD A WHISTLE.
THEN I'M PUTTING YOU IN CHARGE OF FINDING OUT AS MUCH AS CAN BE LEARNED ABOUT HIM.
YOU'LL HAVE EVERY AVAILABLE RESOURCE.
"BUT MAKE NO MISTAKE: I WANT HIM FOUND."

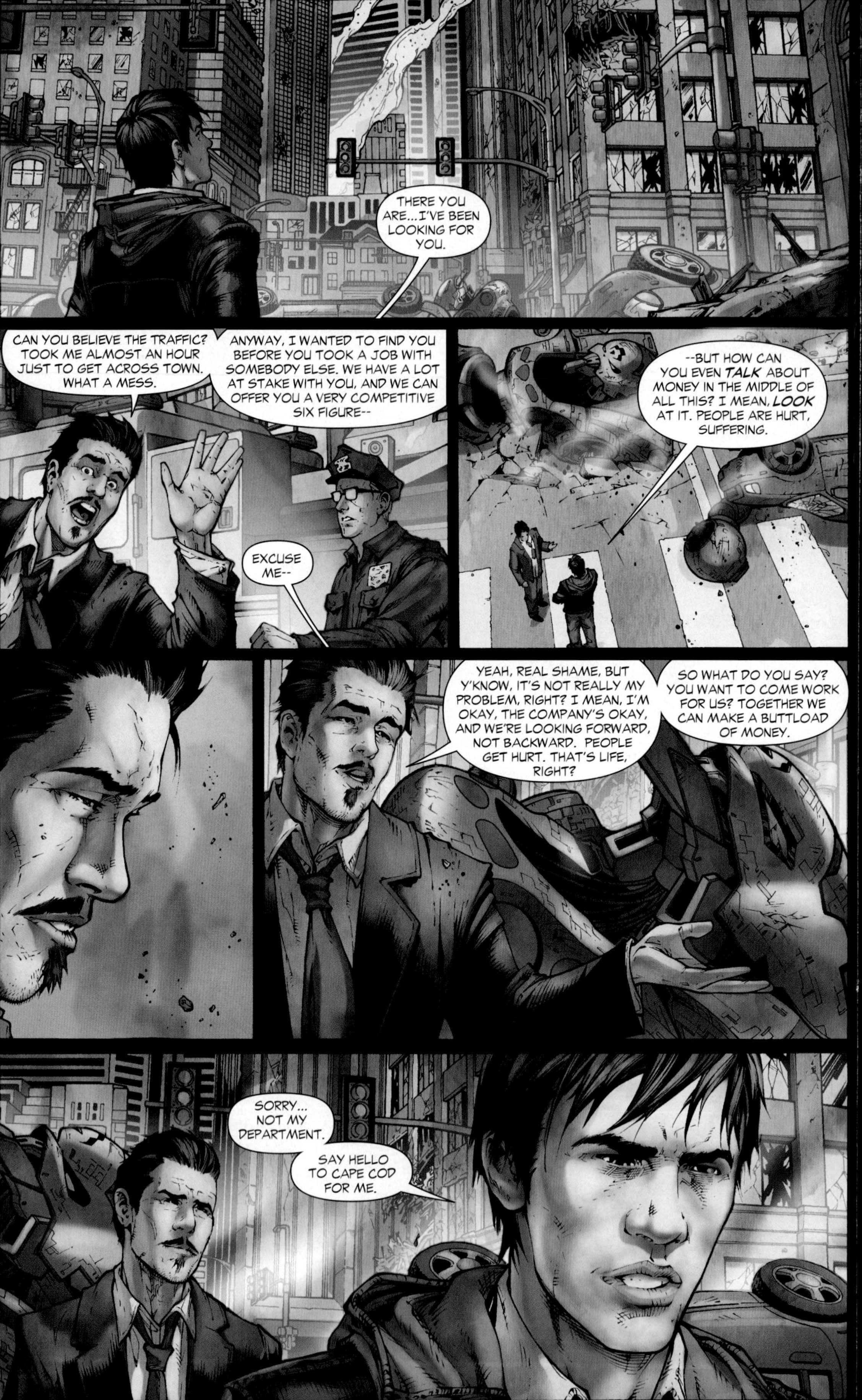
THERE YOU ARE... I'VE BEEN LOOKING FOR YOU.
CAN YOU BELIEVE THE TRAFFIC? TOOK ME ALMOST AN HOUR JUST TO GET ACROSS TOWN. WHAT A MESS.
ANYWAY, I WANTED TO FIND YOU BEFORE YOU TOOK A JOB WITH SOMEBODY ELSE. WE HAVE A LOT AT STAKE WITH YOU, AND WE CAN OFFER YOU A VERY COMPETITIVE SIX FIGURE--
EXCUSE ME--
--BUT HOW CAN YOU EVEN TALK ABOUT MONEY IN THE MIDDLE OF ALL THIS? I MEAN, LOOK AT IT. PEOPLE ARE HURT, SUFFERING.
YEAH, REAL SHAME, BUT Y'KNOW, IT'S NOT REALLY MY PROBLEM, RIGHT? I MEAN, I'M OKAY, THE COMPANY'S OKAY, AND WE'RE LOOKING FORWARD, NOT BACKWARD. PEOPLE GET HURT. THAT'S LIFE, RIGHT?
SO WHAT DO YOU SAY? YOU WANT TO COME WORK FOR US? TOGETHER WE CAN MAKE A BUTTLOAD OF MONEY.
SORRY... NOT MY DEPARTMENT.
SAY HELLO TO CAPE COD FOR ME.

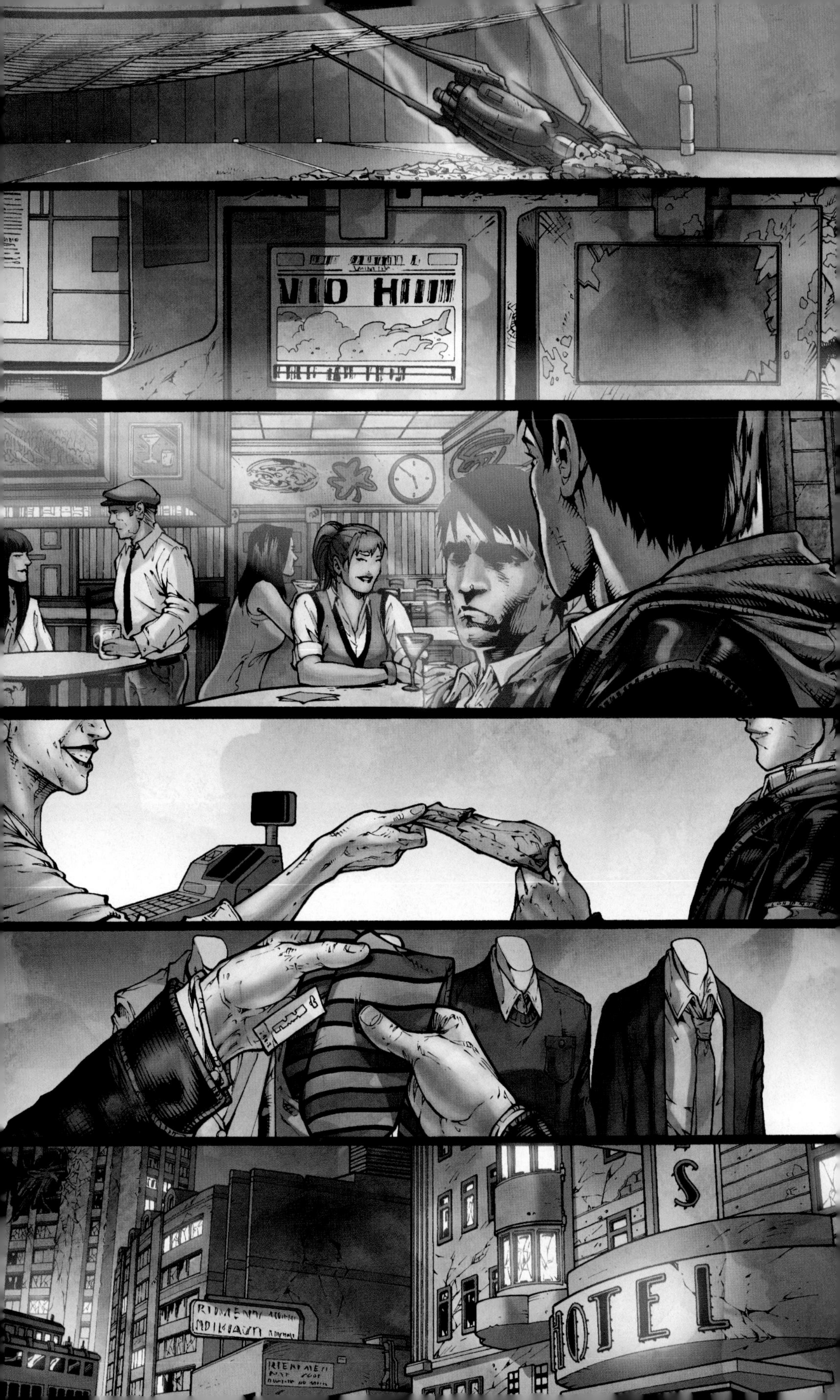

HOTEL

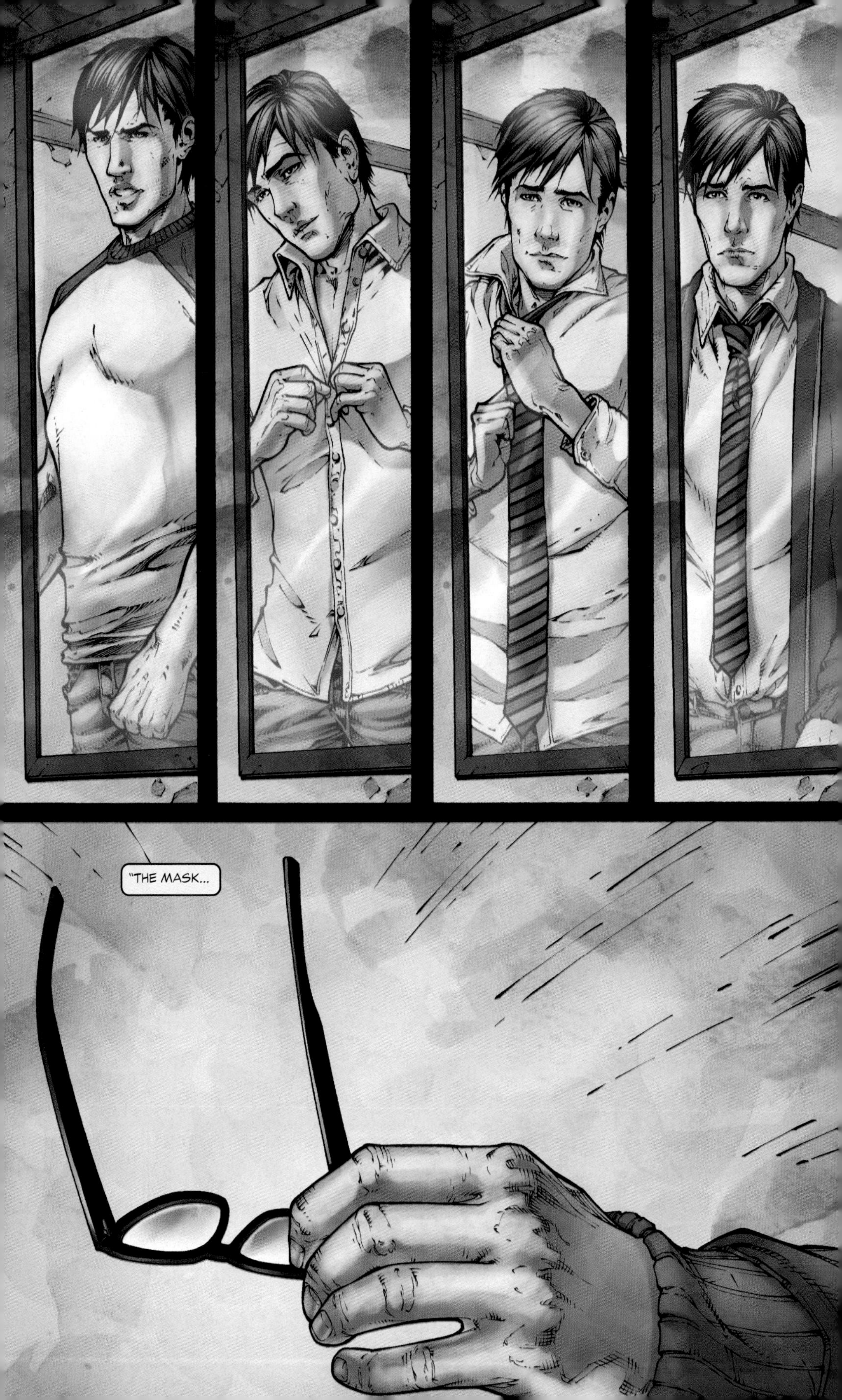
"THE MASK...

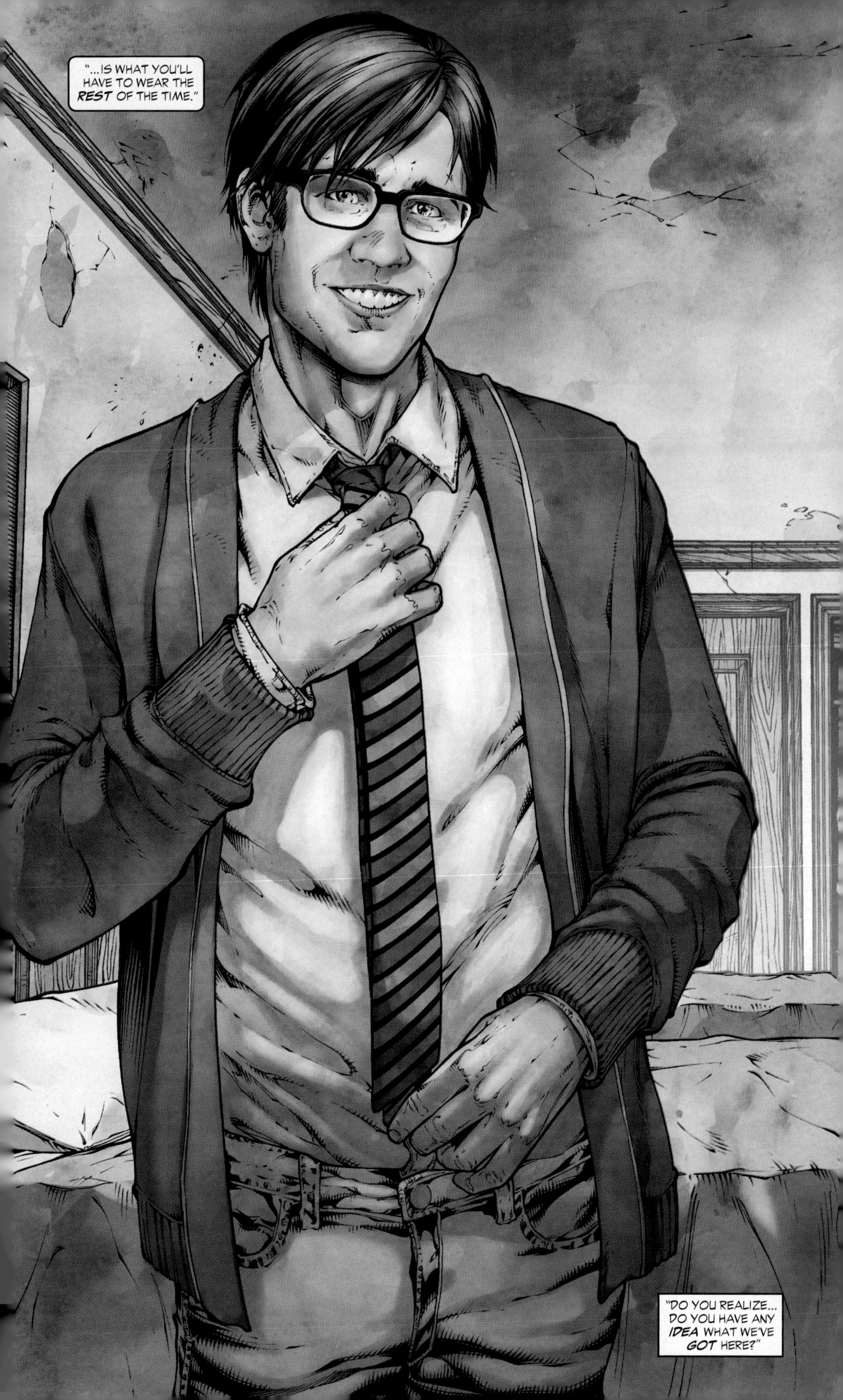
"...IS WHAT YOU'LL HAVE TO WEAR THE REST OF THE TIME."
"DO YOU REALIZE... DO YOU HAVE ANY IDEA WHAT WE'VE GOT HERE?"

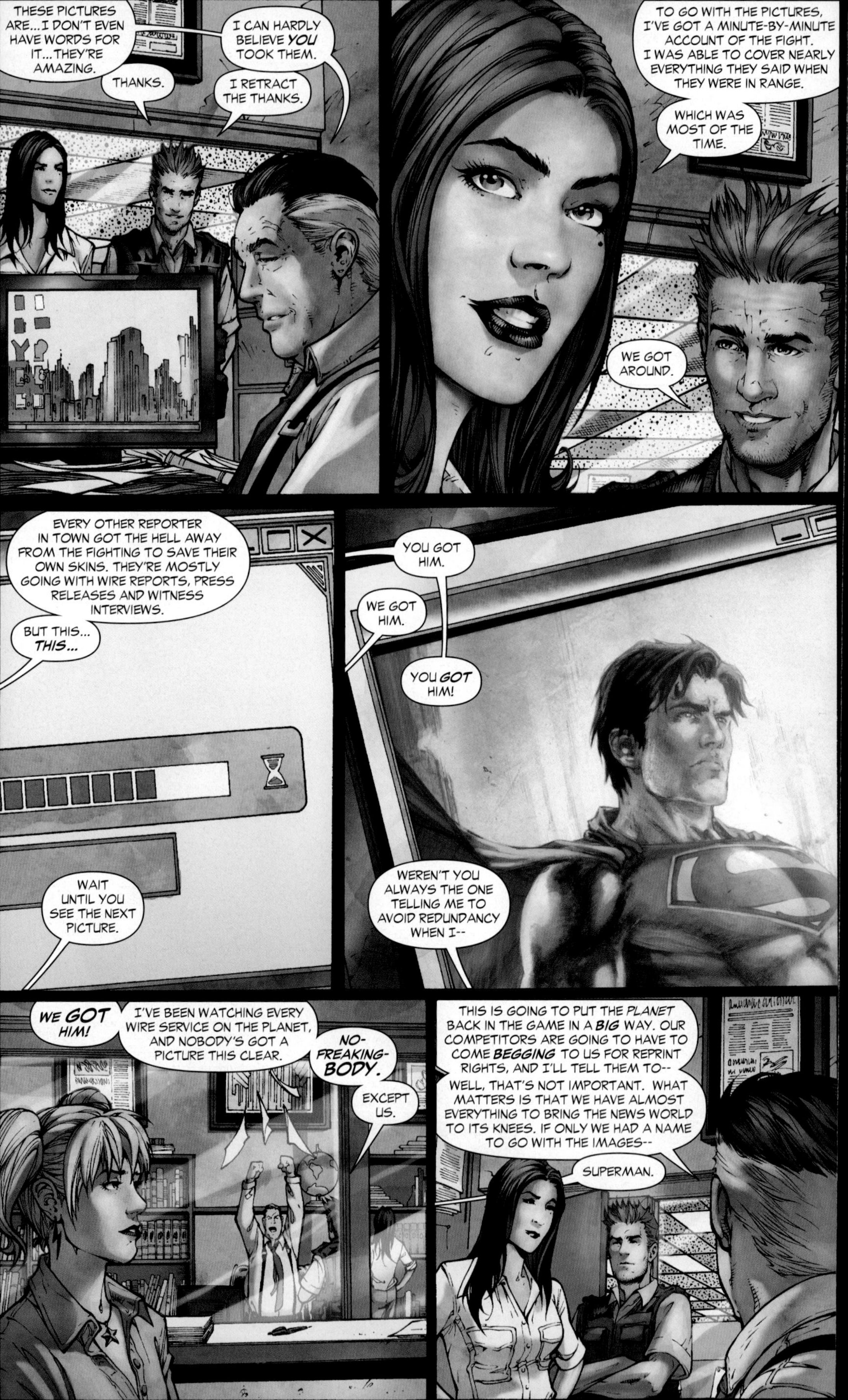
THESE PICTURES ARE...I DON'T EVEN HAVE WORDS FOR IT...THEY'RE AMAZING.
THANKS.
I CAN HARDLY BELIEVE YOU TOOK THEM.
I RETRACT THE THANKS.
TO GO WITH THE PICTURES, I'VE GOT A MINUTE-BY-MINUTE ACCOUNT OF THE FIGHT. I WAS ABLE TO COVER NEARLY EVERYTHING THEY SAID WHEN THEY WERE IN RANGE.
WHICH WAS MOST OF THE TIME.
WE GOT AROUND.
EVERY OTHER REPORTER IN TOWN GOT THE HELL AWAY FROM THE FIGHTING TO SAVE THEIR OWN SKINS. THEY'RE MOSTLY GOING WITH WIRE REPORTS, PRESS RELEASES AND WITNESS INTERVIEWS.
BUT THIS... THIS...
WAIT UNTIL YOU SEE THE NEXT PICTURE.
YOU GOT HIM.
WE GOT HIM.
YOU GOT HIM!
WEREN'T YOU ALWAYS THE ONE TELLING ME TO AVOID REDUNDANCY WHEN I--
WE GOT HIM!
I'VE BEEN WATCHING EVERY WIRE SERVICE ON THE PLANET, AND NOBODY'S GOT A PICTURE THIS CLEAR.
NO-FREAKING-BODY.
EXCEPT US.
THIS IS GOING TO PUT THE PLANET BACK IN THE GAME IN A BIG WAY. OUR COMPETITORS ARE GOING TO HAVE TO COME BEGGING TO US FOR REPRINT RIGHTS, AND I'LL TELL THEM TO--
WELL, THAT'S NOT IMPORTANT. WHAT MATTERS IS THAT WE HAVE ALMOST EVERYTHING TO BRING THE NEWS WORLD TO ITS KNEES. IF ONLY WE HAD A NAME TO GO WITH THE IMAGES--
SUPERMAN.

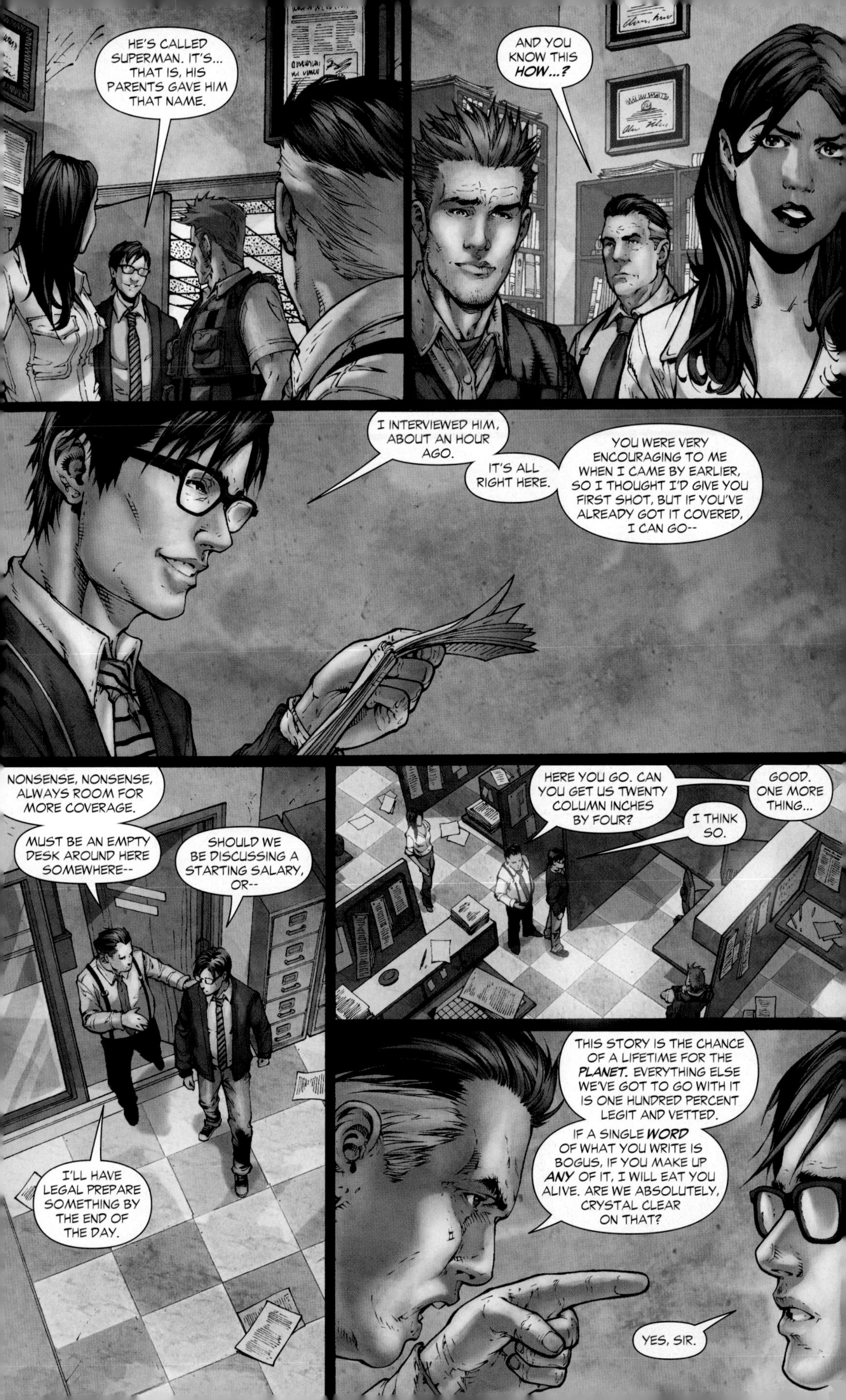

HE'S CALLED SUPERMAN. IT'S... THAT IS, HIS PARENTS GAVE HIM THAT NAME.
AND YOU KNOW THIS *HOW...?*
I INTERVIEWED HIM, ABOUT AN HOUR AGO.
IT'S ALL RIGHT HERE.
YOU WERE VERY ENCOURAGING TO ME WHEN I CAME BY EARLIER, SO I THOUGHT I'D GIVE YOU FIRST SHOT, BUT IF YOU'VE ALREADY GOT IT COVERED, I CAN GO--
NONSENSE, NONSENSE, ALWAYS ROOM FOR MORE COVERAGE.
MUST BE AN EMPTY DESK AROUND HERE SOMEWHERE--
SHOULD WE BE DISCUSSING A STARTING SALARY, OR--
I'LL HAVE LEGAL PREPARE SOMETHING BY THE END OF THE DAY.
HERE YOU GO. CAN YOU GET US TWENTY COLUMN INCHES BY FOUR?
I THINK SO.
GOOD. ONE MORE THING...
THIS STORY IS THE CHANCE OF A LIFETIME FOR THE *PLANET.* EVERYTHING ELSE WE'VE GOT TO GO WITH IT IS ONE HUNDRED PERCENT LEGIT AND VETTED.
IF A SINGLE ***WORD*** OF WHAT YOU WRITE IS BOGUS, IF YOU MAKE UP ***ANY*** OF IT, I WILL EAT YOU ALIVE. ARE WE ABSOLUTELY, CRYSTAL CLEAR ON THAT?
YES, SIR.

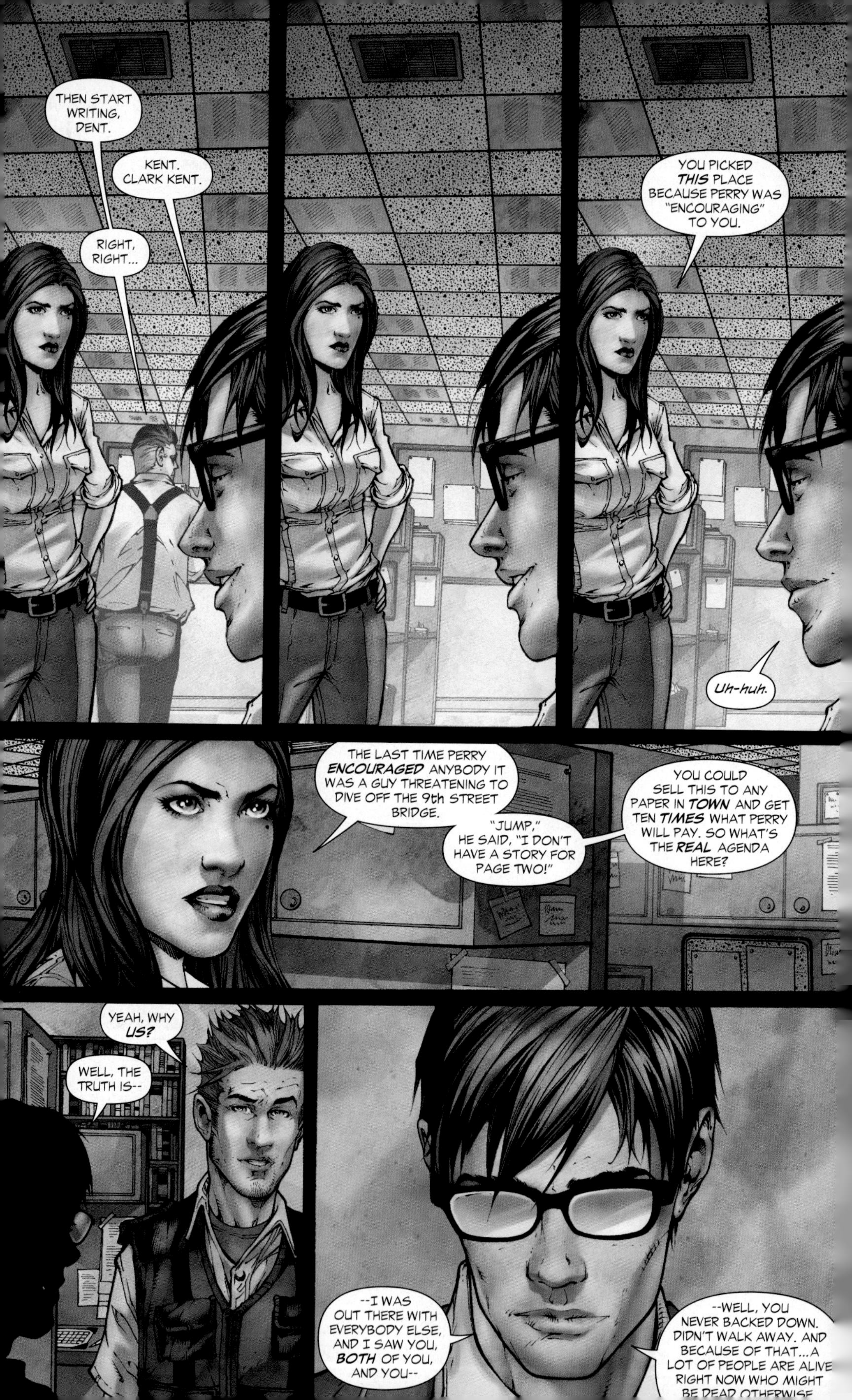
THEN START WRITING, DENT.
KENT. CLARK KENT.
RIGHT, RIGHT...
YOU PICKED THIS PLACE BECAUSE PERRY WAS "ENCOURAGING" TO YOU.
Uh-huh.
THE LAST TIME PERRY ENCOURAGED ANYBODY IT WAS A GUY THREATENING TO DIVE OFF THE 9th STREET BRIDGE.
"JUMP," HE SAID, "I DON'T HAVE A STORY FOR PAGE TWO!"
YOU COULD SELL THIS TO ANY PAPER IN TOWN AND GET TEN TIMES WHAT PERRY WILL PAY. SO WHAT'S THE REAL AGENDA HERE?
YEAH, WHY US?
WELL, THE TRUTH IS--
--I WAS OUT THERE WITH EVERYBODY ELSE, AND I SAW YOU, BOTH OF YOU, AND YOU--
--WELL, YOU NEVER BACKED DOWN. DIDN'T WALK AWAY. AND BECAUSE OF THAT...A LOT OF PEOPLE ARE ALIVE RIGHT NOW WHO MIGHT BE DEAD OTHERWISE.

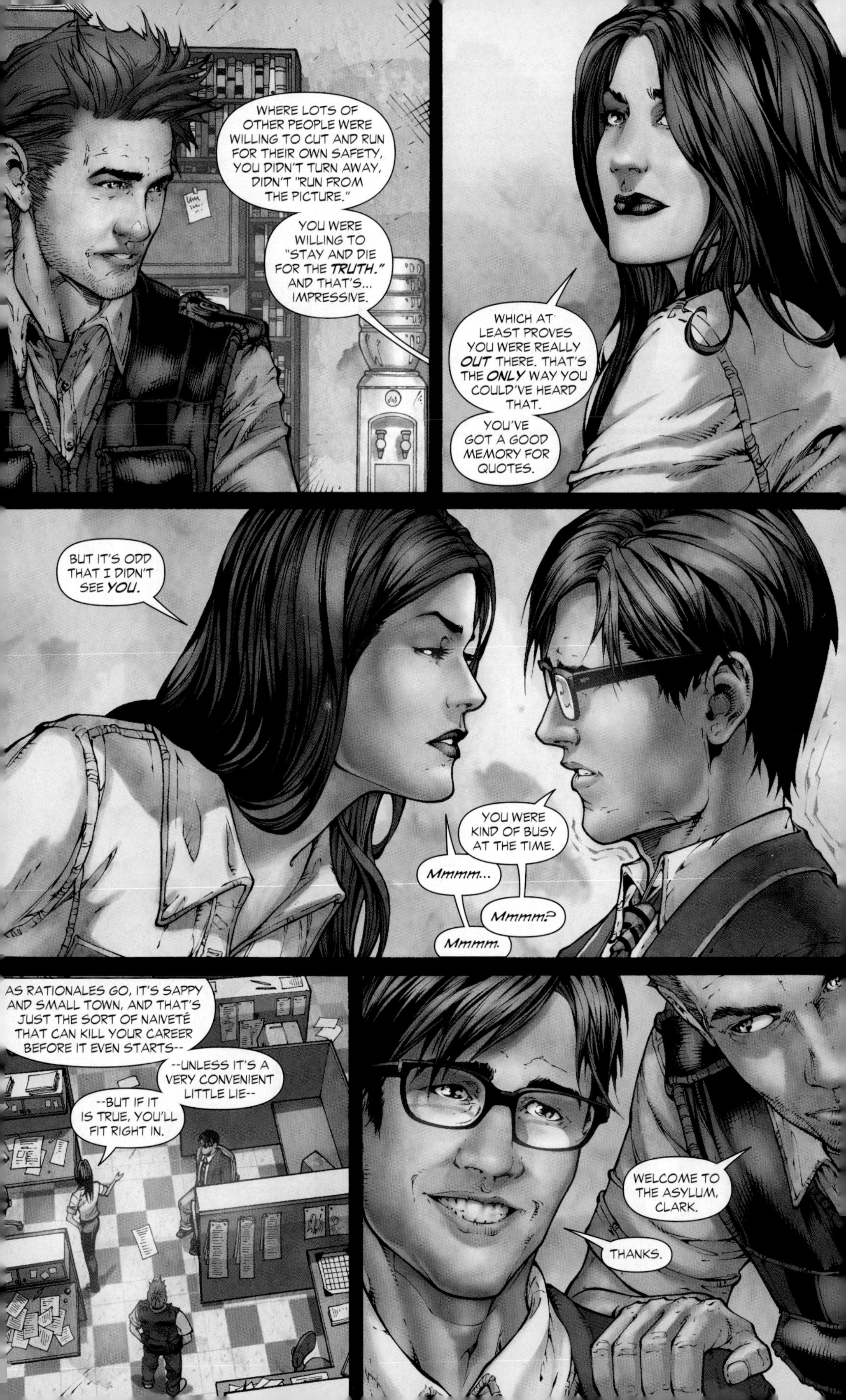
WHERE LOTS OF OTHER PEOPLE WERE WILLING TO CUT AND RUN FOR THEIR OWN SAFETY, YOU DIDN'T TURN AWAY, DIDN'T "RUN FROM THE PICTURE."
YOU WERE WILLING TO "STAY AND DIE FOR THE *TRUTH.*" AND THAT'S... IMPRESSIVE.
WHICH AT LEAST PROVES YOU WERE REALLY *OUT* THERE. THAT'S THE *ONLY* WAY YOU COULD'VE HEARD THAT.
YOU'VE GOT A GOOD MEMORY FOR QUOTES.
BUT IT'S ODD THAT I DIDN'T SEE *YOU.*
YOU WERE KIND OF BUSY AT THE TIME.
Mmmm...
Mmmm?
Mmmm.
AS RATIONALES GO, IT'S SAPPY AND SMALL TOWN, AND THAT'S JUST THE SORT OF NAIVETÉ THAT CAN KILL YOUR CAREER BEFORE IT EVEN STARTS--
--UNLESS IT'S A VERY CONVENIENT LITTLE LIE--
--BUT IF IT IS TRUE, YOU'LL FIT RIGHT IN.
WELCOME TO THE ASYLUM, CLARK.
THANKS.

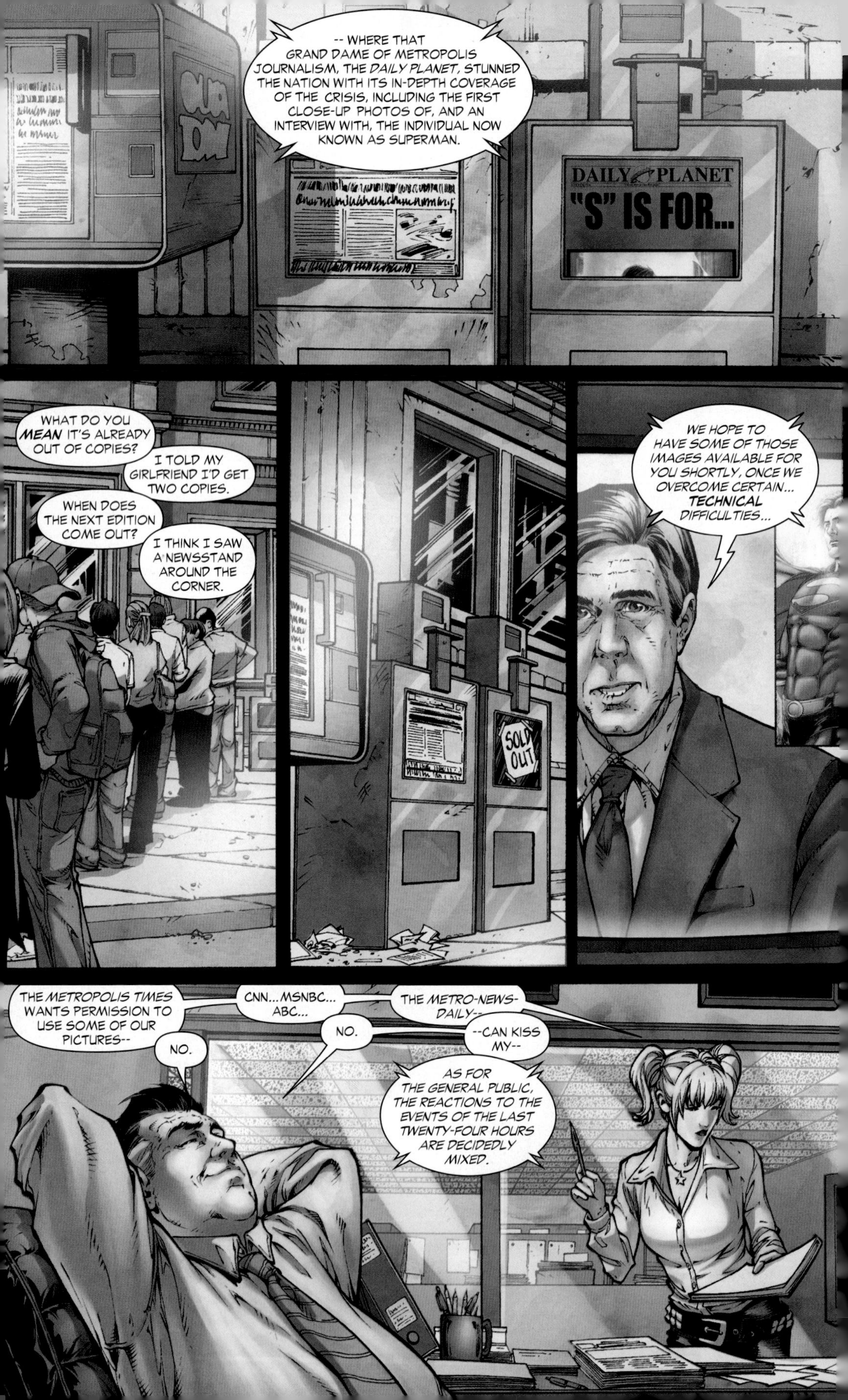
-- WHERE THAT GRAND DAME OF METROPOLIS JOURNALISM, THE DAILY PLANET, STUNNED THE NATION WITH ITS IN-DEPTH COVERAGE OF THE CRISIS, INCLUDING THE FIRST CLOSE-UP PHOTOS OF, AND AN INTERVIEW WITH, THE INDIVIDUAL NOW KNOWN AS SUPERMAN.
DAILY PLANET
"S" IS FOR...
WHAT DO YOU MEAN IT'S ALREADY OUT OF COPIES?
I TOLD MY GIRLFRIEND I'D GET TWO COPIES.
WHEN DOES THE NEXT EDITION COME OUT?
I THINK I SAW A NEWSSTAND AROUND THE CORNER.
SOLD OUT
WE HOPE TO HAVE SOME OF THOSE IMAGES AVAILABLE FOR YOU SHORTLY, ONCE WE OVERCOME CERTAIN... TECHNICAL DIFFICULTIES...
THE METROPOLIS TIMES WANTS PERMISSION TO USE SOME OF OUR PICTURES--
NO.
CNN...MSNBC... ABC...
NO.
THE METRO-NEWS-DAILY--
--CAN KISS MY--
AS FOR THE GENERAL PUBLIC, THE REACTIONS TO THE EVENTS OF THE LAST TWENTY-FOUR HOURS ARE DECIDEDLY MIXED.

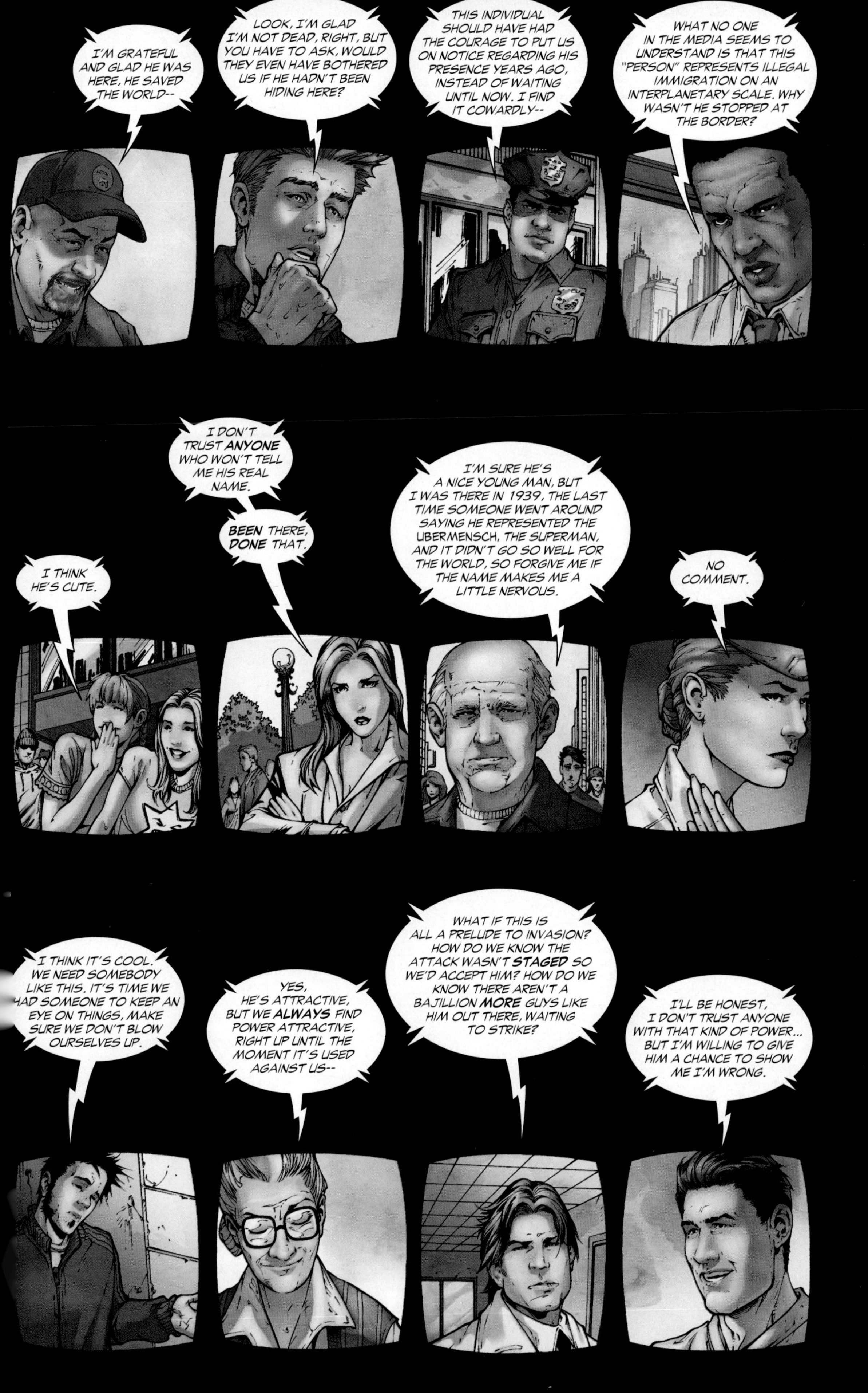
I'M GRATEFUL AND GLAD HE WAS HERE, HE SAVED THE WORLD--
LOOK, I'M GLAD I'M NOT DEAD, RIGHT, BUT YOU HAVE TO ASK, WOULD THEY EVEN HAVE BOTHERED US IF HE HADN'T BEEN HIDING HERE?
THIS INDIVIDUAL SHOULD HAVE HAD THE COURAGE TO PUT US ON NOTICE REGARDING HIS PRESENCE YEARS AGO, INSTEAD OF WAITING UNTIL NOW. I FIND IT COWARDLY--
WHAT NO ONE IN THE MEDIA SEEMS TO UNDERSTAND IS THAT THIS "PERSON" REPRESENTS ILLEGAL IMMIGRATION ON AN INTERPLANETARY SCALE. WHY WASN'T HE STOPPED AT THE BORDER?
I THINK HE'S CUTE.
I DON'T TRUST ANYONE WHO WON'T TELL ME HIS REAL NAME.
BEEN THERE, DONE THAT.
I'M SURE HE'S A NICE YOUNG MAN, BUT I WAS THERE IN 1939, THE LAST TIME SOMEONE WENT AROUND SAYING HE REPRESENTED THE UBERMENSCH, THE SUPERMAN, AND IT DIDN'T GO SO WELL FOR THE WORLD, SO FORGIVE ME IF THE NAME MAKES ME A LITTLE NERVOUS.
NO COMMENT.
I THINK IT'S COOL. WE NEED SOMEBODY LIKE THIS. IT'S TIME WE HAD SOMEONE TO KEEP AN EYE ON THINGS, MAKE SURE WE DON'T BLOW OURSELVES UP.
YES, HE'S ATTRACTIVE, BUT WE ALWAYS FIND POWER ATTRACTIVE, RIGHT UP UNTIL THE MOMENT IT'S USED AGAINST US--
WHAT IF THIS IS ALL A PRELUDE TO INVASION? HOW DO WE KNOW THE ATTACK WASN'T STAGED SO WE'D ACCEPT HIM? HOW DO WE KNOW THERE AREN'T A BAJILLION MORE GUYS LIKE HIM OUT THERE, WAITING TO STRIKE?
I'LL BE HONEST, I DON'T TRUST ANYONE WITH THAT KIND OF POWER... BUT I'M WILLING TO GIVE HIM A CHANCE TO SHOW ME I'M WRONG.

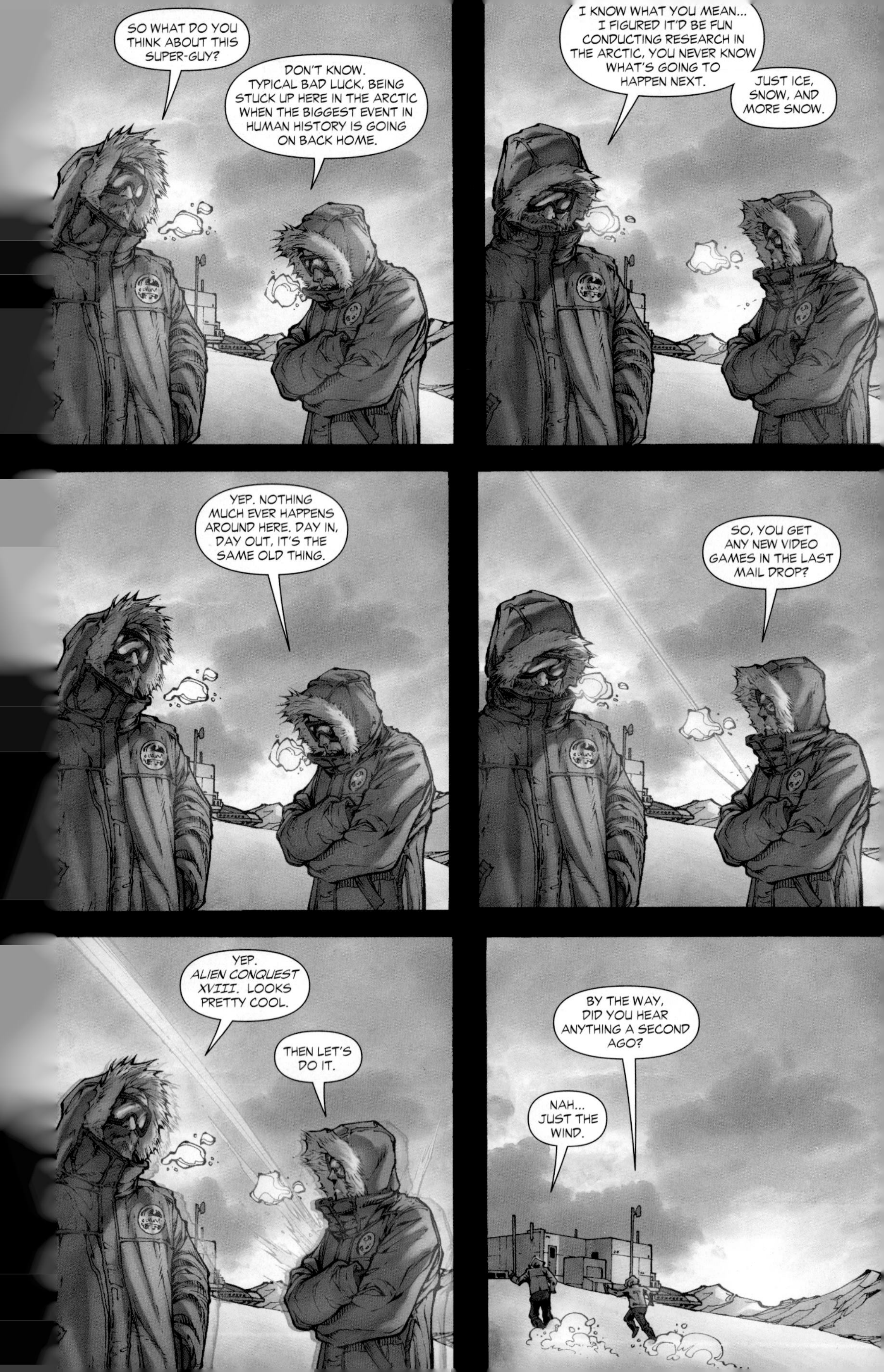
SO WHAT DO YOU THINK ABOUT THIS SUPER-GUY?
DON'T KNOW. TYPICAL BAD LUCK, BEING STUCK UP HERE IN THE ARCTIC WHEN THE BIGGEST EVENT IN HUMAN HISTORY IS GOING ON BACK HOME.
I KNOW WHAT YOU MEAN... I FIGURED IT'D BE FUN CONDUCTING RESEARCH IN THE ARCTIC, YOU NEVER KNOW WHAT'S GOING TO HAPPEN NEXT.
JUST ICE, SNOW, AND MORE SNOW.
YEP. NOTHING MUCH EVER HAPPENS AROUND HERE. DAY IN, DAY OUT, IT'S THE SAME OLD THING.
SO, YOU GET ANY NEW VIDEO GAMES IN THE LAST MAIL DROP?
YEP. ALIEN CONQUEST XVIII. LOOKS PRETTY COOL.
THEN LET'S DO IT.
BY THE WAY, DID YOU HEAR ANYTHING A SECOND AGO?
NAH... JUST THE WIND.

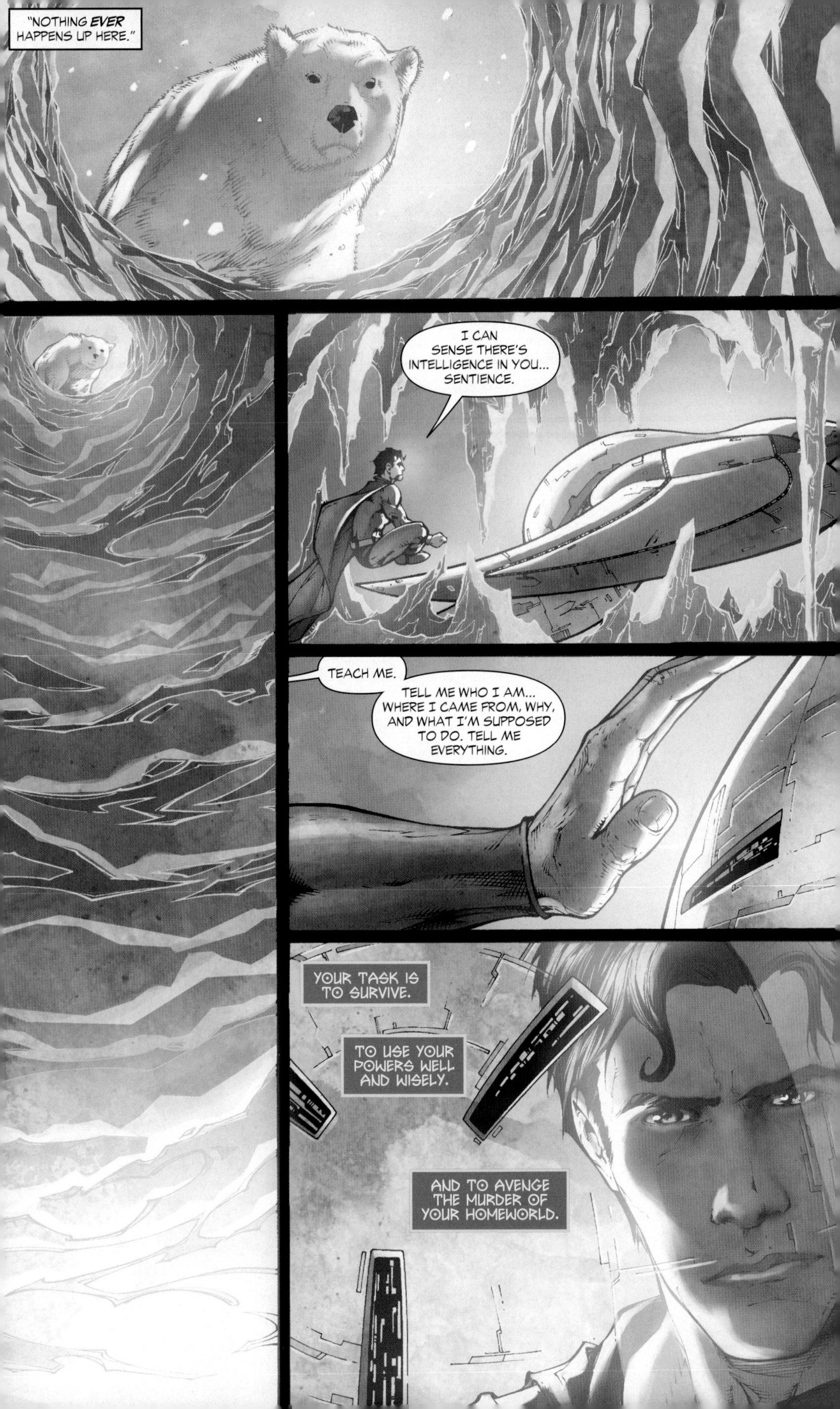
"NOTHING EVER HAPPENS UP HERE."
I CAN SENSE THERE'S INTELLIGENCE IN YOU... SENTIENCE.
TEACH ME.
TELL ME WHO I AM... WHERE I CAME FROM, WHY, AND WHAT I'M SUPPOSED TO DO. TELL ME EVERYTHING.
YOUR TASK IS TO SURVIVE.
TO USE YOUR POWERS WELL AND WISELY.
AND TO AVENGE THE MURDER OF YOUR HOMEWORLD.

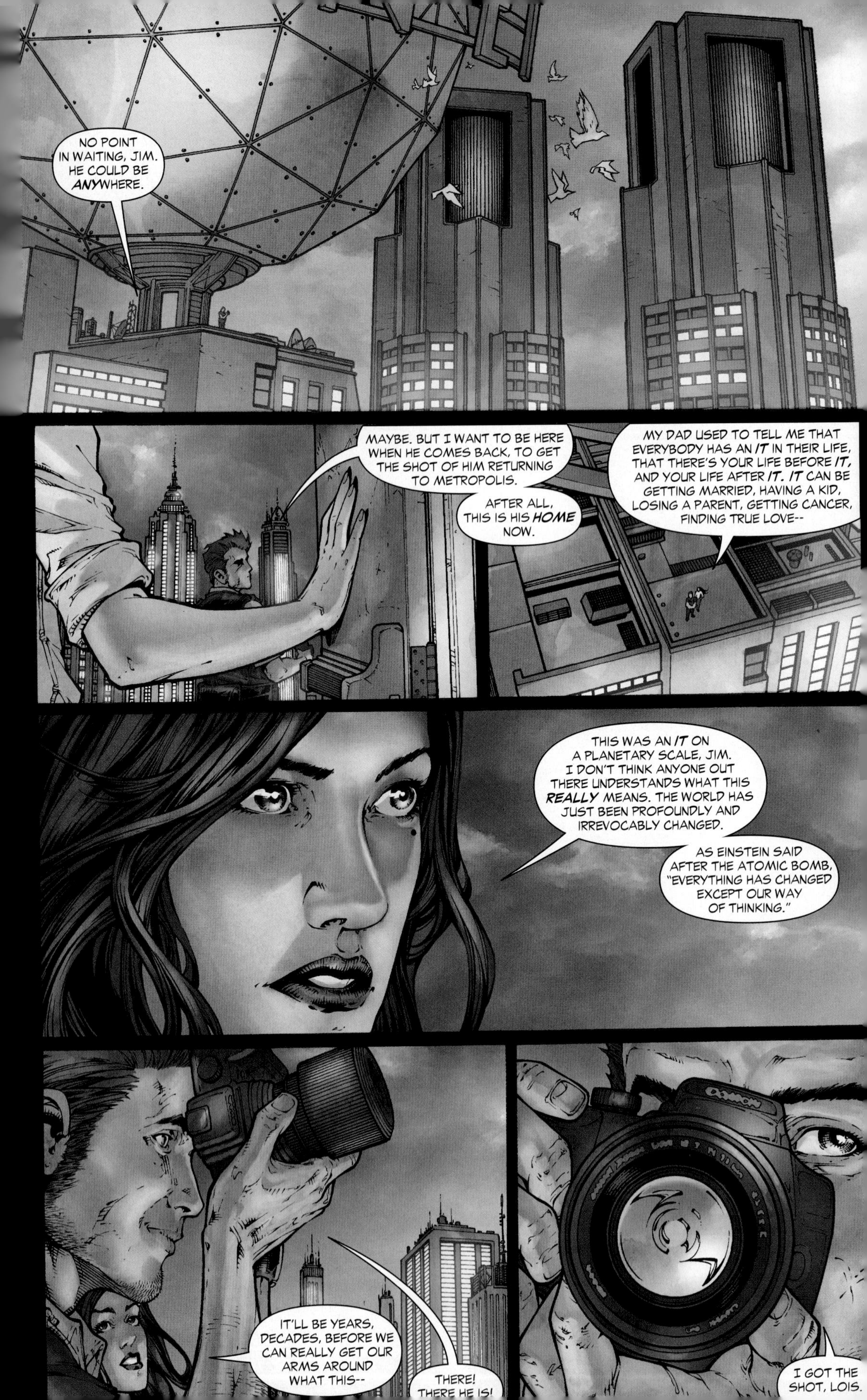
NO POINT IN WAITING, JIM. HE COULD BE ANYWHERE.
MAYBE. BUT I WANT TO BE HERE WHEN HE COMES BACK, TO GET THE SHOT OF HIM RETURNING TO METROPOLIS.
AFTER ALL, THIS IS HIS HOME NOW.
MY DAD USED TO TELL ME THAT EVERYBODY HAS AN IT IN THEIR LIFE, THAT THERE'S YOUR LIFE BEFORE IT, AND YOUR LIFE AFTER IT. IT CAN BE GETTING MARRIED, HAVING A KID, LOSING A PARENT, GETTING CANCER, FINDING TRUE LOVE--
THIS WAS AN IT ON A PLANETARY SCALE, JIM. I DON'T THINK ANYONE OUT THERE UNDERSTANDS WHAT THIS REALLY MEANS. THE WORLD HAS JUST BEEN PROFOUNDLY AND IRREVOCABLY CHANGED.
AS EINSTEIN SAID AFTER THE ATOMIC BOMB, "EVERYTHING HAS CHANGED EXCEPT OUR WAY OF THINKING."
IT'LL BE YEARS, DECADES, BEFORE WE CAN REALLY GET OUR ARMS AROUND WHAT THIS--
THERE! THERE HE IS!
I GOT THE SHOT, LOIS.

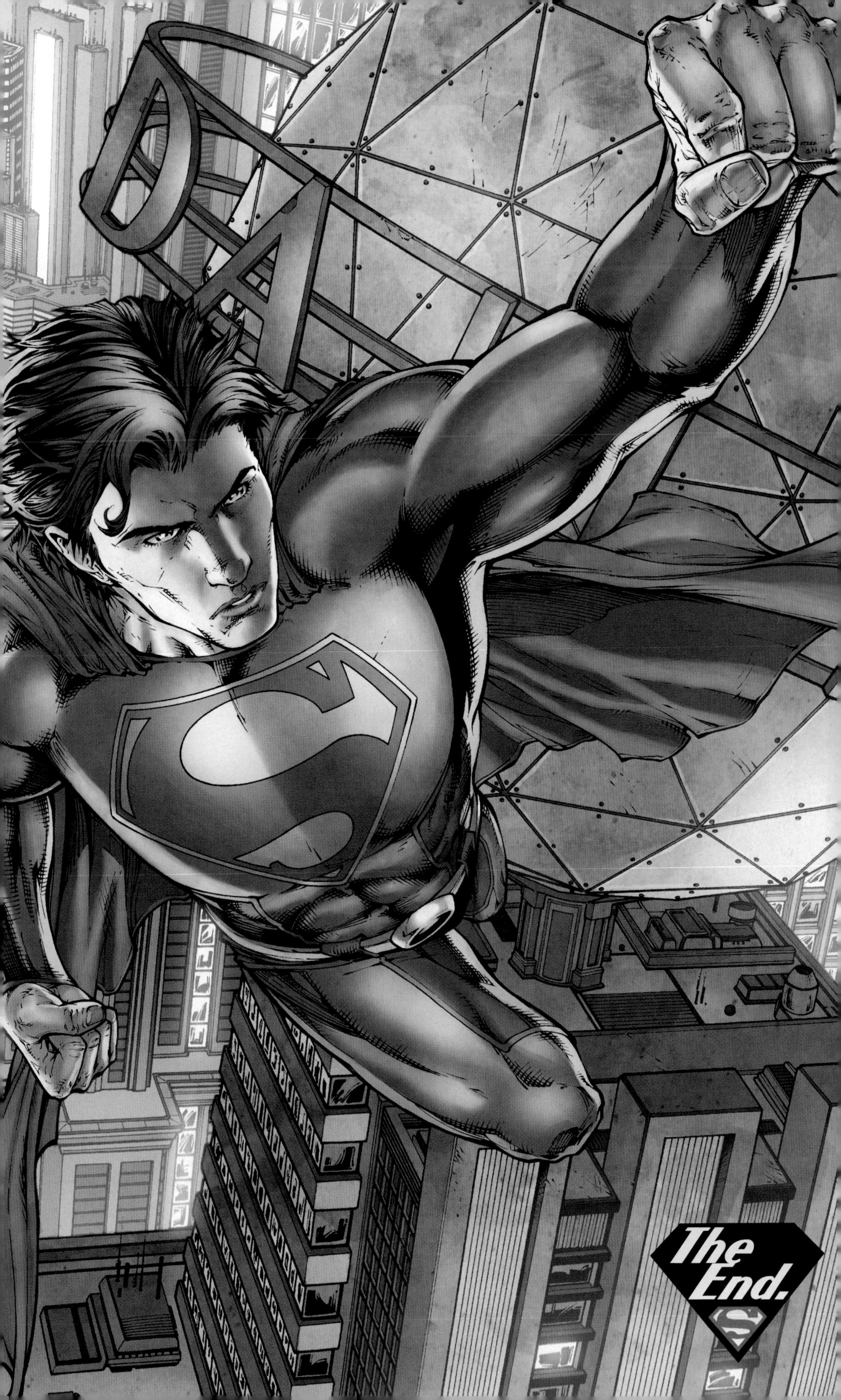
The End.

DAILY PLANET

★★★★ City Extra — "A Great Metropolitan Newspaper" — 75¢

"S" IS FOR...

(DAILY PLANET photo by James Olsen)

...SUPERMAN. At least that's how he identified himself when he sat down for this exclusive interview with the *Daily Planet*, conducted in the aftermath of the recent crisis.

By Clark Kent
Daily Planet
Staff Reporter

Apparently in his twenties, he could be taken for a grad student on his way to Palm Beach for Spring Break except for the blue-and-red uniform, and the fact that he entered the room through the window...and it's a ten story drop.

Coverage continues on page

ontinued from page 1

" Obviously ıperman isn't your al name," I say.

He smiles. "My father ne up with it."

"Aren't you a bit nervous out how that name will be en? I mean, isn't it a bit sumptuous?"

"I don't know, we'll have see," he says. "I guess the portant part is that there y be something super at the rt of that name, but by the e you get to the end, it's l just a man."

He declines a polite request for his real name and the part of the country where he grew up, but from his tone of voice and vernacular, one could come to the conclusion that he was raised along the Eastern Seaboard. But as points of origin go, that's the least interesting one.

"If we can't know where you came from most recently, I suppose the next obvious question is, where were you born?"

"A distant world called Krypton. But understand: I came here as an infant, so I didn't know even that much of my history until recently. I knew I wasn't from around here, but beyond that… nothing."

"Have you had these powers your whole life?"

"Pretty much, yes. I remember the first time I flew, I was looking up at a bird flying overhead, and thinking how amazing that must be. Then I noticed that I was right next to it. For a second I thought it had come down to where I was, then I looked down and discovered that I was about fifty feet off the ground. Scared the heck out of me."

"So why the bright red-and-blue uniform?"

"The fabric, in the form of blankets, is all that came with me from Krypton. They can't be burned, torn, cut…or dyed, unfortunately. They're the only things I can wear without having them ripped off by wind or something else."

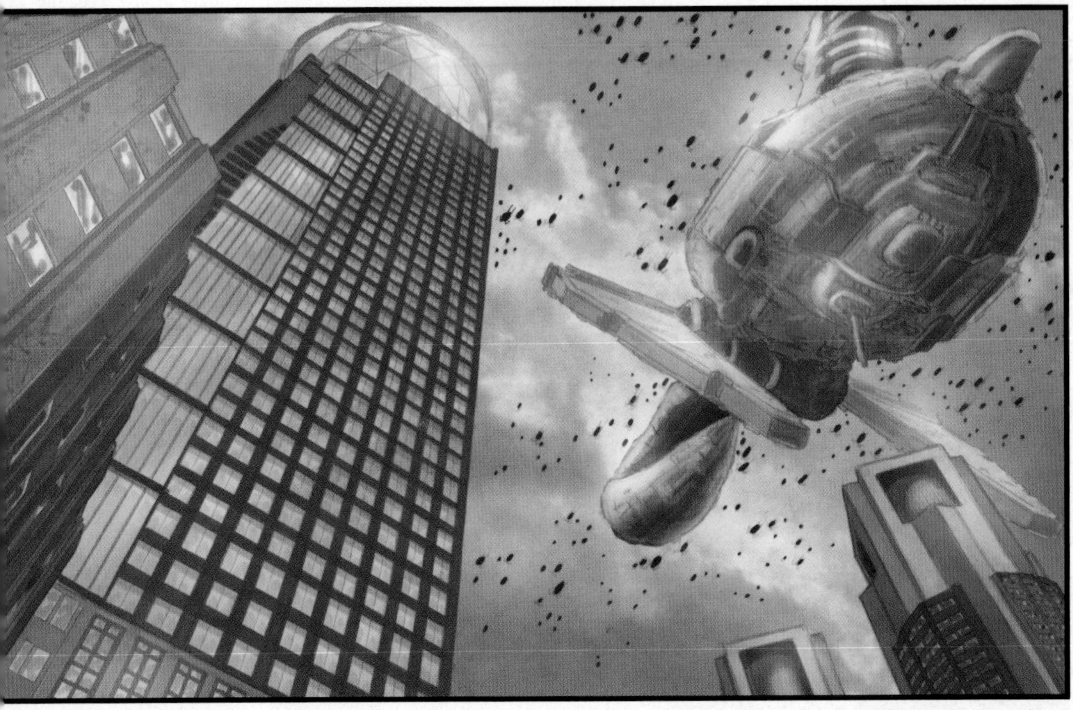

(DAILY PLANET photo by James Olsen)

"Too bad they didn't send ong some blankets made of ay twill, maybe a nice arcoal."

He laughs in the fashion of meone who doesn't seem to it a great deal. "See? That's hat I'm talking about. I'm st lucky I didn't arrive rrounded by plaid blankets, polka dot. That would be ally hard to explain on a first te."

"So you're seeing meone?"

He shrugs. Smiles. "I have y eye on someone."

So why did you wait so long fore revealing yourself?"

"Wasn't any reason to do so earlier. What I can do wasn't needed before then." He hesitates for a moment, trying to find the right words. "Lincoln said that the proper role of government was to do that which individual people couldn't do for themselves. He added, 'you cannot help men permanently by doing for them what they could and should do for themselves.'"

"Sounds like you are advocating trickle-down heroics."

"Not at all. I'm just saying that until that ship showed up over Metropolis, everything that came along in human history to that point could be handled by average men and women who could rise to the occasion. But no amount of rising was going to stop this."

"Like when the Balrog appears, and Gandalf says, 'swords are of no use here.' "

"Right, it's—"

"'This is beyond any of you.'"

I realize that I've revealed myself for the geek that I am, but he's polite enough not to comment on it. "Exactly. If I can help by doing things that the average person can't do for him- or herself, then that's what I want to do."

"So you're not planning on taking over the Earth."

He laughs. "No. I mean, what would I do with it? Where would I put it? Where do you park something like that?"

"Here's the thing," he says, his tone serious again. "I was raised in this country. I believe in this country. Does it have its flaws? Yes. Does it have its moments of greatness? Yes. Bottom line is, it's my home, and I'll always carry those values around with me. But if I do what I can do just for the U.S., it's going to destabilize

See SUPERMAN page 4

Continued from page 3

the whole world. It could even lead to war.

"So I'm here to do what I can, where I can, whether that's in the U.S. or elsewhere. But I can never get involved with politics or policy. There's nothing political about a tsunami, or an earthquake, or a tornado…nothing political about a gunman holding innocent hostages at a bank, or an out-of-control truck barreling down a crowded street. So those are the sorts of things I want to get involved with, where I can make a difference without becoming an instrument of policy."

"A lot of people are going to be unhappy to hear that. I think the Pentagon was already beginning to dream about your walking into China or Afghanistan and taking tanks apart, overthrowing governments and destroying whole fleets."

"And I understand that," he says. "But if I start down that road, then I can't serve humanity as a whole, which is what I feel I'm here to do. If I become an extension of a government or administratic then I lose the rest of t world, and there may be tim when we'll need the rest of t world on board in the event another planetary crisis."

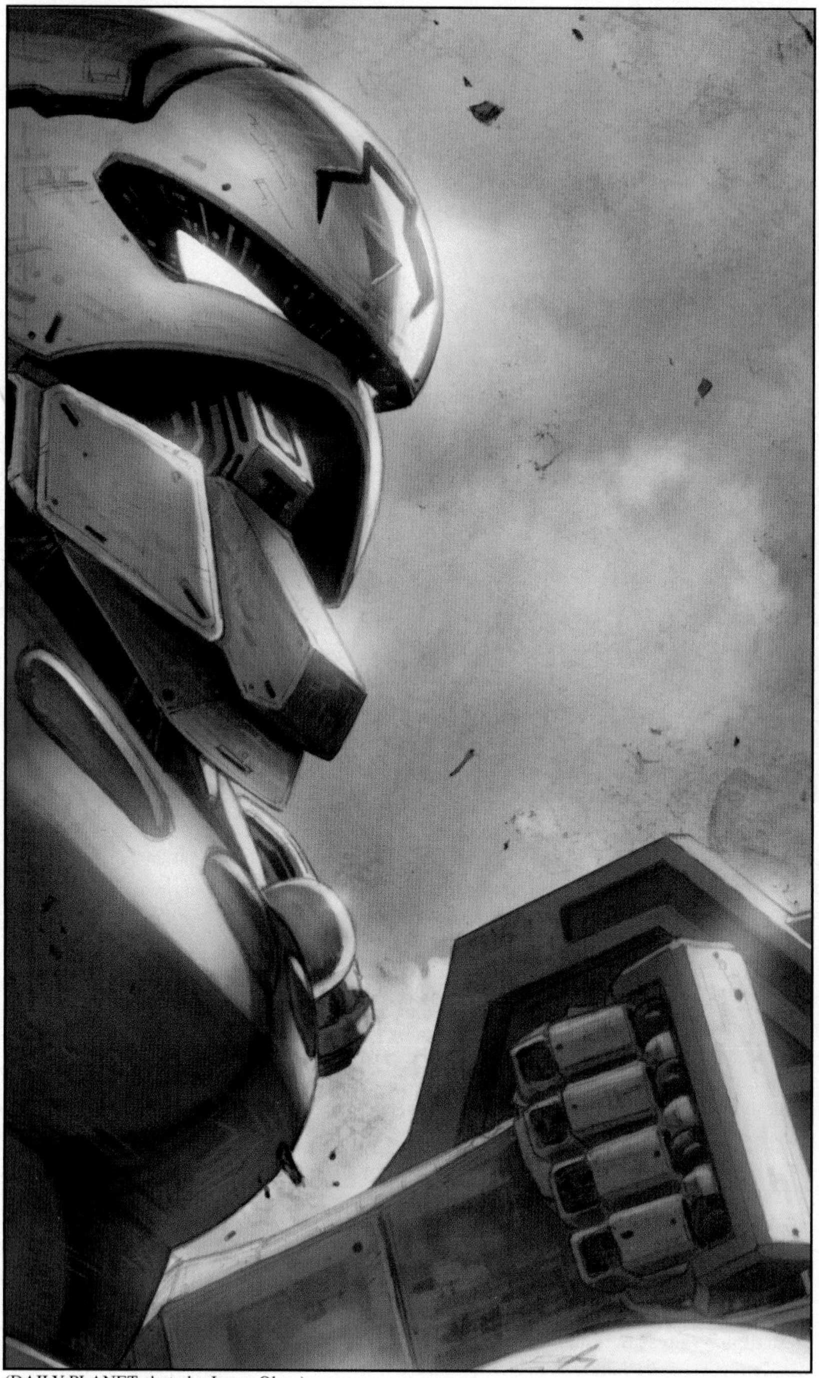

(DAILY PLANET photo by James Olsen)

He pauses for a mome "I saw this documentary a fe years ago about the Briti police force," he say speaking slowly and delibe ately, making his point. "Th interviewed a London bob who said—and I'm not taki sides, I'm just repeating wh he said—that American poli are there to enforce the peac while the British police a there to create the peace.

"I like to think that's w I'm here: to help create t peace by doing what's rig for people without trying change them. Maybe th sounds naive, or superfici but it's the truth."

• WALL STREET REACTS TO RAMPAGE

Aftereffects Felt in Markets Worldwide.

Dollar, Euro, Yen take hit.

In *FINANCE*

• MONARCHS AND METEORS GAMES POSTPONED

Monarchs to play day/nite doubleheader Saturday; Meteors game TBD.

In *SPORTS*

He looks out the windo It's getting dark. "I shou head out, there's still a lot work to be done clearing t streets and digging people o from under the mess."

"One last question, the A hard one. There are going be a lot of people who say th entire incident was your fau After all, they did come he looking for you. What do y say to the families of t civilians, pilots and oth military and police forces wh died fighting those intruders?

See SUPERMAN page

Continued from page 4

He looks at his hands. Hands that could tear down a mountain without even trying. But right now, they seem lost.

"I don't know," he says at last. "I wish I had a good answer. I wish I knew the words that could comfort those who have lost loved ones, or were hurt. Nothing can ever make those wounds go away, ever fill those empty spaces. Which proves that there are some things impossible even for a superman.

"But I will say this. I didn't know they were out there, didn't know they were after me, didn't know any of this until the day they showed up. I found out about it the same time everybody else did. So while what happened may not technically be my fault, it is my responsibility, and I will live with that knowledge every day for the rest of my life. Every morning, when I open my eyes, I'll know that I'm here, and that this world is here, in part because of the sacrifices made by those people on this day. And I will dedicate every breath I take, every action I take, to their memory. I don't know if that scale can ever be truly balanced, but I do know that I'm willing to give my life trying to measure up to their sacrifice.

"See, that's the remarkable thing, and the irony," he says, rising and moving toward the window. "As someone who can look at humanity from the outside, I see your amazing strengths, your stubborn nobility, your greatness and your kindness and your generosity and your willingness to aspire, to sacrifice, to struggle over the mountaintop no matter how big the boulders are coming your way. I am blinded by the light that burns inside every one of you.

"In that light, one truth emerges: if the word 'super' is to be applied to anyone, it should be applied to all of you, to all of mankind. Against that power, against that truth... I'm just a man."

And then he was gone.

(DAILY PLANET photo by James Olsen)

Under a Broken Sky

DAILY PLANET PERSPECTIVE

By Lois Lane
Daily Planet Staff Reporter

METROPOLIS — As a young girl, I was a history nut. In particular I loved reading about Edward R. Murrow, Walter Cronkite and other reporters who chronicled the bombing of London from the inside during the Second World War. I wondered what it would be like to cover a city under seige, and even as a working reporter imagined that the only way I could find out would be to travel somewhere else, to file stories from places like Lebanon or Beirut or Iraq, since after all, those things never happened inside the United States. It was always over there, somewhere.

Yesterday, all that changed.

Yesterday, the sky was broken open, and from that wound something profound and dangerous entered the life of this city, this country, and this world. Yesterday, far-flung, distant peoples in every corner of the globe were united in the possibility of annhilation. Yesterday, we stood at the edge of the abyss.

Yesterday, today seemed impossible. But today has come, and we still stand, in large part due to the arrival of one man, who stood with us against impossible odds.

And because of this man, we now have a tomorrow we did not expect. He is, truly, the man of tomorrow.

■ **For Additional Coverage log on to www.DailyPlanet.com**

Earth One Sketch Book

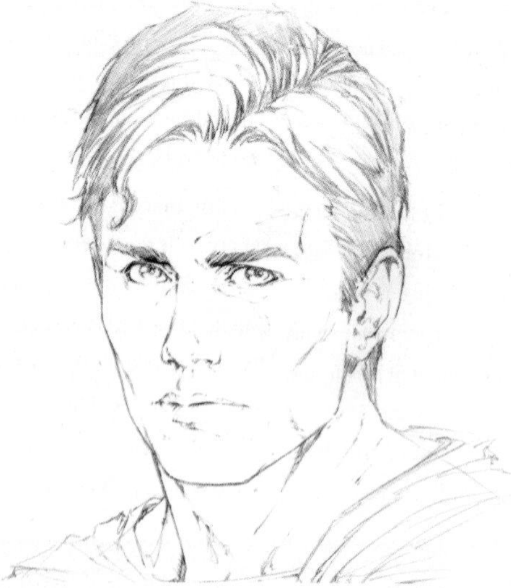

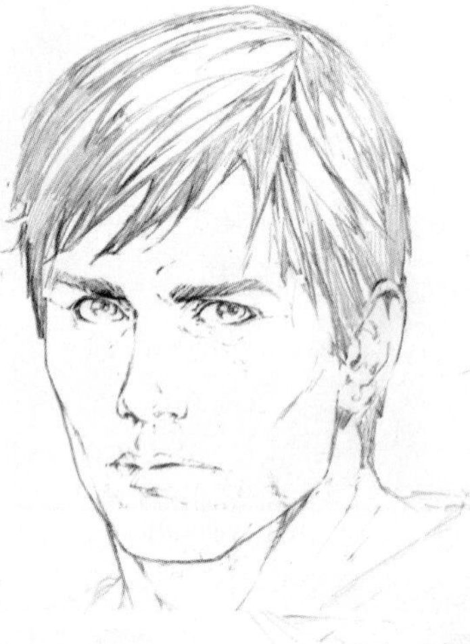

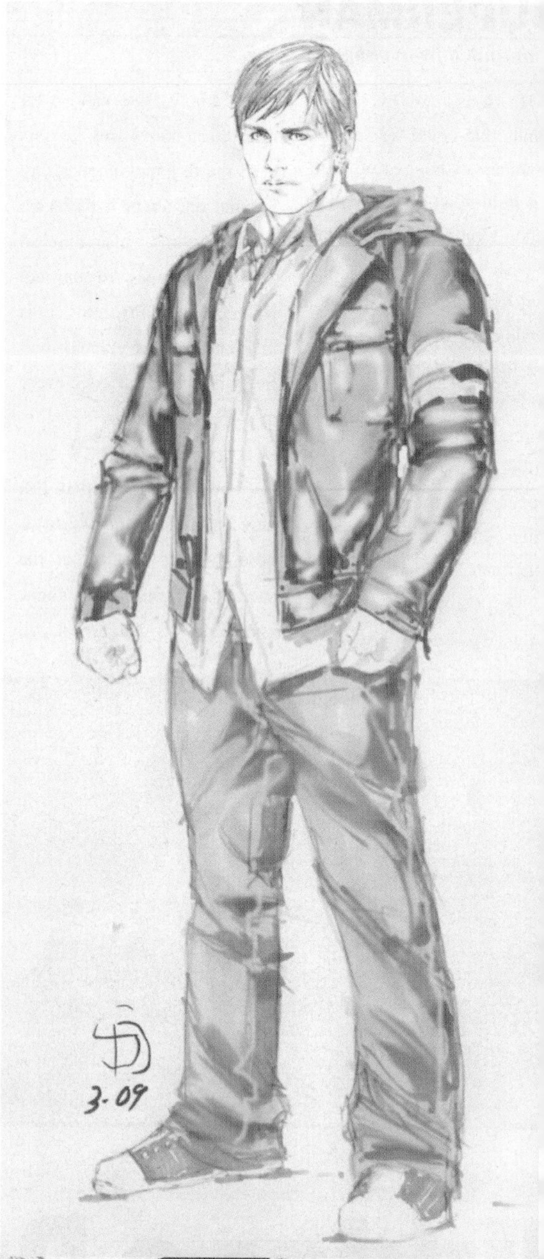
3-09

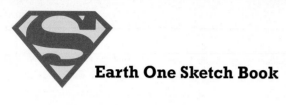

Here and on the preceding pages are Shane Davis's initial design work for Clark Kent, the Man of Steel and his foes.

This was no small undertaking; the artist had to make everything feel fresh and new, while maintaining the iconic look of the character.

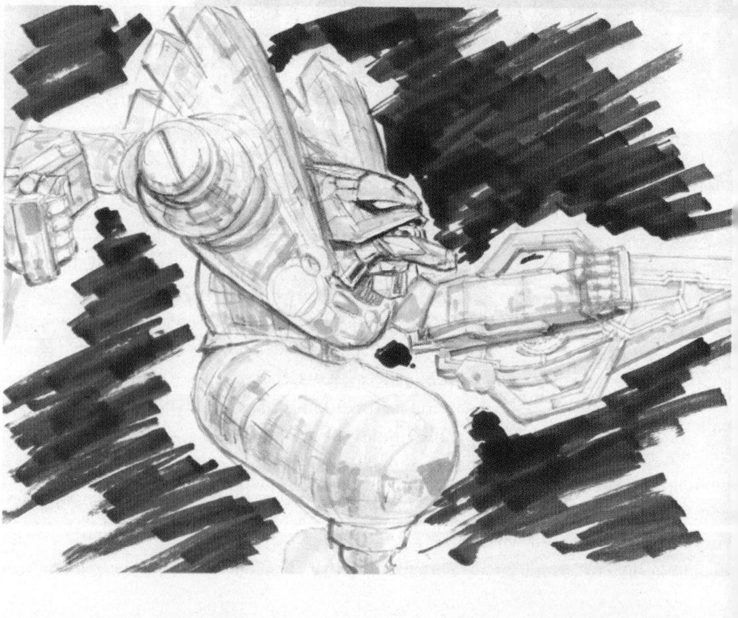

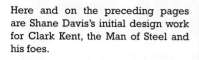

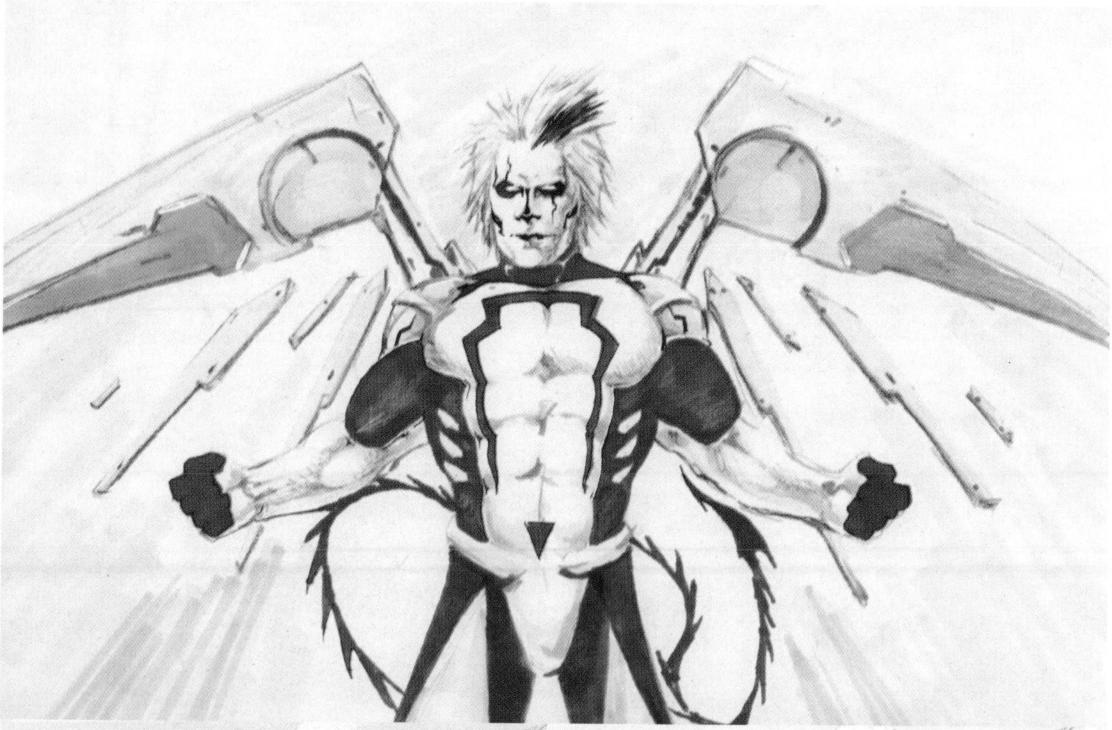

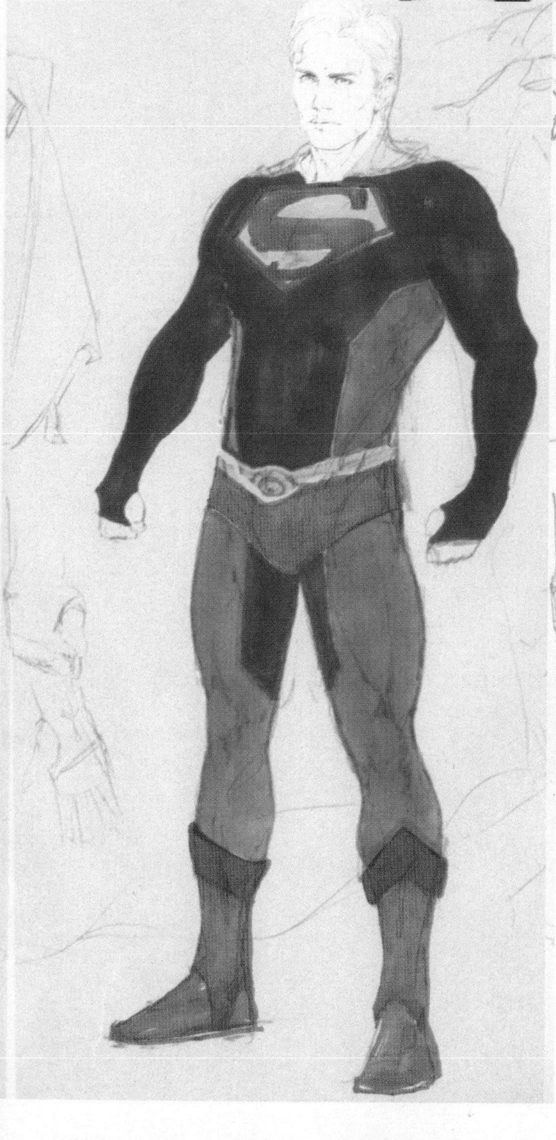

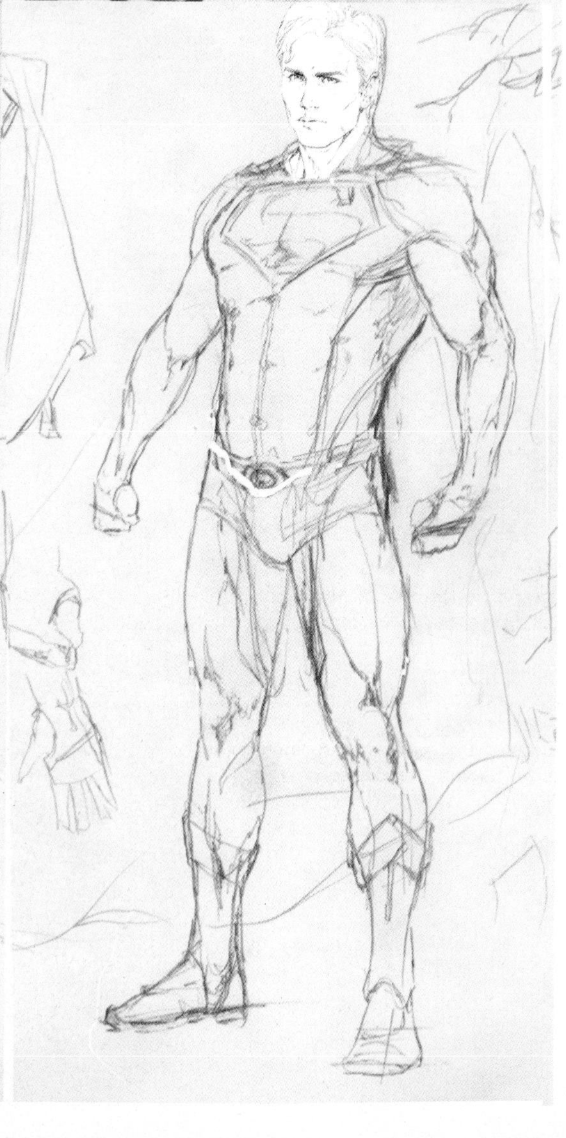

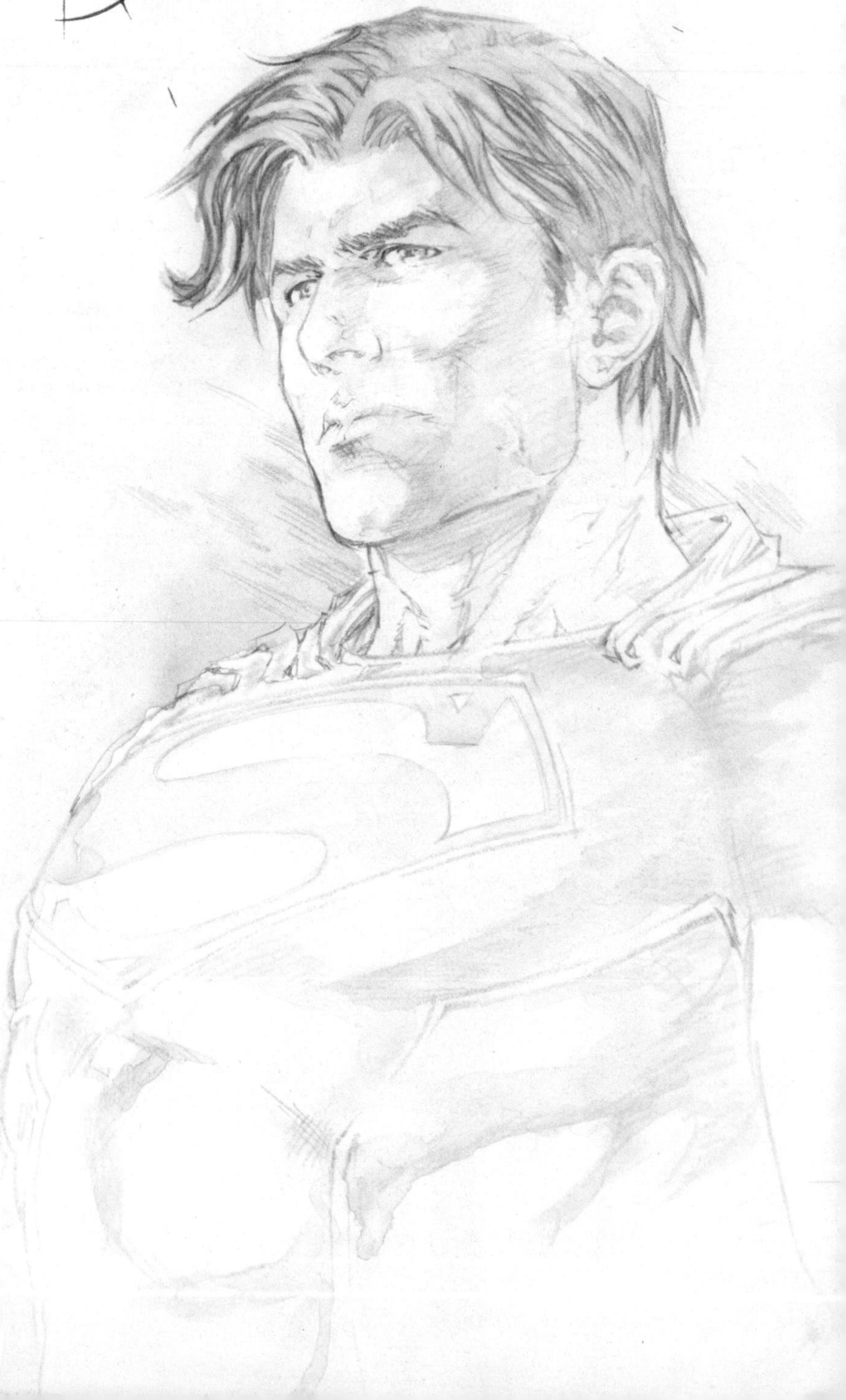